PSYCHOLOGY ON THE ROAD
THE HUMAN FACTOR IN TRAFFIC SAFETY

PSYCHOLOGY ON THE ROAD
THE HUMAN FACTOR IN TRAFFIC SAFETY

DAVID SHINAR
Institute for Research in Public Safety
School of Public and Environmental Affairs
Indiana University

Department of Industrial Engineering and Management
Faculty of Engineering Sciences
Ben Gurion University of the Negev

JOHN WILEY & SONS
New York   Toronto   Santa Barbara   Chichester   Brisbane

Text and Cover Design by Laura C. Ierardi
Production Supervised by Joseph P. Cannizzaro

Library of Congress Cataloging in Publication Data:

Shinar, David.
  Psychology on the road.

    Includes bibliographical references and index.
    1. Automobile drivers—Psychology. 2. Pedestrians—
Psychology. I. Title.

L.C. Call No.	Dewey Classification No.	L.C. Card No.
TL152.3.S54	629.28'3'019	78-18219
ISBN 0-471-03997-7		

Printed in the United States of America

10 9 8 7 6 5 4 3 2 1

To
Eva, Busia, and Pessah

FOREWORD

This book symbolizes the growing interaction of psychologists and engineers. While many scholars attempt to bridge the two professions, few have the advantage of David Shinar who, by nature of his training and research in both psychology and engineering, has been able to utilize the role of both disciplines in highway safety.

This text is one I would have liked to develop for my engineering students with an interest in human factors engineering. It should also be read by traffic safety and driver education students, as well as psychology students with an applied interest and hopefully attract more people to do research in this important area.

Were any scientist to be presented with several million observations he or she would doubtless claim to have little trouble in descriptive and predictive modeling of the process. Why in the case of highway safety do we experience so much casualty data each year and still make so little progress toward problem resolution? The answer is not a simple one as this text demonstrates. I contend that one explanation is the oversimplistic view of driver behavior by safety experts, government decision makers, and automobile and highway designers. Consequently, we are periodically whipsawed by simple solutions such as massive police enforcement, tough-fisted courts, enlightened driver education curricula, or alcohol safety action programs. At the other extreme is the frustration reaction that concedes that changing driver behavior is impossible. This leads to overemphasis on crash injury reduction (e.g., vehicle cockpit design and air bags), which assumes we can protect the driver against any and all erratic performance and subsequent accidents.

Dr. Shinar's view is a balanced one that avoids the above-mentioned extremes. With documentation from recent research, he fully impresses upon the reader the complexities of driver behavior and, at the same time, points out applications of basic human factors engineering principles. Designing the system around the capabilities and limitations of the driver will lead surely and inexorably to imporved highway safety.

This text provides an opportunity for traffic engineers to appreciate better the role of driver behavior in their design, and traffic safety experts to understand the effects of human behavior on the road. The text has the added benefit of Dr. Shinar's experience at

Indiana University in accident reconstruction and analysis. He links behavioral research to the causes of traffic accidents through a systematic analysis of recent accidents.

I have one final observation and a hope for the future of driver behavior research. As an important and well-documented collage of research findings in driver behavior, this text is presented not as a final answer but as a stimulus to continue to study the driver despite and because of his or her complexities and inconsistencies. We must recognize that basic research on the driving process is sorely needed now if applied research is to answer future problems. We must see the potential role of electronic technology to aid the driver in his or her information-seeking decision making and response behavior. In effect, we must design vehicular and highway systems based on the driver.

THOMAS H. ROCKWELL
Professor Ohio State University
Department of Industrial Engineering

PREFACE

While vehicle performance capabilities have been constantly improving over the past several decades, the capabilities of the human controller have remained fairly constant. Consequently, the interaction between the road user (drivers and pedestrians) and the vehicle has been receiving more and more attention from people concerned with highway traffic safety. While the increased awareness of the importance of human factors in highway safety has been reflected in an ever-growing volume of research, no attempt has been made in the recent past to integrate the material in a systematic manner around the human element in the vehicle-highway-road user system. This book hopefully fills this void. To reflect the increased interest and research in this area, I have tried to give this book a state-of-the-art flavor by biasing my selection of references toward more recent ones. Hence, approximately 70 percent of the research cited is from the last decade.

This book introduces the role of psychology in highway safety. It can be used as a textbook in courses on: traffic safety, driver education, and civil and industrial engineering. Parts of this book relate to all of the curricula represented by the experts working in these areas — physicians, industrial and systems engineers, civil engineers, optometrists, educators, and psychologists of various orientations.

I view the road user as a limited-capacity information processor whose efficiency (and safety) is enhanced or degraded by the highway and vehicle design features, as well as by his or her personality, skills, and impairments. This view reflects the influence of my former teacher and co-worker, Thomas H. Rockwell, who introduced me to, and in many ways shaped my thinking in, this area. The discussion of human factors in accident causation (Chapter Five) contains many concepts that I have developed as a result of a fruitful and very pleasant association with John R. Treat, working together on highway traffic accidents research.

The initial stimulus to writing this book came from my friend Peter Kincaid who originally asked me to contribute a chapter to an applied psychology book. That chapter was never written but instead was revised into what became this book. In the process, I was helped by my colleagues, Phil Cornwell, Allen Katz, John Treat, and Nick Tumbas who read, commented on, and — most instructive for me — raised probing questions in various sections of the text. I also received valuable suggestions for improvement from James Noto (San Diego State University) and Eric Van Fleet (Western Illinois University). Most of all, I was helped by my wife, Eva, who critically read all of the drafts and served as a supporting consultant on all of the revisions of this manuscript.

I began this text while working at the Institute for Research in Public Safety, School of Public and Environmental Affairs, Indiana University, and finished it in the Department of Industrial Engineering and Management of Ben Gurion University of the Negev, Israel. It is a pleasure to acknowledge the formal support that both institutions provided me, and, in particular, I thank Rita Fortner, Lili Lang, Claire Penso, and Jody Vaught for readily responding to all my secretarial needs.

Finally, I would like to thank Wiley editors Wayne Anderson and Susan Giniger, and production supervisor Joe Cannizzaro, for bringing this work to its present form.

DAVID SHINAR

CONTENTS

        Driver Improvement   130
        Vehicle Design   141
        Highway Improvements   156
        Summary   165

SEVEN   THE PEDESTRIAN   169
        Identifying the Vulnerable Pedestrian   170
        The Causes of Pedestrian Accidents   175
        The Prevention of Pedestrian   180
           Accidents
        Summary   186

        REFERENCES   189

        AUTHOR INDEX   205

        SUBJECT INDEX   209

ONE
INTRODUCTION

Consider an alien hovering over some great urban center in the United States and watching with curiosity what is happening below. What does he (she, it) see? Well, aside from the smoke rising out from the numerous chimneys, most of the movement appears to be limited to rectangular objects (vehicles) moving in an orderly manner along dark stripes (roads), which are intermittently crossed by bipods (pedestrians). Unknown to our alien, what he is observing is an operations system transporting (mostly unseen) people and goods. This system consists of three elements: the environment (road and signals), vehicles, and people (drivers and pedestrians). In our road-car-driver-pedestrian system the driver/pedestrian is the only decision-making component and therefore it is his or her actions or inactions that make this system go. Thus, our alien, assuming that he has visual capabilities similar to ours, must wonder what makes this system work. What capabilities are required to control the relatively harmonious car movements? How is the movement of vehicles and pedestrians coordinated? And — whenever an accident does occur — what are the causes of the breakdown in that system? These questions concern behavioral scientists engaged in improving our transportation system. Note that the human factors in transportation are not limited to the study of car drivers and pedestrians. It includes pilots, boat captains, train engineers, and the like. However, since the predominant mode in which most of us interact with the various transportation systems, in an active (rather than in a passenger-passive) manner, is in the capacity of drivers and pedestrians, this book deals with these two only.

For initial simplification, we can limit our discussion to the road-car-driver system, that is, assume that there are no pedestrians. As behavioral scientists we have a definite advantage over our observant alien: we know much more about the controlling element — the driver — and about the requirements placed on the driver by the road, traffic, and his or her own car. As the information processor in the system, the driver's role is to process mostly visual inputs from the road, traffic, and his or her own car's behavior, make decisions about appropriate control actions, execute these actions, and observe and respond to the new situation that results. A block diagram of these functions along with some others that will be discussed later is presented in Figure 1.1. While the mere description of these functions seems long and laborious, note that for the most part, as drivers, we are totally unaware of all such internal activities. This is demonstrated by the often-encountered phenomenon, when, after driving uneventfully for some time, we realize that we have no recall at all of the past events and scenery — even though the relevant time period may have been filled with various actions — involving complex decisions — such as passing, stopping, and turning.

The process depicted in Figure 1.1 can best be illustrated with an example. Let us assume that you, as a driver, are following another car and are in the process of deciding whether to pass it or not. To simplify the situation, let us further assume that there is no oncoming traffic and that the field of view is clear. The information you then need concerns the speed of the car ahead, your own speed, and

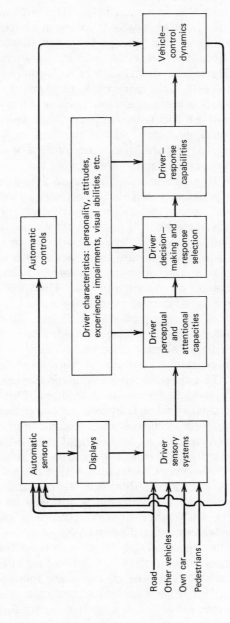

Figure 1.1. A simplified block diagram of the driver functions in the driver-vehicle-road system.

knowledge about your car's performance capabilities: Does it have enough power to pass the other car in a sufficient amount of time? Looking first at the bottom row of boxes, note that you receive sensory information from the road in the form of roadside markers "going" by you, from the vehicle ahead in the form of its relative size, giving an indication of its distance, and from your own car concerning your own speed. This information, however, is useless until it is interpreted by the brain and results in meaningful perceptions of the relative speed of the two vehicles. Once this information is available to you, you make a decision concerning the appropriate responses necessary to perform the maneuver, if you have decided that the maneuver is appropriate. Next, you have to exercise your decision and actually perform the maneuver that you have decided on. Following this process, you finally perform an action that actually affects your car's behavior. Let us say that your decision was to start closing the gap between you and the car ahead. You then accelerate your car. The car, which has its own control dynamics, responds to your action, and you are now faced with a new situation of a new distance and relative speed between you and the car; and again, you go through the same process. This process will go on repeatedly until you have finished your maneuver.

Now let us look at the top part of this figure. To begin, much of the information that you receive is not provided to you directly from the environment, but is already interpreted for you through electronic systems. These are the automatic sensors in the car, such as your speedometer. The speedometer would be useless unless it had a meaningful display, which fortunately it does. This display, then, provides you with quantitative information concerning your speed. The speedometer and other automatic sensors are aids to the driver just as much as (moving further to the right) the automatic controls are. Automatic controls can be as common as automatic gears or as extravagant as "cruise-o-matic" systems, which are velocity regulator systems within the car. The automatic sensors and the automatic controls alleviate some of the load that is imposed on the driver, and provide him or her with more time to attend to other tasks that may be more important or more pleasurable.

Finally, inside the center of the diagram, notice that driver skills, level of arousal, experience, motivation, attitudes, and personality all influence the way we drive. Some of these are relatively stable for a given person, but differ widely among persons, such as driver skills, experience, and personality. Others, such as arousal, motivation, or attitudes, vary both among drivers and within drivers at different times and under different circumstances. All of these affect the way we perceive the information, our decisions at every minute, and our ability to control the car.

This simplified conceptualization of the driver-vehicle-roadway system, is also useful to illustrate how a failure in any of its components can result in a system failure — easily recognized as an accident. The initial event, action, or situation that instigates the accident or makes it imminent may be a human, vehicular, or environmental deficiency — or a mismatch between any two or all three components. Thus, the danger source may be misperceived by the driver because of poor vision or inattention (human failure) low visibility due to glare, fog, or a view obstruction (environmental), or a poorly designed vehicle with many blind areas. In all of these cases the driver is likely to make wrong decisions and responses that — unless corrected in time — will lead to a collision. By knowing more about the way we process all the driving-related information and respond to it we can better understand the circumstances under which accidents occur and, hopefully, we can develop measures that will eliminate these circumstances — through driver selection and training, and improvements in vehicle and environmental design.

Let us return now to the pedestrian, who was temporarily taken out of the system. Contrary to some experiences we have all had from time to time, the relationship between the driver and the pedestrian should be one of coordination rather that competition. The joint objective of both should be to use the road while remaining separated from each other. This requires some agreement on norms and often involves subtle forms of communication between drivers and pedestrians.

In the following chapters we discuss most of the concepts listed within the boxes in Figure 1.1. We begin, however, with a brief review of the different methodologies involved in studying driver behavior (Chapter Two). This discussion provides a better understanding of how driving research results (to be discussed in the succeeding chapters) are obtained, and arms the reader with an ability to critically evaluate conclusions drawn from these results. In Chapter Three we evaluate how various driver characteristics — personality, attitudes, experience, and motivation — and temporary impairments — from drugs and fatigue — may influence driver behavior. The next two chapters discuss how human information processing limitations and capabilities influence the interaction between the driver and the environment (Chapter Four), and the role of information processing failures in accident involvement (Chapter Five). Chapter Six describes how knowledge of driver behavior can (and has been) directed toward improving the driver-vehicle-roadway system through driver regulation, vehicle design, and highway design. Finally, in the last chapter, Chapter Seven, we focus our attention on the pedestrian — often the same person in the new role of the driver without a car. Our discussion of pedestrian behavior is more limited in scope than that of driver behavior and relates to situations in which the "horse-power" and the unassisted "human power" are likely to interact with each other.

TWO
DRIVING RESEARCH METHODOLOGY

This chapter serves as background for the more substantive discussions in the succeeding chapters. The variables investigated, the methods of investigation, and the various advantages and disadvantages associated with these methods are discussed here in detail so that research findings described in this book, and the conclusions derived from them, may be more critically evaluated.

THE VARIABLES: INDEPENDENT, DEPENDENT, AND CONFOUNDING

As in any other research area, at the root of any study in driver/-pedestrian behavior are one or more educated guesses (formally known as hypotheses) that the researcher makes. At the most basic level a hypothesis describes the relationship between two variables: independent and dependent. The independent variable is typically (although not necessarily) the one that we manipulated whereas the dependent variable is a performance measure that may be affected by the manipulation. To illustrate, a hypothesis that smoking marijuana increases the probability of being involved in an accident is an educated guess of the relationship between being intoxicated (the independent variable) and safe driving behavior (the dependent variable). Thus we can describe most research as a hypothesis testing situation, that is, subjecting the researcher's educated guess to a test against empirical reality.

In applied research the variables of key interest are often difficult to study directly. To illustrate, is it ethical to give subjects marijuana — especially if proper research methodology decrees that the subjects be unaware of it? Most university and research organizations now have ethics committees that monitor such research. Thus, while it is possible to conduct marijuana research under strictly controlled conditions, experimental research in which real accidents are used as a dependent variable will hopefully never be conducted.

What, then, are the independent and dependent variables that can be manipulated and measured in highway safety research? How do they relate to the ultimate criteria of safety and/or accidents? We now briefly describe the most commonly studied independent and dependent variables and discuss another kind of variable — confounding variables — factors that, in the context of a given research, are not studied, although their presence may effect the final outcome of the research.

Independent Variables

Any factor that influences the performance of driving-related tasks is of interest as an independent variable in the study of highway safety (e.g., all of the concepts listed in Figure 1.1). In particular, the behavioral scientist is concerned with individual differences that affect driver behavior (see Chapter Three), and the effect of changes in the driver's environment — either in the vehicle or the roadway — that may affect his or her performance (see Chapter Six). Very often the manipulation of the independent variable consists of simply two or more groups of drivers (e.g., sober versus intoxicated) who are given the same experimental task. However, in order to reduce the effects of other individual differences that may influence the results (the two groups may differ in their personality characteristics), the same task is often given repeatedly to the same person under different conditions (one with and one without the drug). There are advantages and disadvantages associated with both approaches and the interested reader is referred to experimental design textbooks (e.g., Edwards, 1968). Very often the approach is dictated by the constraints of reality. This is the case when the variable of interest is a personality characteristic. Obviously, we cannot manipulate a personality characteristic so that the same person on different experimental sessions will assume a different personality. In these cases every attempt is made to manipulate the independent variable by matching groups of people so that they differ on the independent variable but are identical or similar on all other variables that may be of interest (e.g., low- and high-anxiety subjects may be matched in terms of their age, sex, intelligence, perceptual motor skills, etc.).

Dependent Variables

The ultimate criterion of the effectiveness of any manipulation of the driver or environment is the effect of the manipulation on accident reduction. However, as we have just stated, it is very difficult to devise an experiment in which we actually measure the number of people who have accidents as a consequence of a manipulation designed to satisfy a researcher's hypothesis testing curiosity. Therefore, experimental studies of highway safety have often been concerned with the study of *intermediate measures* that are assumed (on the basis of experimental data, a model, or a theory) to be related to safety and/or safe driving. The measures used differ as a function of the level of approximation to real world situations that is achieved in the study. Generally speaking, research may be conducted at one of three levels: *actual* road conditions, in which road users' behaviors (speeds, violations, accidents) are unobtrusively surveyed or measured; on-the-road studies but with volunteer subjects that are aware that they are participating in research and typically drive an instrumented vehicle; and off-the-road research most commonly known as simulation or laboratory research. The range and type of dependent variables that can be measured are most often determined by the environment in which the research is conducted, and we discuss these variables in detail when we direct our attention to the different research methods.

Confounding Variables

As their name implies the presence of these variables often complicates the interpretation of the results. A confounding variable is one
that varies systematically with one or more of the independent variables being investigated. This relationship may or may not be known
to the researcher — but in either case it complicates things. In the
area of driving research a classic example is the relationship between
driver vision and accident involvement. Most of us have a deep-seated
conviction that good vision (whatever that may be — see discussion
in Chapter Three) is necessary for good driving. Yet much of the
early research that correlated driver vision with an accident record
either failed to find a relationship between the two variables, or
indicated that drivers with poor vision had fewer accidents than
drivers with good vision (e.g., Burg, 1967). Had the presence of a
confounding variable not been suspected, would we now have licensing tests that pass only people with poor vision? The confounding
variable in these studies turned out to be the driver's age. Good
vision drivers had more accidents *but were also younger* than poor
vision drivers who had fewer accidents. Age and vision are then said
to *covary*, that is, vary together and be systematically related to each
other. This is why, in our discussion of independent variables (e.g.,
vision) we discussed the needs to match subjects on all variables (e.g.,
age) that might covary with the independent variable of interest, and
thus act as confounding variables. Fortunately, when proper control
of these variables cannot be achieved in the experimental design,
there are statistical procedures that allow for the "control" of their
effects on the dependent variable. Obviously, as long as we are unaware of the presence of a confounding variable, we cannot control
its effects either way.

FROM THE ROAD TO THE LAB: RESEARCH TECHNIQUES

The complexity of human behavior in general, and in the context of
complex systems (such as the vehicle-roadway) in particular, has led
to many different research approaches, and to the realization that
there is no one "best" technique to study all aspects of driver behavior. The span of approaches often involves researchers from different backgrounds, and the concern has been voiced that "just as
there is a tendency for those interested in the driving situation not
to look beyond actual 'driving studies' for pertinent findings, there is
also a tendency to inappropriately generalize findings (from different
areas of basic research) to the driving task" Schori, 1970, p. 157).

Perhaps the greatest distinction is between on-the-road research and research conducted in the sheltered environment of a laboratory. The major advantage of on-the-road research is that results obtained from it may be immediately applicable to the highway environment. Its major disadvantage is that many variables are not under strict experimental control and the results may be due to uncontrolled confounding variables, and/or limited to the specific location where the study was conducted. The reverse holds for laboratory research. Here the environment is strictly controlled and thus the results are more readily attributed to the effects of the manipulated independent variable (or variables). The critical issue is then whether these results or the conclusions derived from them can be generalized to the actual road environment, which is much more complex than the one afforded by the laboratory simulation.

On-the-Road Studies of Unaware Drivers

In studies of this type, the dependent variables may involve the manipulation of the roadway or vehicular environment, or the driver himself. The approach can be illustrated by a study conducted by Shinar, Rockwell, and Malecki (1975), in which pavement markings in a high-accident curve were changed in a manner designed to influence the driver's perception of the degree of curvature. Specifically it was hoped that an approaching driver would perceive the curve as sharper than it is in reality, slow down more before entering the curve, and thus be less likely to be involved in an accident due to loss of control. Instead of waiting for a period of two or more years to evaluate the effect of the markings on the accident frequency in the curve, driver's speeds prior to entering the curve were measured unobstrusively before and after the modification. This type of study is often labeled as "before-after" design. In the particular study, the mean speed observed before the modification was 45 mph whereas the mean speed observed after the modification was 43 mph. Obviously, this is a very small reduction in mean velocity. However, if instead of looking at the mean speed as the dependent measure of performance, we observe the actual speed distribution of cars, reproduced in Figure 2.1, we note that the primary effect of the modification was to drastically reduce the percent of cars that approach the curve at speeds greater than 50 mph (this research was conducted prior to the 55 mph speed limit laws). These results also demonstrate that the mere description of the dependent variable as "driver speed" may not be sufficiently accurate to describe the effects of the independent variable.

A different technique of measuring the behavior of unaware

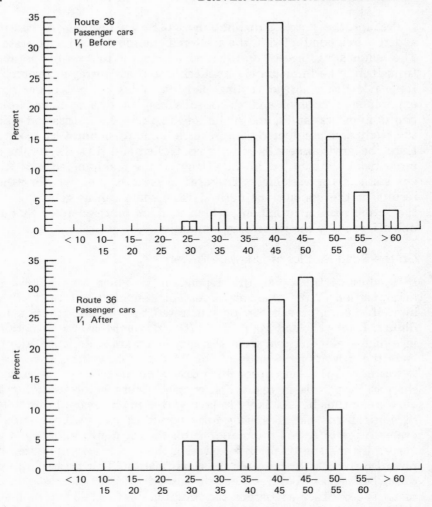

Figure 2.1. Speed distributions of drivers prior to entering a high-accident curve before (top) and after (bottom) a modification in the pavement marking (from shinar et al., 1975).

drivers, originally devised by General Motors researchers (Perkins, 1969) is known as the "traffic conflict" technique. The method involves measuring and tabulating conflicts among vehicles or between vehicles and pedestrians, conflicts that can best be described as "near accidents." These are situations in which an evasive action, such as a sudden braking or swerving, must be made by one or more drivers in order to avoid an accident. The evasive action is typically indicated by either braking or quick lane changing (weaving) — behaviors that can be easily recorded by hidden observers or cameras. The rationale behind this approach is that the same factors that are liable to cause accidents are also liable to cause near accidents. Furthermore, since — as we all know from personal experience — near accidents are much more common than accidents, it should be feasible to be able to predict the accident liability of a given intersection in a relatively short period of time based on observations of traffic conflicts. This hypothesis was, in fact, supported in a recent study conducted in England by Older and Spicer (1976), who demonstrated a high correlation between the number of injury accidents and serious conflicts measured at six intersections. Detailed analysis of the types of conflicts may also provide insights into the problems the drivers encounter and potential countermeasures that could be employed. Thus, signalization at rural intersections has been shown to reduce conflicts between cross-traffic drivers (Baker, 1972).

On-the-Road Studies with Subjects Driving Experimental Vehicles

Common sense would seem to suggest that driver performance might be influenced by a psychological state, visual capabilities, alertness, and the like. Unfortunately, such variables are extremely difficult to observe and measure in the unsuspecting driver. Instead, to evaluate the effect of various experimental manipulations on these variables subjects are asked to drive in an "instrumented vehicle." Perhaps the most widely known instrumented vehicle is the car developed by the Ford Motor Company (Platt, 1970). Sensors, counters, and recorders installed in the car (most of them hidden from the driver's view) are able to measure the driver's steering wheel movements, brake and gas pedal applications, as well as more subtle measures of driver stress, such as the galvanic skin response and heart rate. Some physiological indicators of driver stress (e.g., galvanic skin response) can be measured unobtrusively by simply picking up the body's minute changes in electrical conductivity from the hand gripping the steering wheel. The output of such recordings can be displayed on moving paper tape, as illustrated in Figure 2.2 (from Helander, 1976). In this study the independent variable was driver experience and the dependent variables were those displayed by the trace recording: acceleration, brake application, and electrodermal response (a measure of electrical activity that is associated with stress and risk taking). For each variable, the data obtained from the experienced drivers is displayed above the data obtained from the inexperienced drivers. Information that can be gained from such recordings is also illustrated in this figure. Point A in the figure corresponds to a narrow bridge on the road and is associated with braking behavior and

14

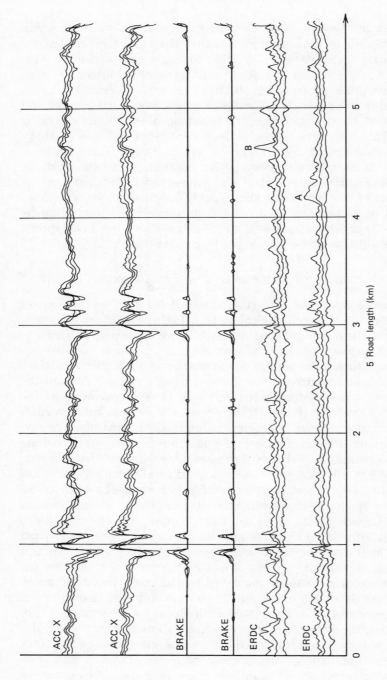

Figure 2.2. Trace recordings of vehicle acceleration (ACCX), brake applications (BRAKE), and electrodermal levels (ERCD) of experienced (upper curves in each pair) and inexperienced drivers (lower curves). In each measure the middle trace recording represents the group's average performance and the lines above and below it and the +1 standard deviations around the mean (from Helander, 1976).

increased electrodermal response of inexperienced drivers. No braking behavior and no increase in the electrodermal response is observed at this point for experienced drivers. On the other hand, point B represents an intersection that was responded to by the experienced drivers with an increase in the electrodermal response and a slight braking action — but appears to have been totally ignored by the inexperienced drivers. With respect to the acceleration it can be easily observed that in crossing the bridge, the variability among the inexperienced drivers was much greater than among the experienced drivers (indicated by the fact that the curves representing +1 standard deviation are closer to the mean for the experienced drivers than for the inexperienced drivers).

Perhaps one of the most potentially informative kinds of behavior that could be observed in driving is that of the driver's visual search behavior. As we view the road ahead our eyes keep darting from one part of the visual scene to another. If we now assume that where a person looks is where his or her attention is (note the use of the phrase "look here" to indicate "pay attention"), then by observing where a driver looks on the road we can infer what information is useful for performing the driving task, or where it might be advisable to place relevant information. Applications of this methodology are discussed in detail in Chapters Three and Six. For the moment, we can simply state that observing a driver's eye movements is feasible through eye movement recording devices such as the one designed by Rockwell, Bhise, and Mourant (1972), illustrated in Figure 2.3. Although the system is quite complex, its output is amazingly simple. By coupling the outputs of TV cameras that monitor the direction at which the eye is pointing (camera 2), and the scene ahead (camera 1 in Figure 2.3) a combined picture is displayed that indicates where on the road the driver looks, for how long, when and for how long does the driver blink, how far do the eyes move between successive looks (known as fixations), and so on. Although it is practically impossible for the driver wearing the special head gear not to be aware that his or her eye movements are being recorded there are several advantages in using eye movement behavior as an indicator of driver's perceptual activity, over other indirect measures. These advantages all have to do with the fact that our visual search is a relatively unconscious process and as such it is relatively bias-free compared to verbal reporting of where a driver looks. Furthermore, subjects in such research are typically not totally aware of the research objectives (e.g., sign-reading behavior) and in any case do not know what a "good" eye movement pattern is. In fact, some of the early research on driver eye movement behavior was specifically directed toward finding what constitutes a good fixation pattern.

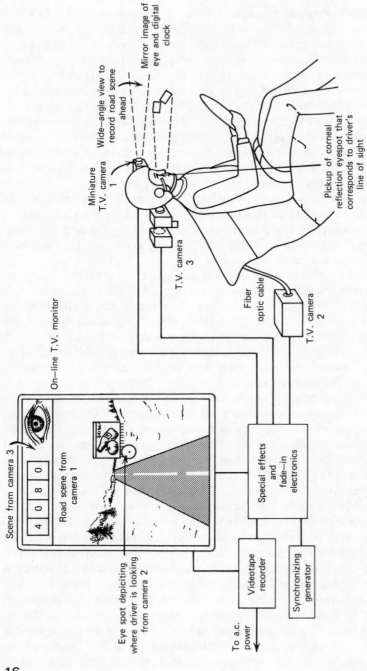

Figure 2.3. A television eye movement recording system for automobile driving (from Rockwell, 1972a).

16

Finally, the recording of eye movements does not require any additional tasks of the subject and therefore eliminates a potential source of artificiality to the driving task. The most recent development in eye movement recording devices is a system that is totally devoid of any headgear. The only clue that the driver has that eye movements are being monitored is the placement of a large camera lens next to the dashboard (Graf & Krebs, 1976). Preliminary studies with this system have been directed at the evaluation of the effects of different headlight beams on the driver's visual search behavior.

The rapid rate at which new electronic systems are being improved and miniaturized will probably make possible the instrumentation of cars with automatic portable units for recording motoric, physiological, and visual aspects of driver behavior. The installation of such systems in, say, rental cars would then make future studies much more realistic since the one important remaining difference between studies involving unsuspecting drivers and studies using volunteer subjects — driver motivation — would disappear.

Laboratory Research: From Driving Simulators to Basic Research

It is safe to say that at least as much of the insight that we have gained about driver behavior comes from research conducted in laboratories as from research conducted on the road. There are several advantages to conducting laboratory research compared to on-the-road research: first, and foremost, it is safe. No one has yet been rushed to a hospital as a result of an "accident" in a driving simulator. Second, the researcher has a much better control of the "environment," which he or she can manipulate almost at will — depending on the sophistication of the experimental apparatus. Third, the cost per data point (observation) is much smaller and the number of observations that can be made in a given period of time is much greater. Finally, only in the sheltered environment of a laboratory are we able to study separate aspects of driving behavior without having to worry about contaminating influences of other factors. In fact, one of the primary objectives of many simulation studies is to isolate a selected number of independent variables for a focused examination.

Simulation or laboratory research is not a panacea. It has its shortcomings: foremost among them is the questionable generalizability of the laboratory findings to the actual highway environment. The limits of the generalizability are due to the fact that the simulation's environment is controlled and the number of variables involved is small; whereas on the actual roadway the number of uncontrolled variables is extremely large, and only a few restricted aspects of the environment are controlled. In order to overcome this shortcoming, it is desirable to make the simulation as close as possible to reality. At a certain point, however, the simulation becomes so complex that it is no longer more cost effective than an actual on-the-road study. Thus, in conducting laboratory research, the first issue that a researcher must resolve concerns "how much simulation?"

Whole-Task Simulator. The whole-task simulator is one in which every attempt is made to create the illusion of driving. This typically constitutes a situation in which a subject sits behind a steering wheel of a stationary car while the visual scene in front of the car "moves" in accordance with the "driver's" gas and brake pedal applications and steering control movements. There are various technical approaches to providing the driver with a realistic visual environment, perhaps the best known of which is the one that employs motion picture displays generated by television or movie projectors. (A comprehensive review of the various types of driving simulators is provided by Hulbert and Wojcik, 1972). Figure 2.4 is a schematic representation of a driving simulator used in the University of California at Los Angeles, Institute of Transportation and Traffic Engineering. In this system, wide-angle projections of two films provide the driver with both the view ahead and the view behind. The "driver's" task is to "drive" on the road projected on the front screen. The movies, incidentally, are originally filmed from a car moving on the road so that the displayed image of the roadway is from the driver's perspective. As the driver accelerates and decelerates in response to the changing roadway, that information is picked up (from the speed of the rear wheel of the vehicle) and conveyed to the two movie projectors that are either speeded up or slowed down, respectively. In addition, whenever the driver turns the steering wheel to the right or left, an experimenter provides a compensatory steering input that rotates the movie projector that provides the view ahead. Thus, the driver's visual environment also changes in accordance with his or her steering inputs. In addition, the system can provide the stimulation of an incline in the road and weather conditions such as rain, wind, and fog. As sophisticated as this system seems, it is still limited to a preprogrammed trip (the one that has been filmed), and as such it does not provide the driver with all the choices and options that exist in the real-world driving. To provide greater freedom "unprogrammed" simulators exist in which the driver, through his or her control actions, manipulates the movement of a TV camera over a scale model of a network of roadways that may contain intersections, winding roads, other traffic, and various levels of visibility (such as day versus night).

An idea of the range of independent variables that can and have

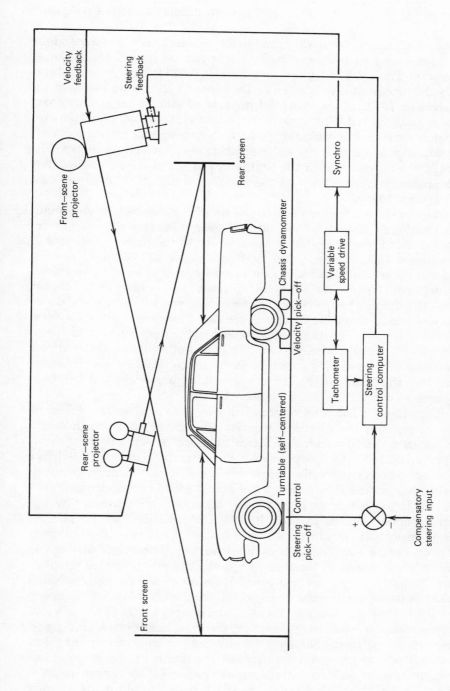

Figure 2.4. A television eye movement recording system for automobile driving (from Hulbert and Wojcik, 1972).

been manipulated in driving simulation research, and the dependent measures used to evaluate their effects can be gained from a brief glance at Table 2.1 (adapted from Barrett, 1971). This table contains only 10 representative studies of the close to 50 studies reviewed by Barrett in 1971. Since then, the number of studies using simulators has at least tripled. The variety of factors studied is truly extensive, ranging from driver variables (e.g., experience, age, stress, alcohol) to situational variables (e.g., overtaking, emergency situations). In fact, the extensive use of the simulator has led to several studies that are primarily concerned with the simulation effects themselves (e.g., Ellingstad, 1970).

The dependent measures that can be picked up by a driving simulator are very similar to the intermediate measures that can be recorded in an instrumented vehicle as far as the driver's behavior is concerned (e.g., brake pedal and gas pedal application, steering control movements, galvanic skin response, and so on), but are more limited with respect to the vehicle's responses to the driver's inputs since the driver's behavior does not produce various vehicle responses such as lateral acceleration (the force that pushes us against the door of the car as we negotiate a high-speed sharp right turn), and longitudinal (forward) acceleration. On the other hand more direct measures of safe driving capabilities are more testable in a simulator than on the road. These include simulated accidents and spinouts (Duggar, Young, Budrose, & Kanter, 1969).

Regardless of the level of sophistication achieved in the design of the simulation, the question remains: Is "driver" performance in a simulator a valid indicator of driver behavior on the road? As previously mentioned, the purpose of a simulator is to provide the driver with an illusion of reality. However, even in the domain of replicating the physical features of the actual roadway environment the success is limited — or in any case unknown (as witnessed by the many "none" entries in the "Fidelity Information" in Table 2.1). More important, however, is the extent to which the psychological environment is simulated: Does the driver enjoy or dislike driving the simulator as much as the real car? Is the driver stressed as much in the simulator as on the real road? Does he or she assume the same risks? Is he or she as concerned with having an accident? The answer to all of these questions is obvious, and consequently the validity of a simulator for evaluating driver on-the-road behavior (according to many experts) is questionable. In any case, there is no dispute that research conducted with the driving simulation has provided many insights toward understanding drivers' responses to various tasks — if not to the total driving task — and has been useful for the training of specific driving skills (Lucas, Heimstra, & Spiegel, 1973).

Table 2.1 A Sample of Automobile Simulator Research Studies

AUTHOR(S)	TYPE OF SIMULATOR	INDEPENDENT VARIABLES	DEPENDENT VARIABLES	FIDELITY INFORMATION
Johnson and Lauer (1937)	Model car on continuous leather belt; fixed base[a]	Effect of one arm on driving errors	Reaction to auditory stimulus; tracking; speed of completing; observational errors	None
Crandall, Duggar, and Fox (1966)	Unprogrammed; point light source; rear projection; fixed base	Experienced and inexperienced drivers	Steering wheel movements; speed; brake; accelerator movement	Visibility; field of view; speed; steering
Barrett, Kobayashi, and Fox (1968)	Unprogrammed; TV projected image; fixed base	Driver behavior during emergency	Speed; brake; steering; lateral and longitudinal position; pedestrian position	Illumination; acceleration; steering; visual angle; field of view; visibility; speed; braking
Crancer, Dillie, Delay, Wallace, and Haykin (1969)	Programmed film; fixed base	Effects of marijuana and alcohol on driving	Errors in speed, steering, brake, accelerator, and signal	None

21

Duggar, Young, Budrose, and Kanter (1969)	Unprogrammed; point light source; rear projection; moving seat	Learning skid control in simulation and real world	Stopping distance; pylons hit; spinouts; number of trials	None
Salvatore (1969)	Programmed film; fixed base	Effects of removing cues on speed judgment	Velocity estimation	None
Beers, Case, and Hulbert (1970)	Programmed film; fixed base	Performance of younger and older drivers	Speed, acceleration; brake; breathing rate; GSR; steering	Field of view
Ellingstad (1970)	Unprogrammed; point light source; rear projection; fixed base	Real world and simulated driving behavior	Steering reversals; speed; speed change	None
Wojcik and Weir (1970)	Unprogrammed; TV projected image; fixed base	Overtaking, passing, and car following in field and simulator	Steering, acceleration; heading rate and angle; forward and lateral velocity	Field of view; sight distance; control functions
Heimstra (1970)	Control element on continuous rubber belt; fixed base	Effect of stress on driving errors	Tracking error; speed; brake reaction time; vigilance	None

From Barrett, 1971.
[a] In this simulator the subject sits outside of the simulator and peers, typically through a small aperture, at a model car on a moving belt.

Part-Task Simulators. Because of the expense associated with whole-task simulators, part-task simulators have been developed to investigate limited aspects of driving behavior. Such simulators may often involve a mockup of a vehicle in which a "driver" sits and responds through steering and foot movements to static displays such as slides. It is then assumed that the various tasks that the subject performs correspond to the information processing and motoric tasks required in actual driving. To a much greater extent than in whole-tasks simulator, the subject involved in such tasks does not have the "experience" of driving, and therefore the validity of the results is even more questionable than in the case of a whole-task simulator.

Most of the knowledge that we have about driving performance that has come out of laboratories, is based on performance in part-task simulators. A part-task simulator is considered appropriate for a given research purpose as long as it can be demonstrated that the specific aspects under investigation are, in fact, a simulation of the real environment in some sense. The utility of such studies can be illustrated with an example of a study conducted by Mihal and Barrett (1976) in which the effect of a personality characteristic (field dependence) on the speed of responding to various highway signs was evaluated. In this study, the subjects were seated in a simulated driver seat with standard controls and asked to make the response indicated by a sign as soon as the sign was perceived. Thus the appropriate response to a "stop" sign would be depression of the brake pedal and the appropriate response to a green right-turn arrow would be to turn the steering wheel to the right. The signs were all displayed via slides in two modes: In one mode, the slide contained only an image of the sign, while in the other mode, the slide contained a photograph of the actual roadway environment in which the sign was embedded. The results indicated that individual differences along the personality characteristic evaluated influenced the reaction time to the picture of the sign embedded in the natural environment but not to the picture of the sign alone. Thus, even though the display was static rather than moving (as it would be in a whole-task simulator), and the subject's responses had no effect on the visual feedback from the environment, the mere inclusion of the complete visual display to which a driver would be responding on the road was sufficient to demonstrate the effect of the independent variable (field dependence) on reaction time.

Basic Research on Driving-Related Component Skills. As we indicated in the introductory chapter, a common view of the driver is that of an information processor who must respond to visual inputs from the environment with control movements that effect the behavior of the vehicle. Much of our knowledge about the driver's information processing capabilities biases and limitations, comes from basic research conducted in areas as diverse as personality, motivation, perception, reaction time, risk taking, and perceptual-motor coordination. Typically, the subject participating in such a study is not even aware of its implications for driving and the researcher conducting the study is more interested in the basic processes he is investigating than in their implications for the driving task.

Obviously the remoteness of basic laboratory research from the actual driving situation makes the direct generalization to on-the-road driving behavior very difficult (or perhaps more accurately, foolhardy). The study just discussed by Mihal and Barrett (1976) illustrates this point. The hypothesis concerning the relationship between field dependence and reaction time to road signs was verified only when the road sign was displayed in the context of the naturalistic roadway environment, and the possibility remains that the relationship may change in the actual dynamic driving environment.

In our discussions of the effects of driver characteristics, capabilities, and limitations on driver behavior, we attempt to integrate studies from all levels of research. It has been suggested that to the extent possible, laboratory research should serve as a prelude to on-the-road research. Very often, however, all our knowledge is based on basic research that has yet to be evaluated (if this is at all possible) in the context of the actual driving environment. You can and should exercise your own judgment as to the applicability of the various results discussed to driver behavior: at one extreme, we can ask whether an effect observed in one state, county, or road site is generalizable to a different roadway environment, and at the other extreme we can speculate as to whether the result obtained in a sheltered laboratory environment is relevant to driving at all!

Observational versus Experimental Studies

All the research methods described above belong to a particular approach known as the experimental approach. This approach involves — as we have already stated — the manipulation of the independent variables. It is, however, extremely difficult to imagine the kind of experimental research methodology that would yield the often-cited (true) statement that alcohol is involved in approximately 50 percent of all fatal crashes. Obviously, no program has ever been devised in which a controlled group of people was given alcohol and then sent out to the road to get killed. Instead, to obtain this kind of information, we use what may be described as an observational technique rather than an experimental one. This technique involves measuring the variations along some variables of interest and then correlating them. Thus, to support the above statement, researchers rely on autopsy reports containing blood alcohol levels of all fatal accident victims, and then compare the number of accidents in which the driver was intoxicated to the number of accidents in which the driver was not intoxicated.

There is a pitfall that must be avoided in interpreting results obtained from observational studies. Since variables are not manipulated but only measured, it is always likely that the relationship that is observed is spurious, that is, it is due to the effect of a confounding variable that may not have been measured at all. To illustrate, concluding from the above statement that "alcohol causes accidents" may be inappropriate since it is possible (though this is not the case) that at any one time half the drivers on the road are intoxicated and thus the drunk driver is really not overinvolved in accidents. Similarly, the fact that young drivers are overinvolved in accidents (per miles driven) does not imply that being young causes accidents. More likely it implies that young people have certain characteristics that cause them to be overinvolved in accidents.

There are two justifications for the use of observational techniques rather than experimental ones: (1) when the dependent measures of interest (e.g., accidents) cannot be readily measured in an experimentally controlled situation and (2) when there exists an a priori reason to suspect a causal relationship between two variables. This a priori reason typically stems from a theory about driver behavior or accident involvement. Thus, in the case of alcohol, the overinvolvement of drunk drivers in accidents essentially corroborates the theoretical formulations of what driver behavior involves (e.g., the processes described in Figure 1.1) and the experimental data that has already been gathered concerning the effect of alcohol on these component processes. Nonetheless, in interpreting results obtained in observational studies, it is always judicious to question the validity of drawing cause-effect conclusions based on these data. A case in point is the above statement that young drivers are overinvolved in accidents, and the explanation that we have just given that this is probably due to attitudinal-, personality-, and information-processing characteristics of young drivers. While this explanation appears to be reasonable and is definitely consistent with much of the experimental data available about young driver behavior, it is also true that young drivers (less than 30 years old) are "greatly overrepresented on the highway during the high-risk nighttime hours. Thus, they are overexposed during these high-risk hours" (U.S. Department of Transportation, 1975, p. 10). While this observation does not necessarily imply that the characteristics of young drivers are not the reasons for the overinvolvement in accidents, at least part of the reason lies in other factors such as exposure to conditions associated with higher accident rates.

Because accidents are essentially the ultimate criterion in evaluating any safety program, the factors that are associated with them are of extreme importance. Unfortunately, since the study of accidents is limited to observational approaches, the cause-and-effect conclusions drawn from such studies can never be as well supported as conclusions drawn from experimental studies. It is also for this reason that relations obtained in observational studies are much more enlightening when they are consistent with, or have been predicted from, experimental studies and theoretical formulations than when they just "appear" in the data. In the latter case the best use that can be made of such relationships is to use them as hypotheses for future studies.

Driver Performance Versus Driver Behavior

Another dichotomy that has implications for evaluating the results obtained in a study is whether it involved voluntary subjects (in either artificial or on-the-road environment) or nonvolunteer drivers unaware of being observed. Studies with voluntary subjects have been characterized by Näätänen and Summala (1976) as dealing with driving performance: typically measuring peak abilities and emphasizing the perceptual motor aspects of driving. In contrast, these researchers believe that the more important aspects of driving — the motivational and cognitive aspects — have been largely ignored. Driving behavior, they claim, is often much more influenced by these aspects than by our perceptual-motor capabilities. Driving performance is probably more indicative of the limits of our capabilities, while driving behavior determines actual behavior somewhere below these limits.

The two approaches may often lead to different conclusions in response to the same problem. An example is in the area of road-sign perception. When sign perception is evaluated under laboratory conditions in which pictures of signs are presented tachistoscopically (i.e., for a brief period of time), the likelihood of correctly identifying the sign is function of the physical attributes of the sign and its similarity to other signs with which it may be confused. Thus, a sign is more conspicuous — and therefore easier to identify correctly — the brighter it is, the simpler its configuration, and the more it differs from other signs (Eklund, 1968). Conspicuity is thus determined by physical characteristics that have a direct relationship to sensory processing. While this sounds intuitively reasonable — or perhaps almost obvious — it appears that a sign perception in actual road condition is mostly governed by motivational-cognitive conditions. In roadside surveys conducted in Sweden, people were stopped immediately after they passed a sign and asked to identify the last sign they saw. The accuracy of reporting the sign under these conditions was as low as 30 percent for some signs and could be described as a function of the "subjective importance" of the sign to the driver, or the amount of risk involved in ignoring the sign (Johansson & Backlund, 1970). After reviewing the road and laboratory studies, Näätänen and Summala (1976), point out that "the most interesting outcome of the (Eklund) study is the fact that the conspicuity rank order of the signs does not at all coincide with their 'registration' order found in the field study" (p. 127).

Returning now to the driver performance versus driver behavior issue, the results of the Eklund (1968) study were obtained under conditions in which every sign was "important," total attention was devoted to it, and the subject actually tried to "do his best" on each trial. When similar criteria of importance of signs were applied in an experimental on-the-road study, subjects, driving a total distance of 160 miles on a two-lane road with heavy traffic, missed on the average only 3 percent of the 581 traffic signs (Summala and Näätänen, 1974). What was therefore measured in both studies is "performance" rather than behavior. Performance criteria are probably most relevant under conditions of reduced visibility (threshold conditions) in which the driver is in fact trying to identify the sign. However, in daylight and under normal driving conditions, Johansson and Backlund's (1970) results suggest that sign visibility is sufficiently high (suprathreshold) so that psychophysical concepts such as conspicuity are overridden by motivational factors that determine the actual driver behavior.

The purpose of this somewhat lengthy discussion of the distinction between driver behavior and performance is not to show that driver performance is irrelevant, but to demonstrate that the conditions under which it is relevant may be more restricted than at first realized. Thus it is likely that the concept of conspicuity may be more relevant to sign perception at night driving when visibility is degraded, the driver visual search is more concentrated on the road, and the driver visual acuity is more critical to the safe driving task, than during most daylight driving conditions.

SUMMARY

This chapter introduced some of the common methodologies, concepts, and problems associated with the study of driver behavior. A distinction was made between the independent variables that are manipulated by the experimenter and the dependent variables, on which we observe the effects of the independent variables. The need to be aware of the presence of any confounding variables that may give rise to spurious relationships was also stressed.

Research methodologies can be described as a continuum ranging from the strictly applied to the basic. Driving, being an applied domain of human behavior, is therefore studied with a wide range of approaches from laboratory experiments to on-the-road, unobtrusive, observations of drivers. One of the more popular approaches, that lies somewhere between the two extremes, is the simulation study that affords many of the conveniences of the laboratory and some of the reality of the actual roadway environment. The simulation is therefore an attempt to make the results more valid for application purposes without sacrificing the capability to isolate a few independent variables of interest.

Most research can be described as being either experimental or observational. The key difference between the two is that in experimental research the researcher can exercise control of the independent variables and manipulate them, whereas in the observational study they must simply be observed. Consequently, experimental research generally measures cause-and-effect relationships while observational research yields associations and correlations between variables, and its conclusions concerning cause and effect weaker.

An issue specific to studying driver behavior centers around the problem of the driver's awareness of being studied or observed. Much of the research on driving has been conducted on volunteer subjects, and can be said to have measured drivers' capabilities (labeled here as driver performance) under conditions likely to generate best performance instead of driver behavior as it actually occurs on the road. The distinction between the two is important since driver behavior and driver performance may be completely different even when responding to the same thing (e.g., stop light).

THREE

INDIVIDUAL DIFFERENCES: PERSONALITY CHARACTERISTICS, TEMPORARY IMPAIRMENTS, AND RELEVANT CAPABILITIES

The search for driver characteristics that can distinguish the safe driver from what we often call others (never ourselves) the "nut behind the wheel" is based on the desire to identify the "problem driver." Insurance companies, which for obvious reasons are more concerned with staying in business than with satisfying scientific curiosity, identify problem drivers in relation to demographic variables that in the past have been shown to be related to accident involvement. These variables are often not of the kind that allow the drivers any freedom in improving their standing (e.g., age and sex). While these variables are repeatedly found to be related to accident involvment, it is hard to see how they can be viewed as independent variables that *cause* accidents.

The search for driver characteristics that may actually *affect* or *influence* driving behavior has generated a long list of such factors. Unfortunately these cannot simply be listed since they are often interrelated and difficult to isolate experimentally. To illustrate, one would expect that driving performance improves with experience and level of driving skill, and this may be reflected in safer driver behavior and a lower accident rate. Yet in a comprehensive study in which registered race drivers in the states of Florida, New York, and Texas were compared to "normal" drivers in the same states, the race drivers had a significantly higher number of both accidents and violations (Williams & O'Neill, 1974). It is possible that this result — which, incidentally, runs counter to the popular myth that race car drivers are safer drivers — is due to the fact that these highly skilled drivers are also used to taking high risks that most drivers do not take. These risks can become particularly hazardous when assumed in the presence of less skillful (i.e., nonracing) drivers.

Nonetheless, to simplify the presentation, the various characteristics are described individually, although interactions between various factors are occasionally pointed out.

DRIVER PERSONALITY

Personality is a hypothetical construct that implies the existence of a relatively enduring set of characteristics that influences the way a person behaves in different situations. As such it is a rather broad term that is difficult to apply directly to applied research, such as driving research. Nonetheless, certain characteristics, which are relatively stable for a given person but along which people tend to differ from each other, have been studied in relation to driving and accident involvement. The purpose of the discussion below is not to be exhaustive but to illustrate the rationale, study approach, and results of studies in three areas that can be considered a part of the broad definition of personality: personal maladjustment, social maladjustment, and perceptual style and a related concept known as accident proneness.

Accident Proneness

The term accident proneness was first used to describe an early statistical phenomenon noted by Greenwood and Woods (1919) in their study of the distribution of accidents among women working in a munitions factory. Basically they found that some women had many accidents while others had none. Thus it was felt that if we could only identify accident-prone people we could reduce accidents in general and "protect" these people from themselves in particular. While the accident-prone concept was very appealing — so much so that it became a synonym of clumsy — its validity, and therefore its usefulness, turned out to be almost nil. First, with respect to driving accidents, it was found that although at any given period a minority of the population may have the majority of accidents, if these people were to be removed from the driving population, that would have almost no impact on accidents in any subsequent period. Thus, the high-accident drivers at one period of time are not the same ones who are high-accident in another period (Forbes, 1939). Second, accident proneness explains nothing. There still remains the problem of finding out what makes some people accident prone — if such a trait exits at all. In a recent review of the role of personality factors in highway accidents McGuire (1976) concluded that "certain people *are* accident-prone, but sometimes only for short periods of time, and that there are others who are accident prone over extended periods of time, perhaps for several years or most of their remaining lifetime. Furthermore, different persons are accident-prone for different reasons, and the same person may move in and out of a state of accident-proneness each time because of different circumstances" (p. 439). What remains, then, is to find the *reasons* that may make a person accident prone and the *times* when a person is likely to be overinvolved in accidents. A partial answer to these questions is provided by studies that have investigated the relationship between accident involvement and social and personal maladjustment.

Social Maladjustment

For a system as complex as our highway transportation system to operate properly, it is necessary that all drivers follow the same rules. In fact, many accidents happen when one or more drivers fail to do so. Violations like speeding and failing to stop at stop signs are often the causes of collisions. Of interest here is the answer to the following question: Can people who violate the traffic laws and norms be identified on the basis of a more general characteristic, such as inadequate adjustment to society's norms in other areas? In one of the earliest investigations in this area, Tillmann and Hobbs (1949) published, in the *American Journal of Psychiatry*, the results of a study comparing 96 taxi drivers who had four or more accidents to 100 taxi drivers matched for age and sex without any previous accidents. The results, reproduced in Table 3.1 indicated that accident repeaters were more likely to have a history of involvement with criminal

Table 3.1 Relative Frequency of Contact with Social Agencies for High-Accident and Accident-Free Taxi Drivers (in percent)

	Adult Court	Juvenile Court	Public Health	Social Service	Credit Bureau	At Least One Agency
High-accident taxi drivers	34	17	14	18	34	66
Accident-free taxi drivers	1	1	0	1	6	9

Adapted from Tillmann and Hobbs, 1949.

courts, social service, public health agencies, and credit bureaus than accident-free drivers. Tillmann and Hobbs concluded that "It would appear that the driving hazards and the high accident record are simply one manifestation of a method of living that has been demonstrated in their personal lives. Truly it may be said that a man drives as he lives. If his personal life is marked by caution, tolerance, foresight, and consideration for others, then he would drive in the same manner. If his personal life is devoid of these desirable characteristics then his driving will be characterized by aggressiveness, and over a long period of time he will have a much higher accident rate than his stable companion" (p. 329).

Somewhat similar results were obtained in more recent studies for other groups of driver populations, all indicating that a history of antisocial behavior is related — although not necessarily causal — to driving behavior (See McGuire, 1976, for a review).

Perhaps the most extreme form of support for Tillmann and Hobbs' notion that a person "drives as he lives" comes from a recent study by Haviland and Wiseman (1974) who compared the driving records of 114 jailed criminals with those of the normal population. The criminal driver was found to have, on the average, 3.25 as many citations for traffic violations, and be involved in 19.5 as many fatal accidents as the average noncriminal driver. Furthermore, "criminals who were involved in major traffic offenses were likely to have been involved in major crime and those involved in minor traffic offenses in minor crime, (suggesting that) the degree of an individual's deviation from societal norms is similar in divergent areas" (p. 432). Not noted by Haviland and Wiseman, but obviously of great relevance, is whether or not the traffic offenses were independent of the crimes for which these people were convicted. Obviously, for a person who has just committed an armed robbery, speeding the wrong way in a one-way street and crossing red traffic signals in order to flee from police is almost a "reasonable" and adaptive thing to do.

Table 3.2

Selected questions used to measure social maladjustment, that were found to be significant correlates of accident involvement (adapted from Mayer and Treat, 1977).

- How many times have you moved from one residence to another in the past five years? How long have you lived at the present address?

- Are you registered to vote? How many times have you voted in the last four years?

- How active a member are you (from being a member to holding office) in church? A social club? A union? A political party? A sports team?

- While in school how often did you play hooky? Wanted to drop out? Received awards? Was suspended? Went out on dates? Was a loner?

- Were you a regular cigarette smoker before the age of 17? Did you fail one or more grades before grade 8? Were you ever arrested for something other than driving? Did you run away from home as a child?

- Do you feel that:
  Your way of doing things is apt to be misunderstood by others?
  You have often gone against your parents' wishes?
  It is pretty easy for people to win arguments with you?
  Even the idea of giving a talk in public makes you afraid?

The relative contribution of various personality characteristics to accident involvement was most recently explored in a study by Mayer and Treat (1977). In this study a battery of questions and tests, pertaining to 20 personality characteristics previously hypothesized to be related to driving behavior, was administered to a sample of students divided into two groups: accident-free (control) group and with three or more accidents during the past three years (accident) group. The two groups were matched in terms of their age, sex, and average annual mileage, so that the higher accident rate could not be an artifact of these variables. Using a statistical procedure known as discriminant analysis they found that of the six tests that best distinguished the control group from the accident group, five measured social maladjustment. These tests indicated that the accident group drivers were (in that order) poorer in their citizenship, had more antisocial tendencies had a more negativistic attitude, attributed responsibility and control for events to external sources (known as external locus of control), and had a more negative schooling experience (school socialization). Selected items representing these scales are presented in Table 3.2. In a follow-up study by the same authors the discriminant function (on the basis of which one may predict accident involvement from the personality charac-

Table 3.3 Frequencies of Personal Maladjustment Indicators for Drivers Killed in Accidents vs. Control-Matched Drivers (in percent)

	Interpersonal Problem	Loss of a Dear One	Job Problems	Financial Problems	At Least One Stress
Fatalities	36	10	31	16	58
Control	8	4	5	7	16

Combined data from Selzer, Rogers, and Kern, 1968, and Brown and Bohnert, 1968.

teristics) was shown to be sufficiently valid to correctly assign 12 out of 14 new subjects into accident-involved and accident-free groups.

In Mayer and Treat's (1977) study all the subjects were young college students, and so one might question the applicability of their results to the general driving population. However in a recently completed detailed study of 310 fatal and injury-producing accidents, Schmidt, Shaffer, Zlotowitz, and Fisher (1976) reached similar conclusions concerning the role of social maladjustment characteristics in accident involvement. Furthermore, they found that whether the driver possessed these characteristics or not did not correlate with sociodemographic variables such as age, positive blood alcohol levels, or whether or not the driver was killed.

If poor social maladjustment is characteristic of the "bad" driver, what characterizes the "good" accident free driver? A highly detailed study of six truck drivers who had received the National Safety Council Safe Driving Award for 20 years or more found that these drivers did not differ from the average driver in their IQ or physical capabilities but were much more "loyal, dependable, sober, saving and cautious husbands and fathers, as well as dependable, loyal and hard-working employees" (Malfetti & Fine, 1962, p. 6). These drivers were also considerate of others and unagressive both off the road as well as on the road. This was manifested even in the way they entered elevators: letting everyone else get in first and then looking behind them (to see if anyone else is coming) before stepping in themselves. This study together with the studies of high accident involvement strongly support Tillmann's original claim that "a man drives as he lives," driving simply being another manifestation of the style of interacting with other people.

Personal Maladjustment

Many of us have experienced the urge to "really step on the gas" when we are angry, "drive around" when we are depressed, or drive dangerously just to impress someone. This tendency to use driving as

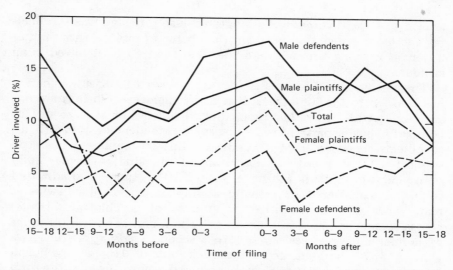

Figure 3.1. Percentage of drivers involved in accidents and violations before and after filing for divorce (from McMurray, 1970).

a coping mechanism for personal problems is obviously not a healthy one. However, acknowledging the existence of such relationships, leads to the hypothesis that people under personal stress are likely to have dangerous driving habits and as a result be involved in more accidents. This hypothesis was verified by several studies which compared the accident rates of people going through a difficult period in their lives versus "normal" people. Table 3.3 illustrates the difference in fatalities in highway accidents between people under stress and a control group for various stressful situations.

The effects of divorce on accident involvement have received close attention — perhaps because it's an experience that is being shared by more and more people. The effects of divorce are relatively easy to evaluate through an examination at the time pattern of accidents relative to the divorce date. One such plot is illustrated in Figure 3.1 (from McMurray, 1970). This study was conducted on 410 persons who filed for divorce in the State of Washington. Both the graphs and the statistical analyses clearly indicated that during the year of the divorce — from six months before to six months after filing for the divorce — the percentage of drivers involved in accidents was greater than average. A similar pattern was obtained when the dependent variable was violations rather than accidents. Note that the time of greatest accident (and violation) involvement is in the three months following the filing for divorce. It is probably not just coincidental that the minimum elapsed time between the filing and the granting of the divorce in Washington is also three months — reflecting the close association between the degree of internal turmoil that a person is going through, and the likelihood to be involved in an accident.

The notion that life stresses may be reflected in driving behavior has also led to the hypothesis that many highway collisions are not accidents at all but rather premeditated suicides or at least an outcome of behavior patterns reflecting suicidal tendencies. It is difficult to objectively assess such a hypothesis but the argument has been supported by at least three observational-type studies. In one study of psychiatric patients (Selzer & Payne, 1962) those who admitted to having considered or actually attempted suicide, had twice as many accidents as a control group (also of psychiatric patients) whose socioeconomic level, age distribution, and exposure (in terms of annual mileage) was similar. In a second study (by Crancer & Quiring, 1970) accident and violation records of 915 persons hospitalized for suicidal gestures were compared against those of the total driving population registered in the same county. The results were striking: the suicidal patients had an 81 percent higher accident rate and 146 percent higher violation rate. A closer look at the kind of violations in which the suicidal patients were involved was also enlightening. It revealed an overinvolvement in "drunken driving, reckless driving, driving while suspended, and negligent driving" and an underinvolvement in speeding and improper turns. This is a pattern of behavior that clearly supports the correlation between accident involvement and personal problems, rather than a relationship between accident involvement and a pervasive tendency to violate the specific traffic laws.

Finally, the most compelling evidence that some people resort to highway collisions in order to commit suicide comes from a very recent study by Phillips (1977) who demonstrated first that the number of suicides increases sharply after a suicide is publicized by newspapers, and the increase is related to the amount of publicity. Second, and more important for our discussion, a similar increase — by as much as 35 percent — was observed in California highway fatalities three days after well-publicized suicide stories. The explanation for this rise in fatalities, according to Phillips, is the imitative nature of suicides: people with suicidal tendencies are more likely to actually commit suicide after reading about one. The rise in highway fatalities simply reflects one method.

The observational (versus experimental) nature of these three studies and the awareness that many variables in these studies remained uncontrolled requires that caution be applied — and more

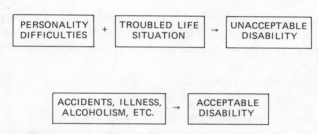

Figure 3.2.   The role of personal maladjustment in accident involvement (adopted from Hirschfeld & Behan, 1966).

studies be conducted — before the *causal* relationship between suicidal tendencies and deviant driving behavior can be stated unequivocally.

Notwithstanding the final qualification, if some people do tend to resort to highway collisions as means of committing suicide, the question is then why. A rational (although being rational may be irrelevant in this context) explanation is that within our social norms, where suicide is euphemistically called a "tragic accident," death in a car crash allows the driver an honorable way out, without embarrassing the family or forfeiting their insurance compensation. A somewhat Freudian explanation has been offered by Hirschfeld and Behan (1966) who suggested that self-destruction as a causal factor in highway accidents may be described by the model presented in Figure 3.2. According to this model the experience of personality difficulties coupled with a troubled life situation leads to a disability that is socially (and possibly personally) unacceptable. However this disability can be made acceptable — and therefore more tolerable — if it can be blamed on an accident or physical illness, a cause that is perceived as definitely outside the control of the person. According to this model, therefore, the goal of the person is not self-destruction, but some degree of physical disablement that — paradoxically — would make life easier. Unfortunately using the car to achieve this goal often ends up in an "overkill."

Using Driving as a Means to Satisfy Nondriving Needs

Clem began screaming into the roaring wind, "Go ahead! Kill us, you bastard! I dare you to!" Gradually Clem's hysteria spread itself to me, and I was barely able to prevent myself from joining in screaming and jeering at the gods. I was far too caught up in the thrill of the fatal high speed, and the wind howling in my bouffant hairdo lashing my face, to worry about

*the likelihood of being smeared all across the highway like
peanut butter on bread. Or to question the mental make-up
of the boy to whom I was entrusting my precious and pre-
carious life.*
(From Kinflicks *by Alther, 1975, p. 135.)*

While highway designers and traffic engineers keep trying to improve roadways so that they can serve their stated objective — moving people and goods — more quickly and safely, many people are
on the road for totally different reasons. It appears that driving provides us with the opportunity to satisfy needs such as excitement,
risk, power, and status. In this light, it is very reasonable to accept
Hirshfield and Behan's model of the suicidal driver as just another
means of using driving as a way to satisfy one's needs for acceptable
disabilities.

There are various indications that our driving behavior is influenced by nontransporting motives. To begin with, the desire to "feel
the wind" — perhaps not as extremely as in the above quote from
Alther's book — is common to most of us. Second, automobile advertisements sell cars on the basis of their power (who really needs it
on our crowded urban highways and new speed limits?), "sexy"
look, "slim and elegant contours," and "the people who drive" it.
Not too long ago, car manufacturers tried to argue that bumpers are
a "design feature" of a car rather than a safety feature that should
conform to government standards. Third, there is some psychological
research to support the notion that people's unconscious attitudes
toward driving are radically different from their overtly stated concerns and attitudes.

The above-mentioned research was conducted by Black (1966) in
England when car design concepts were undergoing some radical
changes. His subjects were a cross section of people of different ages
and different professions. Common to all of them was the fact that
they were suitable and willing hypnotic subjects. When interviewed
consciously they thought that safety was an important issue in car
design and wearing safety belts was a "good thing." Accidents were a
source of anxiety and were most often blamed on the driver — particularly the speeding driver. However, when interviewed under hypno-
sis, a totally different picture emerged: the spontaneous comments
hardly ever referred to the "technical details of design," the desired
dream car was one that was "sleek, fast and low" and "looked good
in town." Road safety was not an important issue, and the blame for
accidents was shifted to the slow driver. Wearing safety belts was
considered "sissy" and the greatest virtues of the car were the feel-

ings of "freedom, power, a sense of superiority, a feeling of being master of it all" (Black, 1966, pp. 64-66).

Perceptual Style

People vary in the way they perceive the world and objects that surround them. One dimension along which this variation has been explored is the degree of independence with which they can perceive an object relative to its surrounding. This ability to *disembed* a perceptual target from its surrounding underlies the skill that is needed in the children's puzzles that require finding "the bird in the tree." A person who can easily locate a target independently of the background in which it is embedded is labeled field independent while a person who has difficulties ignoring the context in order to perceive the target is labeled as field dependent. The theoretical concept and a formal psychological test to measure the degree of field dependence that a person possesses have been developed by Witkin and his associates (Witkin et al., 1954). The test — called the Embedded Figures Test — is similar to a children's puzzle in that it requires the subject to identify a relatively simple target (e.g., "cross" sign) embedded in a complex pattern of lines. The time it takes the subject to disembed a set of targets is then used as the measure of the degree of field dependence.

In the roadway environment an occluded sign, an obscured car moving out of a row of parked cars, or a child jumping off the curb may often constitute such an "embedded figure." It is therefore reasonable to suspect that people who have difficulties in disembedding a target from its background may encounter problems in driving. To test this hypothesis several researchers administered the Embedded Figures Test to high- and low-accident drivers and found that low-accident drivers are indeed more field independent (i.e., identify the embedded figures fast) while high-accident drivers are more field dependent (i.e., need more time to identify the embedded figures) (see Goodenough, 1976, for a review). The specific driver performance measures underlying the increased accident involvement of field dependent drivers may be the longer times they require to recognize developing hazards and partially obscured (or "camouflaged") signals. These effects were demonstrated in two simulation studies. In one study (Barrett, Thornton, and Cabe, 1969) a dummy pedestrian moved into the driver's path from behind a shed and the driver's response was measured. The field-dependent subject "struck" the pedestrian more often, braked later, and decelerated more slowly than the field-independent driver. In the second study (briefly described in Chapter 2), field-dependent drivers were found to have longer reaction times to road signs or signals than field-independent drivers, but only when the signs and signals were presented in their natural context (Mihal & Barrett, 1976).

To understand why the field-dependent drivers have these difficulties, Shinar, McDowell, Rackoff, and Rockwell (1977) in two experiments measured how field-dependent drivers actually scan the roadway compared to field-independent drivers. Using the eye movement recording system depicted in Figure 2.3, they found that "the more field-dependent a driver is, the longer his eye fixation durations, indicating longer time necessary to pick up relevant information; and more importantly the less adaptive the eye fixation pattern." This lack of adaptivity in surveilling the relevant areas of the visual field was also demonstrated in an actual car-following driving task (Olson, 1974). In this study the subject drove the car behind two other cars. Whenever the first car slowed, the second car did too (in order to avoid a collision), and so did the subject in the third car whose braking reaction time was measured. When the lead car was not visible no difference in reaction time was observed between the field-independent and field-dependent subjects. However, when the lead car was in view, field-independent subjects braked sooner than field-dependent subjects. Thus field-independent subjects were apparently able to look at and respond to the lead car while field-dependent subjects were unable to utilize information beyond the very compelling view of the car immediately in front of them. Note that in this study, as well as in the study by Mihal and Barrett (1976), the difference in performance capabilities appeared only in the context of the total relevant visual field. In its absence, no difference in information processing time (as measured by reaction time) was observed between the two groups of subjects.

Given the apparent handicap of being field dependent, is a person doomed to be a higher accident risk? If the reduced visual search efficiency of field-dependent drivers is the reason for their poorer performance, rather than just another by-product of being field dependent, then it may be possible to *train* people to improve their visual search behavior and thus increase their safety.

TEMPORARY IMPAIRMENTS

While our personality, like our shadow, is always with us, we do not always enter the driver's seat with the same capacities. We may be only half awake in the morning or half asleep driving late at night. We may be relaxed or tense, feeling high or low, sober, or (unfortunately all too often) intoxicated. In our highly mobile society, in which the average licensed driver in America drives 22.4 miles every week, people are very reluctant to let driving get in the way of their other activities. And so, as a result, many of us often drive while so tired as to barely be able to keep our eyes open, so drunk as to barely be able to walk, so upset or preoccupied as to barely be able to concentrate, and so on. Under all these conditions, are we still the same drivers? The answer is a qualified no. Within limits, we can compensate for various deficiencies by harnessing inner resources — but at a cost. Thus, when tired we often actually *feel* the effort that goes into just keeping our eyes open, wary of letting a blink turn into a wink.

How far can we still "push" ourselves? What are our limits? How is our driving affected when we exceed them? In this section we examine the two most common conditions of impairments, fatigue and alcohol intoxication, and a rapidly rising phenomenon of driving while under the influence of one drug or another, often under the influence of marijuana.

Fatigue

I was returning from a long drive . . . I was nodding out. Dozing off, you know, and I thought once, you know, should I stop or should I keep going? And I thought, well, I'm close to home, I was within five miles, and I rolled my window down and turned the tape player up real loud and shut the heat off. And it was a pretty chilly night, and I thought that would do it, and it did; and the closer I got to home, the colder I got; so I rolled the window up and turned the tape player down and I was within about a half a mile from my house, and then that is just about the last thing I remember until I hit the tree.
(Indiana University In-Depth Accident Case Report #260, 1975.)

The above quotation, from an interview with a driver following his accident, is self-explanatory. Falling asleep while driving is the most extreme end result of fatigue. However, the effect of fatigue on driver behavior is not a simple two-step process in which we are fully alert at one moment, and then totally oblivious to the visual environment the next. The effects of fatigue on driving behavior can be observed in experimental situations long before the driver starts dozing. In observing the eye movements of drivers who drove continuously for 9 hours after having gone without any sleep in the previous 24 hours, Kaluger and Smith (1970) found that the fatigued drivers exhibited a less-responsive eye movement pattern. Instead of looking way ahead down the road and monitoring other vehicles and signs, the fatigued drivers tended to fixate their gaze on the right road edge as if totally absorbed in the task of keeping the car within the lane. This conclusion is consistent with Safford and Rockwell's (1967) findings, that drivers who have been continuously driving for 24 hours were unable to do a satisfactory job of both maintaining a constant speed and a constant position within the lane. The drivers could do either one by itself, but could not perform both tasks simultaneously. Using the driving simulator described in Figure 2.3 Hulbert (1972) found that, when requested to "drive" after 24 hours without sleep, people actually started to doze off within 60 minutes.

The experience of dozing at the wheel has been shared by all too many drivers. Why do we experience fatigue while driving "effortlessly" in modern cars? The answer appears to be that driving, while it may not require excessive muscular work, does require mental work (Wyss, 1971). In the previously mentioned study on sign perception by Summala and Näätänen (1974), even though the accuracy of sign perception was very high, the drivers missed progressively more signs as they drove over the 160 miles route. Furthermore, by the time they finished the task most of them complained of severe fatigue.

To understand the effects of fatigue on driving, an analogy is often used in which driving is viewed as a vigilance task — a task requiring continuous monitoring of a display for an infrequently occurring target. In such laboratory tasks the consistent result is that "performance in most tasks can be maintained for a few minutes in face of quite severe loss of sleep, but as soon as the duration of a repetitive task is extended to half an hour or more it seems impossible to sustain concentration" (Wilkinson, 1969, p. 261). All of these tasks can be described as extremely boring (as sometimes driving is). In contrast when involved in complex and interesting work people have been known to perform without any apparent decrements for after as many as 60 hours of sleep deprivation (Wilkinson, 1964). Where do the automobile driving tasks fall relative to these two extreme situations? The key to the answer appears to be the level of attention that we allocate to the driving task. Under normal driving situations, despite alarming accident statistics, most drivers do not feel at risk and do not allocate all their attentional capacities to the driving task (hence, when they do, as in Näätänen and Summala's study, they feel very fatigued). As a result, some performance degradations can be observed in experimental road studies, and a small but significant percent of the highway accidents can be attributed to fatigue. Yet the possibility of an accident is probably a sufficient motivator to cause drivers to allocate more attention to driving on the road than to a meaningless target in a vigilance task (or, for that matter, to the road in a simulator).

For practical purposes, the issues of greatest interest are when we become fatigued, and how often we need to take breaks in our driving. Because of the key role of motivation, there are no simple answers to these questions. Fortunately, as drivers, we are often aware of the early signs of fatigue in the form of lapses in attention. Other behaviors that have been shown to precede the final stage of actually falling asleep are (Hulbert, 1972):

1. Longer and delayed deceleration reactions in response to the changing road demands.
2. Fewer steering corrections.
3. Reduced galvanic skin response (GSR) to emerging traffic events.
4. More body movements such as rubbing the face, closing the eyes, and stretching.

If all of these signs do not cue us to our critically reduced level of attention, then we might still be able to recover as we catch ourselves drifting of the road into the shoulders.

There is only one sure way to overcome the effect of fatigue — take a nap. When this is unrealistic, the driver can energize himself or herself by continuously shifting his or her eyes from one side of the road to the other, chewing gum, by singing, by opening windows to let fresh air come in, and the like. The benefits of stimulants such as amphetamines and caffeine have been demonstrated in vigilance tasks and in tracking tasks (Sanders and Bunt, 1971). Both tasks are assumed to involve processes common to driving. However, these drugs also have side effects, and on the road the benefits of these drugs still remain to be determined. The potential danger in excessive use of stimulants — that of making the driver agitated — certainly merits consideration. In any case, when used in moderation the effect of coffee is probably positive, since, as Rodger (1956) comments, it involves both stops to get it and then later stops to get rid of it . . . .

Alcohol

It is almost impossible to discuss the effects of alcohol on driving without appearing to be sermonizing. Various studies (see Buttigliere, Brunse, & Case, 1972, for a review) have shown that alcohol is the most common single factor involved in fatal accidents, contributing to perhaps up to 50 percent of the highway fatalities. The awareness of alcohol creating a serious safety problem in the context of driving

Table 3.4 Estimating the Blood Alcohol Level (BAL) on the Basis of Number of Drinks Ingested and Driver's Weight

	BODY WEIGHT IN POUNDS								
DRINKS	100	120	140	160	180	200	220	240	IMPAIRMENT
1	0.04	0.03	0.03	0.02	0.02	0.02	0.02	0.02	
2	0.08	0.06	0.05	0.05	0.04	0.04	0.03	0.03	Rarely
3	0.11	0.09	0.08	0.07	0.05	0.06	0.05	0.05	
4	0.15	0.12	0.11	0.09	0.08	0.08	0.07	0.06	
5	0.19	0.16	0.13	0.12	0.11	0.09	0.09	0.08	Possibly
6	0.23	0.19	0.16	0.14	0.13	0.11	0.10	0.09	
7	0.26	0.22	0.19	0.16	0.15	0.13	0.12	0.11	
8	0.30	0.25	0.21	0.19	0.17	0.15	0.14	0.13	Definitely
9	0.34	0.28	0.24	0.21	0.19	0.17	0.15	0.14	
10	0.38	0.31	0.27	0.23	0.21	0.19	0.17	0.16	

Subtract 0.01 percent for each 40 minutes of drinking. One drink is 1 ounce of liquor, 12 ounces of beer, or a 3.5-ounce glass of wine.

Source: Adapted from *Indiana's Driver Manual.* Indiana Bureau of Motor Vehicles, November, 1974.

has been recorded as early as 1904, when in an analysis of 25 fatal accidents, 19 of the drivers were found to have ingested alcohol within an hour of the accident. At the time, it was predicted that "accidents would increase dramatically and that only total abstainers would be permitted to drive" (Buttigliere et al., 1972). Unfortunately, only the first of the two predictions has materialized.

As the most commonly used tranquilizer, alcohol affects the central nervous system, and its effect on performance is directly proportional to the level of alcohol present in the blood system. This direct relationship between the amount of alcohol in the blood and the deterioration of driving related perceptual-motor capabilities, has led many states to legislate that people having a blood alcohol level (BAL) of 0.10 percent or greater be considered as legally drunk. This figure may be meaningless to most people until they realize that it takes very little alcohol to get to that level. To satisfy your own curiosity, look at Table 3.4, from which you might note that if you are an average person, weighing approximately 160 pounds, you need only five drinks or five cans of beer to become legally drunk and behaviorally unsafe on the road.

Note that there is nothing magical about the 0.10 BAL; only the convincing empirical fact that of the alcohol-related highway fatalities, approximately 80 percent have a BAL of 0.10 or higher (U. S. Department of Transportation, 1972). Also, in a landmark study conducted in Grand Rapids, Michigan, Borkenstein, Crowther, Shumate, Ziel, and Zylman (1964) compared the BALs of 5985 accident involved drivers with the BALs of a control group of 7590 drivers. Their results indicated that more accident involved drivers had BALs greater than 0.08 percent than control drivers. From 0.00 to 0.08 percent BAL the frequency of each alcohol level was similar for the two groups, or slightly higher for the control group. However, in another part of the same study, Borkenstein et al. (1964) compared the BALs of at-fault and not-at-fault drivers involved in multiple-vehicle accidents. They found that drivers with BALs less than 0.05 percent were as likely (or less likely) to *cause* an accident as sober drivers. However, with 0.06 percent BAL, the probability of causing an accident was twice as high as with 0.00 percent and at 0.10 percent BAL the likelihood of causing an accident was six to seven times higher than with 0.00 percent BAL.

As the BAL increases, more and more driving-related functions are impaired, beginning with visual and perceptual judgment abilities at low alcohol levels, through cognitive decision making capabilities at intermediate levels, and ending with gross motor incoordination at levels 0.15 or higher. In the driving task, all of these abilities interact to impair the driver's performance (Levine, Kramer, & Levine, 1975). Thus, in a driving simulator, Jex, DiMarco, and Wade (1974) were able to demonstrate that for moderate drinkers, the probability of inadvertent lane crossing increased from .0001 when sober to 0.05 with BAL = 0.11 percent — an increase by 500 fold! How these results can be transferred to the actual road situation is demonstrated in Figure 3.3.

Other driving impairments that have been observed for people with BAL $\geq$ 0.10 include poor detection of roadway signs in a simulator (Jex et al., 1974), and in actual nighttime driving (Hicks, 1976); misjudgment of speed and distance, and running signal lights and stop signs. These reduced judgmental and perceptual capabilities are eventually manifested in the kind of accidents that intoxicated drivers have. These are typically nighttime (when more people are drunk) single-car accidents in which the driver runs the car off the road, overturns it, or strikes a fixed object (U. S. Department of Transportation, 1975) — hardly the kind of accident for which "the other driver" can be blamed.

Another effect of alcohol, that is highly relevant to driving, has been labeled as "tunnel vision" effect — the narrowing of the field of view to objects directly ahead of the driver. In light of the importance of peripheral vision (to be discussed later) this reduction in the effective size of the peripheral visual field is very critical. Furthermore, it appears that the inability to detect peripheral targets is

After one drink

After three drinks

After five drinks

Figure 3.3. Loss in vehicular control due to alcohol. The drivers in these pictures are all professional, and as such are probably better drivers than most people. But, after three drinks they could no longer drive safely. After five drinks, each lost the ability to think clearly, see well, and control the car. They were able to walk and talk well enough, but they had a hard time driving.

aggravated by alcohol only in the presence of attention demanding events that occur simultaneously in the central visual field (Moskowitz & Sharma, 1974). Thus alcohol reduces our ability to effectively allocate our attention — something that is constantly required in driving. This is also manifested in the change in the way people visually scan the road when sober versus when under the influence of alcohol. The visual scanning of the intoxicated driver is less active, more limited to the center of the road (probably the same tunnel vision effect), and less affected by the presence of other objects or cars on the road (Belt, 1969; Moskowitz, Ziedman, & Sharma, 1976).

There are many effects of alcohol that can be observed by almost anyone. These effects provide physicians and accident investigators with rough ideas of how drunk a person is. Clinical tests based on these behavioral impairments can serve to illustrate how prevasive the effects of alcohol are. Thus, moderate intoxication can cause slurring of speech (try saying "Methodist Episcopal" after five or six drinks), gross deterioration of handwriting, inability to touch the nose with a finger with the eyes closed, inability to walk heel-to-toe in a straight line, and eventually inability to remain upright (without trying to "push" the wall) with the eyes closed (Bridge, 1972). Perhaps, this is why the drunk driver often feels that all he or she needs is a little help to get *to* the car .... Once in it he or she feels quite all right. It is unfortunate that we are not as acutely aware of our reduced cognitive and perceptual-motor capabilities that are so critical to the accomplishment of the safe driving task as we are aware of the other impairments.

As long as socialized drinking remains a social norm, how can we still drink and then drive? This is where myths are generated. To begin, "I can handle it" is more a mixture of arrogance and ignorance than a reflection of skill. True, there are large individual differences, and it is also true that given the same level of BAL, heavy drinkers perform better than moderate drinkers (Jex et al., 1974), but then they tend to drink more to begin with. What may be a related myth is that it is the occasional drinker, who cannot "handle" alcohol, and whose driving performance is affected, who is most frequently arrested for driving while intoxicated. The (questionable) rationale behind this belief is that the alcoholic who has learned to hide his or her "problem" in most public situations, is able to do the same while driving. Both the belief and the rationale may however be completely unjustified according to an in-depth clinical evaluation of several hundred drivers arrested for driving while under the influence of alcohol. On the basis of clinical tests, interviews with the drivers, their families and friends, and checking various records, Bridge (1972) concluded:

In the three years in which I did many DWI (Driving While Intoxicated) examinations . . . I could find no respondent who was definitely not an alcoholic. At the time of arrest, however, there were a few very convincing suspects who said with as much honest appearance as they could muster that they had only a couple of beers, and that they certainly had no alcohol problem. Then almost invariably this couple of beers produced a blood level of over 0.2 percent, indicating a very heavy intake of alcohol, and when I inquired Alcoholic Anonymous (AA) people or others around the town who knew them, they were found to have drinking problems (pp. 6-7).

In his study, in response to his question of "how much did you have to drink?" Bridge (1972) found that drivers with BAL levels greater than 0.15 percent were just as likely to say that they had no drink at all as they were willing to admit to having eight or more beers or five or more drinks of liquor. One reason, perhaps, for the previously undetected overinvolvement of the chronic alcoholic in alcohol related driving violations and accidents may be the pervasive network of denial of the problem — beginning with the drivers themselves and extending to their immediate family and friends; all trying to "shield" the driver. Nonetheless, even conservative estimates indicate that at least 50 percent of the people arrested for driving while intoxicated can be classified as problem drinkers who are frequently on the road at high BALs (U. S. Department of Transportation, 1975).

The ingestion of coffee does not reduce the BAL, and therefore does not improve driving. Coffee may, nonetheless, combat the fatigue inducing effects of alcohol since alcohol, like fatigue, has been shown to increase the duration of blinks (Beidman & Stern, 1977). Food on the other hand, while it does not reduce the BAL, slows down the rate at which alcohol is absorbed, and thus slows down its effects. As most people who have experienced a "hangover" know, there is only one way to sober up — wait. Just as alcohol requires time to be absorbed into the blood and affect the central nervous system, so it requires time — and, for that matter, more time — to dissipate. Characteristic absorption and dissipation curves are given in Figure 3.4. A convenient rule of thumb to stay under 0.10 BAL is to limit oneself to one drink an hour.

The final myth and a word of caution. Many people feel that they can "tell" how strong a drink is, and thus control their drinking. In a direct test of this issue, Staak and Brillinger (1975) gave college students, who were accustomed to drinking, grapefruit juice mixed with various amounts of ethanol (alcohol) from 0 to 10 percent.

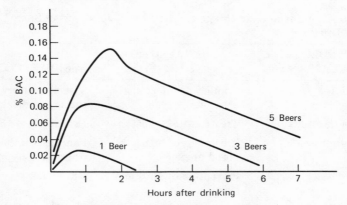

Figure 3.4. Absorption and dissipation rates of alcohol in the blood. The smoothed graphs are for a 150-pound man (from Heimstra & McDonald, 1973. Copyright 1973 by Wadsworth Publishing Co. Inc. Reproduced with permission from Brooks/Cole Publishing Co.).

Their findings, as summarized by the authors, showed that "the assessment of the strongest beverages was extremely erroneous; the number of errors was higher during intoxication and increased with increasing BALs. These results suggest that the strength of unconventional beverages of unknown alcohol concentration, such as fruit punches, can easily be misjudged even in sober condition." A recent attempt to train heavy drinkers to utilize internal cues to discriminate their own blood alcohol level was also unsuccessful (Maisto & Adesso, 1977), suggesting that internal control of drinking through sensitization to BAL is not a practical solution to the problem. On the positive side, however, it appears that with low BALs ($\leqslant 0.05$) for many people, feelings of intoxication precede most of the sensorimotor skills deterioration (Springer, Staak, & Raff, 1973), so that if they choose to do so, they can stop drinking before their driving capabilities are significantly impaired.

Other Drugs

The drug culture is not a phenomenon limited to the younger generation; it only takes a look in any family's medicine chest to realize that. Current surveys indicate that up to 20 percent of the driving population is under the influence of some prescription or nonprescription drug at any time. While the awareness of the potential dangers from different drugs is high, the data on their actual effects on driving are still meager.

Before we can discuss the effects of drugs on driver behavior, we

Table 3.5   The Therapeutic Usages and Negative Side Effects of Some Common
Types of Drugs

PHARMACOLOGICAL CLASS	THERAPEUTIC USAGE(S)	SIDE EFFECT(S)
Antibiotics	Combating infections	Visual, auditory disturbances, dizziness
Antidiabetic agents	Treatment of diabetes	Fainting
Antihypertensives	Treatment of high blood pressure	Fainting, dizziness, orthostatic hypotension
Antimotion sickness agents	Prevention of motion sickness	Drowsiness
Antispasmodics	Treatment of ulcers, "nervous stomach"	Visual disturbances
Antitussives	Relief of cough	Drowsiness
Cardiac glycosides	Treatment of congestive heart failure	Visual disturbances, muscular weakness
Diuretics	Treatment of edema, hypertension	Fainting, muscular weakness
Ophthalmic diagnostic agents	Refraction, visual testing	Visual disturbances

From Joscelyn and Maickel, 1975.

must attend to several of the problems that plague this area. First, is
the definition of a drug, which according to the World Health Organization, is "any substance that, when taken into a living organism,
may modify one or more of its functions." This definition includes
both therapeutic drugs (of which there are over 20,000 listed in the
American Drug Index) and nontherapeutic drugs, food additives, and
chemical pollutants. Second, different drugs metabolize in the body
in different ways and at different rates. Third, the relationship between the amount of drug that can be measured in the body fluids
(blood or urine) and its behavioral effects is typically not a simple
one. In this respect, alcohol is an exception since there is a relatively
straightforward relationship between the BAL and the measurable
level of deterioration of various information-processing and perceptual-motor functions. Fourth, many drugs, in addition to their
therapeutic effects, produce negative side effects, that could impair
driving performance. Thus, drivers taking these drugs may be
"damned if they do and damned if they don't." Table 3.5 contains a
list of the major kinds of commonly administered drugs along with
their therapeutic and side effects. Individual differences in these side

effects are very large — unfortunately, most people discover their sensitivities to these side effects only by trial and error. Fifth, many drugs produce residual effects that appear only after the main effects have disappeared and the drug is no longer detectable. The "morning-after hangover" from alcohol and "withdrawal" symptoms from heroin are familiar examples.

Finally, all too often, we are under the influence of more than one drug: alcohol and marijuana, alcohol and coffee, or even coffee and aspirin. This is where most of the complications arise. The combined effects of two or more drugs on our perceptual, mental, or motor functioning may be *additive* (the sum of the individual drug effects), *antagonistic* (one drug reduces the effects of the other), or *synergistic* (the combined effect is greater than the sum of the individual drug effects). Which of the three possibilities will result in a combination of any two drugs is almost impossible to predict (it also changes as a function of the amounts of the drugs ingested). Reconsider now all the potential combinations between 20,000 or more different drugs, and you have an idea of the scope of the problem.

A methodological complication specific to the interpretation of drug research is that most often the research is conducted on young healthy subjects who are given a single (acute) dosage of the drug, and thus the results may have no bearing on the effects of the drug on the chronic user who benefits from the drug's therapeutic effects and may have developed compensatory behaviors to counteract its negative side effects or residual effects.

Still, it is useful to briefly review the potential effects of some of the more commonly used drugs and toxins on driver behavior and driving-related skills.

Amphetamines.   Amphetamines are powerful stimulants of the central nervous system that counteract deteriorations that would accompany fatigue. Laboratory findings on the effects of amphetamines have been summarized as follows: "They don't impair performance, they enhance it! The degree of enhancement is generally greater in fatigued subjects and in simple and repetitive as opposed to complex tasks such as reasoning or I.Q. tests. When subjects are not previously deprived of sleep the effect is not a large one. Driver-related behaviors, such as simple and disjunctive reaction time and various measures of vigilance and psychomotor performance are among those showing positive effects" (Hurst, 1976, p. 10). Some studies have also shown an antagonistic effect of amphetamine on alcohol — thereby reducing some of the detrimental effects of alcohol (Hurst, 1976). The awareness of these potential benefits has resulted in the abuse of amphetamines by students, business executives, and professional drivers — all trying to stretch the day a little longer. However, since all the laboratory studies involve small doses, and administration is not repetitive to the point of habit formation, it is impossible to say what are the actual benefits or dangers to the drug abuser.

Barbiturates. Barbiturates produce a generalized depression in the central nervous system and are among the most widely used mood-modifying drugs. One recent survey estimated their use by 17 percent of the college students (Holroyd & Kahn, 1974). Although there are no conclusive data to indicate that the proportion of drivers with barbiturates in their blood is greater among the accident-involved drivers than in the general driving population, experimental studies have demonstrated that barbiturates degrade various driving related skills such as reaction time, tracking, and division of attention, as well as actual vehicle handling skills. Furthermore, barbiturate intoxication disrupts the ability to visually track moving targets — an ability critical for an important driving visual skill known as dynamic visual acuity (discussed later in this chapter). Finally, in combination with alcohol, the effects of barbiturates on psychomotor abilities are further amplified (cf. Sharma, 1976, for a review).

Tranquilizers. Tranquilizers are psychotropic drugs (drugs typically used to treat mental illness), whose use has more than doubled during the past decade (Clayton, 1976). The effects of various tranquilizers have been studied on both basic psychomotor skills as well as in simulators and actual car driving. Taken by themselves at commonly used levels tranquilizers appear to have very little significant effects, however when a tranquilizer is taken with alcohol (to help it go down?) the two drugs often have a synergistic effect. Depending on the specific tranquilizer used and the dosage, the combination of the drug with alcohol can impair attention, choice reaction time, and motor coordination. Beyond this, in a simulator, the combined intoxication was shown to increase the number of "collisions," inattention to signs and signals, and steering errors (Linnoila & Mattila, 1973). In most of the studies reviewed, however, the drugs were given in acute dosages to healthy people (the ones who otherwise would not use this drug), and so the extent of their long term effects in the actual driving situations is still to be determined (Clayton, 1976).

Psychotropic Agents. Like psychotropic drugs, these too affect the mind (hence the prefix psycho), but since their use is not medicinal, they are technically labeled as agents. Of these, the combination of extensive usage, illegality, and psychological effects, put marijuana (or rather its psychoactive ingredient THC) high on the list of research priorities. Several studies have shown that marijuana can impair performance on vision tests, learning tasks, divided attention tasks, memory and perception tasks, and time estimation tasks (see Joscelyn & Maickel, 1975, for a review). More to the point is a recent study that assessed the effects of marijuana in the real driving environment (Klonoff, 1975). Klonoff compared the driving behavior, in a closed course as well as in traffic, of two groups of subjects, one group under the influence of marijuana and the other under the influence of a placebo (any substance that has the appearance of the drug being tested but does not have its chemical effects). During the actual testing, neither the subjects nor the experimenter knew whether they were participating in the placebo condition or in the marijuana condition. In driving through traffic, Klonoff found that after smoking marijuana, drivers often forgot the instructions for the drive, missed more traffic lights and stop signs, made more passes without sufficient caution, were less aware of the presence of pedestrians and stationary vehicles, and were slower to respond to green lights at intersections than subjects who smoked the placebo. However, being a very mild hallucinogen, the effects of marijuana were often masked by individual differences and motivational factors, resulting in some subjects showing no change or even improving their performance when under the influence of marijuana. Nonetheless, in summarizing his data, Klonoff concluded that "it is evident that the smoking of marijuana by human subjects does have a detrimental effect on their driving skills and performance in a restricted driving area, and that this effect is even greater under the normal conditions of driving on city streets" (p. 323). These conclusions may be qualified somewhat by the fact that, as with alcohol, the chronic marijuana smoker who has learned to compensate for its effects, is less affected by the drug than the novice or naive user (Weil, Zinberg, & Nelson, 1968).

Psychotropic drugs in general, and marijuana in particular provide a good case for emphasizing the need to understand the effects of drug combinations on behavior. Surveys of college students have repeatedly shown that of the close to 50 percent students who occasionally smoke marijuana (Waller, Lamborn, & Steffenhagen, 1974; Mortimer, 1976), the majority also consume alcohol at the same time. Furthermore, most of those who smoke regularly drive while "high," and of these approximately one-quarter are legally drunk from alcohol at the same time (Waller et al., 1974). What, then, are the combined effects of the two drugs? At least one study (Ling, 1973) indicates that the joint effects of the two drugs are much worse than the effects of either drug alone. However, the types of impairments observed and their magnitude vary for the two drugs, and when combined, there are large individual differences.

The concern about the ever-growing use of psychotropic drugs has prompted several surveys to determine their impact on actual accident involvement. In one study in New York State (Babst et al., 1969), of 1245 known drug users who had a driver license, 77 percent had one or more accidents during the previous two-year period compared to 20 percent in the general driving population. However, as in many observational studies, it is likely that chronic drug users differ from the general driving population in more than just drug usage. Neither the accident rates nor the conviction rates were higher for the drug user groups in two independent studies. In one study (Moser, Bressler and Williams, 1971) both the users and the nonusers were selected from a population of people arrested for serious crimes, so that in a sense they were somewhat similar in their personality characteristics. In the second study (Blomberg & Preusser, 1972) patients in a methadone maintenance program were compared to their nonaddicted friends. No significant differences between the two groups were found despite the fact that most methadone patients reported driving immediately after receiving the drug!

In summary, despite the fact that at any one time over 20 percent of the people on the roads in the United States may be under the influence of one drug or another and despite the fact that many of these drugs have detrimental effects on driving-related skills, the role of these drugs in causing accidents is still unknown.

Toxins

While the alcohol and drug intoxication is something we bring with us to the car, other toxins are freely provided by our car themselves. Chief among them is carbon monoxide. When inhaled, it replaces oxygen in the blood and causes asphyxiation, including death. The traffic congestion on the highway during rush-hour traffic often raises the carbon monoxide in the air in the cars to levels that, under controlled experimental conditions have been shown to cause degradations in various driving behaviors (Rockwell & Balasubramanian, 1975). In fact, following the 1977 Fourth of July parade in the city of Philadelphia 60 drivers and passengers waiting in a line of idling cars to get out of a parking garage, had to be rushed to the hospital after being overcome by carbon monoxide inhalation. When combined with alcohol (driving home after "happy hour"), the two agents seem to interact synergistically (Rockwell & Weir, 1975), at least under conditions that place high information processing demands such as curve negotiation.

Smoking also increases the levels of carbon monoxide in the air (and eventually the carboxyhemoglobin in the blood), though the little research done in this area suggests that habitual smokers might be better off smoking while driving than experiencing the effects of withdrawal (Myrsten, Post, Frankenhauser, & Johansson, 1972; Schori & Jones, 1977). Apparently it *is* hard to kick the habit.

DRIVING-RELATED CAPABILITIES

We all tend to assume that some skills and abilities are helpful to driving, and, by implication, people who score high on these abilities are good/safe drivers. This is often difficult to demonstrate since people who may score high on a desired capability often also have some undesirable characteristics that may nullify the gains of the former. Two driver characteristics examined here are experience and vision. We know that performance on most driving tasks improves with practice, and we know that the blind cannot drive. Still, as we see below, it is difficult to demonstrate how experience and good vision improve driving safety.

Experience

Although for most readers of this book driving comes as easy as walking, try and reflect back on the very first time you sat behind the wheel. The driving task appeared immeasurably complex; controlling acceleration and deceleration while maintaining proper position in the lane and at the same time watching out for other cars, pedestrians, signs, and signals. That complexity is reflected in the results of a study by McKnight and Adams (1970) who identified approximately 1500 different perceptual-motor tasks that the driver must master in order to negotiate safely on our highways.

The realization that driving is a complex task is the cornerstone for the various driver education programs now in use in all 50 states. What do people learn as they gain driving experience? One large part of the learning process, of which most of us are aware is the automation of the various motor procedures such as shifting gears, braking, and steering. A more subtle learning is concerned with the perceptual information gathering task. As can be seen in Figure 1.1, one of the driver's primary tasks is to gather information about the position of the car relative to the direction of the road and position of other cars, and to use that information to safely guide the vehicle within the lane through traffic. It now appears, that in order to perform these perceptual-motor tasks the driver actually has to learn how to look. By observing where on the road drivers look, Mourant and Rockwell (1972) found that "novice drivers looked closer in front of the vehicle and more to the right of the vehicle's direction of travel than the experienced drivers (and), sampled their mirrors less frequently than the experienced drivers" (p. 325). These results indicate that the first few times behind the wheel almost all of the driver's information processing capacity is absorbed in simply maintaining the car's position in the lane. Apparently, the novice drivers feel that unless they constantly monitor the land and/or the road edges (close to the right) the car will go off the road. As they gain more experience, they learn to rely more on their peripheral vision to maintain their position in the lane, and direct their gaze further down the road to maximize the time available to process the visual information. The relative ineffectiveness of the looking behavior of the novice drivers probably accounts for Summala and Näätänen's (1974) finding that even when specifically instructed to pay attention to road signs, inexperienced drivers miss significantly more signs than experienced drivers. Finally the results of recent in-depth investigations of accidents suggest that the novice driver's fears of not being able to control the car's position in the lane, may be justified. In comparing the accident causes observed for experienced versus inexperienced drivers, it was found that inexperienced drivers are more likely to be involved in accidents due to improper directional control of their car than experienced drivers (Shinar, McDonald, & Treat, 1977).

The importance of experience is also reflected in the high accident involvement of inexperienced motorcycle riders. In motorcycle riding, where the importance of sensorimotor coordination is probably greater (or in any case more apparent) then in driving a car, a significantly high percentage of the people having accidents, have less than six months of experience. In fact many of the crashes occur on the first ride and often on borrowed vehicles (U. S. Department of Transportation, 1975). Even in car driving, after controlling for the confounding effect of driver age, inexperience is still associated with higher accident involvement (Brezina, 1969).

What then can we say about the other extreme — the highly skilled and experienced driver? Here the relationship is more complicated, as may be recalled from the study mentioned before that found that registered race drivers are involved in more accidents and violations than "normal" drivers (Williams and O'Neill, 1974). This is probably because as we gain experience we tend to change our driving habits. The risks that are perceived by the novice drivers prevent them from making many of the truly risky maneuvers that the experienced drivers often make. Thus, many of the benefits that we gain from our increased skills are offset by the higher risks that we take (Näätänen and Summala, 1976).

Visual Abilities and Requirements

Of all the sensory systems, vision is the most important for driving. While it is obvious that the blind cannot drive, it is not so obvious how much or what kind of vision is needed for safe driving. Consider the following two case histories. The first case was reported by McGuire and Kersh (1969, pp. 79-80).

> The driver was an "older man who attempted to hide from his family the fact that he was going blind. For more than a year he drove his car to work and home again every day, using the hazy shadows of parked cars to guide him during the day and the headlights of other cars at night. He never had an accident during this period of time, and when his family discovered his condition and made him give up driving, it was found that he legally qualified for aid for the blind."

Apparently, this driver was able to compensate for his deteriorating vision by driving at slower speeds, avoiding heavy traffic situations, or taking other defensive driving actions. However not all drivers are aware of their limitations as can be seen from the second case history, taken from the files of a study by Shinar (1977).

> The driver was 46 years old with normal driving habits who admitted to having been involved in four accidents over the past five years. Although two of the accidents were judged by the researchers to be vision caused or related, the driver believed he had normal vision. Upon examination, this driver was found to have poor vision in many specialized driver-related vision tests — most of which are typically not administered in the context of driver licensing. He was referred to an opthalmologist, who promptly fitted him with new glasses (and also discovered some pathology). When encountered a month later this driver was very thankful for the vision test since "before it," he stated, "I didn't realize how much I wasn't seeing." (Case No. 775)

The confusion surrounding the issue of what kind of visual capabilities are required for safe driving, is reflected in the large differences existing between states in their vision requirements for licensing. Consider the one test administered in all states: the requirement to read, under optimal illumination, a line of small letters. The size of these letters is measured in degrees of visual angle rather than inches or centimeters. If one thinks of the total visual world surrounding us as having 360 degrees, then the angle subtended by the letters in the critical row on most licensing vision charts is 0.17 degrees. On a chart 20 feet away from the observer this angle equals 0.7 inches and reading these letters signifies a 20/40 Snellen acuity or "twenty forty" static acuity (20/20 static acuity is the ability to resolve details of 1/60 of one degree, coresponding to letter height of 0.08 degrees).

How do the state-imposed requirements relate to the actual driving task requirements? The extensive amount of research on the relationship between static acuity and accident involvement, surveyed in Table 3.6, suggest that there probably is a correlation between the two variables but it is very low. A more logical approach would be to examine the driver's visual environment, and then in light of what we know about the human visual system, determine what visual capabilities and limitations are likely to influence driving.

First, however, it may be appropriate to digress into an extremely rudimentary discussion of the human visual system. The lenses at the front of our eyeballs act to focus images of the outside world on the light-sensitive cells that are distributed on the inside surface of the back of the eyes, known as the retina. The retina is made up of two types of cells: The cones — of which there are approximately 5 million — are concentrated mostly in the center of the retina, known as the fovea. The rods — of which there are approximately 120 million — are distributed all over the retina, except the fovea where they are totally absent. The density of all light-sensitive cells is greatest in the fovea and diminishes towards the periphery of the eye. The two types of cells serve different functions: The rods are only sensitive to difference in brightness but not to color. They are however sensitive to low levels of illumination, hence for night vision we often rely primarily on the rods (Have you ever noticed how difficult it is to tell the color of cars at night?). The cones provide us with color vision and also with the high ability that we have to resolve spatial details (20/20 vision). Now, the farther away from the fovea (where the cones are concentrated) that an image falls, the more blurred it is. The drop in acuity is so sharp that in order to read a letter that is projected only 10 degrees from the fovea its size must be five times as big as needed to read it when it is projected on the fovea (see Figure 3.5). Thus whenever we want to see something in sharp focus we must turn our eyes toward it. The role of the peripheral part of the retina (known simply as the periphery), is to aid the visual search behavior by detecting images that may need a closer look, so to speak.

Returning now to our driver, as he or she drives down the road, a good part of their attention and along with it their eyes, are pointed

Table 3.6 Summary of Studies on the Relationship between Static Visual Acuity and Accident Involvement

AUTHOR	SUBJECT POPULATION	MEASURES OF PERFORMANCE	RESULTS	COMMENTS
Weiss and Lauer (1930)	24 accidents drivers vs. 24 nonaccident drivers	Accident group vs. visual acuity	No difference between groups in acuity	
Silver (1936)	Drivers grouped by acuity levels	Acuity as function of "accident index" (no. of accidents per driver in each acuity category)	Very high accident index associated with poorer acuity; but for all index levels, mean acuity is still 20/30 or better	
Lauer (1937)	Availability sample of 848 drivers	"Accident index" and acuity	Drivers with *less* than 20/40 had slightly *more* accidents	
Lauer, DeSilva, and Forbes (1939)			Higher acuity–less accidents	Original report not available
Cobb (1939)	Availability sample of 3000 Connecticut drivers, given nine acuity tests	Correlated acuity with number of accidents	Significant but low correlations between acuity and number of accidents per year ($.03 < r < .06$)	Sample probably not representative of driving population, and the availability of minor accident data was inconsistent
Brody (1941)	26 accident repeaters vs. 26 control drivers	Compared groups on acuity	No difference between groups	Groups were not matched
Fletcher (1942)		Acuity vs. driving record	One percent of good drivers failed vision test vs. 5% of "poor" drivers	

Study	Sample	Variable	Results	Comments
Fletcher (1947)	200 "good" (professional) vs. 321 "poor" (involved in fatal accident or 3 or more personal injury accidents)	Differences in visual acuity between groups	Visual acuity better in the "good" drivers group	Matching was partial in terms of age, sex, exposure, and vehicle type
Eno Foundation (1948)	Two sets of matched groups in Michigan (100 pairs) and Connecticut	Proportion of drivers having 20/20 or better acuity	Significant differences in the proportion found for the Michigan group only	
Fletcher (1949)	181 fatal accident drivers, vs. 135 "volunteers," vs. 100 accident-free habitual violators	Visual acuity as function of group	No differences between groups	For the fatally injured drivers only, those killed in intersection accidents had poorer acuity than those killed in nonintersection accidents
Brody (1957)	375 chronic violators, 133 accident repeaters, and 124 control drivers	Mean visual acuity in each group	No differences found	
Henderson, Burg, and Brazelton (1971)	206 optometry clinic patients with 20/40 or better vision	Absolute number of DMV accidents and violations and Snellen acuity, hexobar acuity and checker-board acuity	Only monocular (OS) Snellen acuity was significantly related to accidents, but the correlation was low ($r = .15$)	Absolute number of accidents is confounded with exposure and acuity is confounded with age effects
Burg (1974)	12,211 California drivers of all ages	Absolute number of accidents (broken down by day/night and front/side/rear angle of impact) vs. binocular and monocular acuity	Correlations between acuity and accidents all $\leq .02$. Acuity was not significant in any of the regression analysis	No exposure data were available so accident rates could not be derived.

Table 3.6 Continued

AUTHOR	SUBJECT POPULATION	MEASURES OF PERFORMANCE	RESULTS	COMMENTS
Henderson and Burg (1974)	669 California drivers mostly applicants for license renewal	Multiple analyses. Frequency and rate of convictions and accidents as a function of acuity	Significant correlation between Snellen Acuity and accident rate only for drivers 25-49 years old ($r = .22$)	The acuity test was part of a battery containing 12 different vision tests, some of which appeared to be related more to accident involvement
Hofstetter (1976)	13,786 drivers from 27 states	Number of accidents vs. binocular visual acuity	Percentage of drivers with poor acuity who had 3+ accidents was twice as large as that of drivers with good acuity, for all age groups above 19	Good and poor acuity defined as above median and in lowest quartile, respectively. Actual acuity varied depending on the specific instrument used in each state

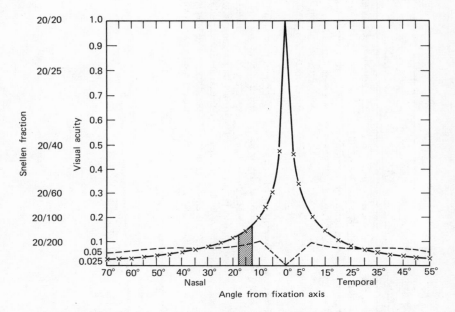

Figure 3.5. The relative acuity of vision in central and peripheral fields of the retina. The acuity of the central fovea has been taken as 1. The solid line represents acuity of cone vision (light-adapted eye), and the dotted line represents acuity of rod vision (approximate). The black area is the blind spot (after Ruch & Patton, 1965).

straight ahead toward the "end" of the road. Events there provide the driver with cues about cars ahead, signal light changes, cars or pedestrians ready to cross the intersection, or messages on any one of the highway signs. In all of these tasks, the driver and the environment are in motion relative to each other. In addition, the drivers typically do not have the luxury of optimal illumination. During the day, they may be exposed to glare from the sun, while at night they are operating under low levels of illumination coupled with glare from the headlights of oncoming cars. Finally, relevant events may occur in the driver's peripheral visual field such as a car coming behind a corner, a child jumping into the street, and so on. All of these considerations suggest that for safe driving purposes it is important to have adequate (what is adequate is yet unknown) visual acuity for both static as well as dynamic (i.e., moving) targets, under good as well as degraded conditions of illumination, and in both the central (foveal) and the peripheral visual field. In contrast, the traditionally administered test screens drivers on the basis of static (versus dynamic) acuity, under optimal illumination, and in the central field only.

The awareness of this discrepancy has led various researchers to study more driving-related visual abilities with very promising results. In a large scale investigation of over 17,000 California drivers, Burg (1967) showed that dynamic visual acuity — the ability to correctly identify a moving, rather than a stationary, target — was more closely related to drivers' accident histories than the traditional measure of static visual acuity. In more recent studies, dynamic visual acuity and other visual skills important for driving such as movement threshold (the ability to detect movement), and acuity under low levels of illumination (nighttime illumination) have again been shown to correlate with drivers' accident rates (Henderson & Burg, 1974; Shinar, Mayer & Treat, 1975; Shinar, 1977).

Because of the differential sensitivity of the fovea and the periphery, the process by which we pick up information from the visual scene is selective; we must select small areas on which we decide to focus. Thus it appears that another visual skill that would influence driving effectiveness is the ability to rapidly shift our gaze to the more informative areas in the visual field. We have already noted that the effectiveness of the visual search changes with practice (Mourant & Rockwell, 1972), and may be related to the personality characteristic of field dependence (Shinar, McDowell, & Rockwell, 1972). Thus it is not surprising that with a vision test specifically designed to measure the ability to rapidly and accurately shift the eyes and focus them on important areas in the visual field, Henderson and Burg (1974) found that those people who were slower in moving their eyes to targets appearing unexpectedly in their peripheral field also had worse accident histories than people who performed well on the test. Furthermore, using the same test device, Shinar, Mayer, and Treat (1975) found that people who were poor in responding to these peripheral targets were more likely to have right-angle accidents than rear-end accidents, indicating their susceptibility to potentially dangerous events that occur in their peripheral field.

How do the new, less conventional, measures of visual abilities compare with the traditional measure of static acuity? The relationship is not simple or straightforward, and often the different abilities are totally independent of each other. Figure 3.6 is a scatter plot illustrating the relationship between static acuity and dynamic acuity for 356 subjects ranging in age from 16 to 80 years old. In this plot, all the numbers above the diagonal line represent people whose dynamic visual acuity was poorer than their static acuity. In particular, note that of the 277 people who had static acuity of 20/20, more than half had dynamic visual acuity of 20/40 or less. These data indicate that while good static acuity is a prerequisite for good dynamic visual acuity, having good static acuity in no way guarantees good

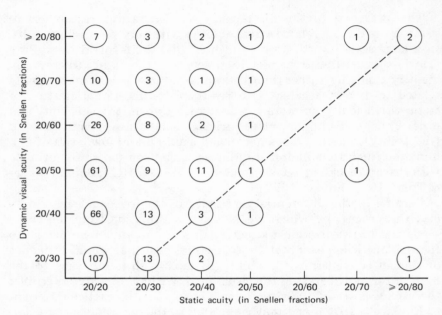

Figure 3.6. Scatter plot of the Snellen acuity of 351 drivers on static acuity under normal illumination and dynamic visual acuity for a target moving at the speed of 50° per second (most difficult static acuity target = 20/20; most difficult dynamic visual acuity target = 20/30; from unpublished data from Shinar et al., 1975).

dynamic visual acuity which is much more relevant to the driving needs. Poor dynamic visual acuity accompanied by good static acuity is especially prevalent among older people. These people, through the use of glasses, are able to retain adequate static acuity but not dynamic acuity, which is also a function of the ability to move the eyes synchronously with moving targets (Shinar, 1977).

These results, may explain why, despite the numerous studies that have examined the relationships between static acuity and accident involvement, only few have come up with significant relationships between these variables. Perhaps a much better understanding of the role of vision in driving may be gained from the new line of research that is focused on specific driving-related visual skills (Shinar, 1977). Once definite relationships between these visual skills and accident involvement is established we might even have standardized tests and required minimum levels of performance common to all states.

Another promising measure of driving-related vision is that of acuity measured specifically under low levels of illumination, such as those typical of nighttime driving. It turns out that acuity under such conditions is relatively independent of daytime acuity. In other words the loss of acuity due to low illumination cannot be predicted from the acuity measured in daylight. The decreased acuity, from which many people suffer, is called night myopia — nearsightedness limited to nighttime lighting conditions. The potential hazard of such an impairment is underscored by the results of a recent and extensive study in which it was found that nighttime accident involvement is related to poor visual acuity under nighttime levels of illumination, but unrelated to visual acuity under high (daytime) levels of illuminations (Shinar, 1977). Together, these findings cast serious doubts on the logic behind the present practice of restricting driving to daylight hours solely on the basis of low daytime acuity. On the more positive side, Owens and Leibowitz (1976) found that night myopia can be improved by specially corrected lenses (that correct for the accommodation error of the human lens under nighttime conditions). Indeed, in one small-scale field study, eight of the nine drivers fitted with the corrective lenses reported improved vision during their nighttime driving.

SUMMARY

Various driver characteristics have been found to be related to driving behavior and accident involvement. These can be descriptors of the driver's personality, temporary impairments caused by fatigue or drugs, and driving-related skills or capabilities such as driving experience and vision.

Personality attributes are relatively permanent traits that influence the way we behave. Studies concerned with the effects of personality on driving behavior have led researchers to conclude that people drive the way they live. People who are socially maladjusted in other areas of life (based on their interactions with various public agencies) tend to be overinvolved in violating traffic laws and in causing accidents. Furthermore, it appears that fluctuations in personal adjustment — reflected in crisis situations such as loss of a loved one or attempted suicide — correspond closely to fluctuations in the likelihood of being involved in a traffic accident. The reflection of social maladjustment and personal maladjustment in accident involvement, indicates that our driving behavior is often influenced by moods and motives not necessarily related to getting from one place to another. High-speed driving is used by some people to release pressure from other matters and to have a sense of power — a sensation often based on misperception of the actual amount of control a driver has on a speeding car.

Another personality attribute that appears to distinguish between good and bad drivers is their degree of field independence. People who are field independent are better at detecting visual cues in a complex visual environment (e.g., a partially hidden stop sign). Different studies have indicated that field dependent people are less effective than field independent people in the way they visually search their environment, and in their ability to detect and respond to emergency situations. Consequently field independent people appear to have fewer traffic accidents than field dependent people.

Temporary impairments that have been studied in relationship to driving ability include fatigue and intoxication from alcohol and other drugs. Aside from the anecdotal evidence of sleeping drivers waking up (or not) after an accident, scientific research has shown the effects of fatigue on driving related skills such as visual search behavior, braking behavior and maintaining a car's position in its lane. The only sure prescription to overcoming fatigue is sleep.

Temporary impairments due to drugs have been studied most extensively with the most commonly taken drug — alcohol. The evidence of the impact of alcohol on both driving-related skills and on accident involvement has been sufficiently convincing to cause most states to enact laws prohibiting driving with blood alcohol levels greater than 0.10 percent. At this point the severity of impairment is such that the likelihood of causing an accident is six to seven times higher than with 0.00 percent (i.e., without any alcohol). The effects of other drugs on driving have been studied less and have been more elusive to establish. Of the several categories of drugs including amphetamines, barbiturates, tranquilizers, and marijuana; barbiturates and marijuana produce the most consistent impairments in driving-related skills such as reaction time and vision. The effects of these drugs are further amplified when taken together with alcohol. Nevertheless, the impact of these drugs on the actual accident statistics is yet undetermined. Finally toxins in the air, such as carbon monoxide, also reduce drivers' information processing capabilities and may interfere with driving behavior.

Individual differences in areas directly related to driving, have been studied with respect to driving experience (typically presumed to be reflected in years of driving), and driver vision. Experience per se, while it is important to the acquisition and refinement of many driving skills does not correlate well with reduced accident involvement. While drivers with less than one year of experience tend to be overinvolved in accidents, highly skilled drivers with many hours of experience — such as race drivers — have been shown to be more involved in accidents than "normal" drivers. The underlying mechanism that accounts for this phenomenon is probably the increase in risk taking that accompanies the increase in confidence gained through experience.

Good vision is considered an axiomatic requirement for safe driving, and accident case histories as well as extensive research have provided some support for this belief. However, recent analyses of the visual requirements in driving suggest that the present visual examination, which measures visual acuity for stationary targets under optimal illumination may not be the best test for measuring driving-related visual capability. A more appropriate test may be one that measures dynamic visual acuity, that is, the visual acuity for moving targets, and acuity under low (nighttime) levels of illumination.

FOUR
THE DRIVER AS AN INFORMATION PROCESSOR

Imagine yourself entering the freeway during the rush hour simultaneously driving and talking to a friend or listening to the radio. As you get on the entrance ramp, you start shifting your eyes back and forth, checking for gaps in the traffic flow so that you may enter the stream of vehicles. Finally, you make your decision and you enter the main flow of traffic. However, somewhere in that process, your mind became so occupied in making the transition that you completely stopped listening to your friend or to the radio only to realize it once you were again in the main flow of traffic. This inability to divide our attention between different tasks illustrates the very limited capacity that we have for processing information. Note that in this particular case, one source of the information was visual (i.e., for the driving) while the other one was auditory (i.e., the conversation). Yet, somewhere in our brain we are unable to simultaneously process all the inputs from the two different sensory modalities. We are then faced with a situation known as information overload in which we must make a decision to attend to some of the information available and to reject, or not attend to, other information. This is the first step in the information processing sequence that we continuously engage in while driving.

If the object or event that attracts our attention is not in the center of our visual field, then a frequent next step is to direct our eyes to the relevant area in the visual field in order to perceive better the information to which we have attended. Then, depending on the information we have perceived, we have to decide whether or not to make a change in our driving behavior (turn the wheel, accelerate, or decelerate). Finally, once a response is selected it must be executed appropriately. To complicate matters somewhat, all of these information processing functions are not totally sequential. In reality, some of these functions are performed partially in parallel. Thus in the process of executing one response we may be already attending to a new source of information that may require a different response. In this section, however, for the sake of simplifying things, we discuss these component processes individually.

Another point that must be considered is the fact that all of these processes are often performed under severe time constraints. As an information processor the driver's limit is not so much a function of the total amount of information that can be absorbed or handled but rather the rate at which the information can be processed. To illustrate, given a sufficient amount of time, anyone can read a sign posted over a freeway listing five different exits. However, when driving at 55 miles an hour, drivers have available to them only a short period of time in which to extract the information relevant to their needs before passing under the sign. In attempting to perform an adequate task, the driver often finds it necessary to slow down so that the amount of information that has to be processed *per unit of time* (i.e., the rate of information flow) is reduced.

The limit on the rate at which we can process information makes the role of the attentional and visual search mechanisms extremely important. Those situations or events to which we do not attend are forever lost to our consciousness and, perhaps more important for driving, never responded to. While there may be many events and objects to which we respond on the basis of low-level processing only such that they are soon forgotten (e.g., signs), those that are totally unattended to (e.g., those outside our visual search area) cannot be responded to at all. Thus, an unattended billboard advertisement probably has no significance for the conduct of safe driving, while an unattended stop sign may lead to an accident. In summary, the driver can best be thought of as an information processing channel in which the central decision-making component is rate limited, and the peripheral attentional and perceptual mechanisms function to select the most important cues to be processed by that central decision mechanism. Although this model is very simplistic and falls short of explaining some behaviors, the notion of hierarchical stages of selection and reduction of information is supported by the evidence presented in the section below and much of the current thinking about human information processing (Norman, 1976).

Before we begin to discuss the component processes that we assume are incorporated within the broader context of information processing it is important to emphasize that the driver is an active component in the driver-roadway-vehicle system rather than a passive one. Thus the driver does not just respond to emerging situations but also is often the one who creates them; the stress of driving can be reduced if the driver chooses to do so (e.g., by driving more slowly). Conversely, the stress and risk may be increased if the driver seeks the excitement of the greater risk. Thus, depending on the driver's mood, personality, needs, and capabilities, the driver performance level fluctuates over time. Also fluctuating over time (as far as the moving driver is concerned) are the environmental demands on the driver. When the two are combined, we have the situation that is qualitatively displayed in Figure 4.1 (adapted from Blumenthal, 1968). Accidents are prevented as long as the driver's performance level remains above the environmental demands level. Thus in congested high-speed driving the environmental demands may be high but the driver's information processing capabilities are probably more focused on the driving task, as illustrated by point A. Conversely when the demands are low — or when the driver reduces the demands by driving slowly — the driver may allocate much of the information processing capacity to nondriving tasks, as illustrated by point B. A characteristic common to most emergency situations is that they place high demands on an unprepared driver — leading to the situation depicted by point C in which the two curves cross each other, and an accident results. In the following discussion we consider some of the interactions between the environmental demands and drivers' primary information processing functions: attending to, fixating on, deciding, and responding to the different driving-relevant stimuli.

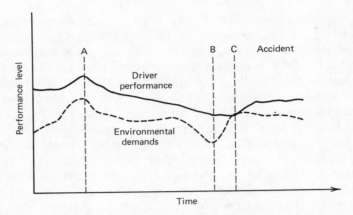

Figure 4.1. The interaction between the environmental demands and driver performance levels. For explanation of points A, B, and C see text (adapted from Blumenthal, 1968).

ATTENTION

The need to constantly pay attention to events that occur, both on the road and off the road, is a very demanding task. Although we have become accustomed to consider driving as a fairly nonstrenuous activity (otherwise, how could we drive for several hours without a break), the accident statistics suggest that as many as 45 percent of the accidents could possibly be prevented if all of the involved drivers were attentive to the critical events immediately preceeding the accident (Treat, Tumbas, McDonald, Shinar, Hume, Mayer, Stanisfer, & Castellan, 1977). These lapses in attention are manifested in failure to observe stop signs and signals because of internal (inside the car) and external (outside of the car) distractions, as well as preoccupation with non-driving thoughts. Even perceptually conspicuous information is often unattended to. To understand how attention affects our driving we must discuss in some detail two of its more important characteristics: the level or amount of attention and the distribution of attention.

Level of Attention

The amount of attention that we allocate to any task is a variable. Its fluctuations are a function of the external environment and situational demands and/or our internal state of arousal and motivation. Consider the difference between driving on a long, straight, undivided highway with no other traffic in sight and driving on the same highway but in an urban area in rush-hour traffic. One of the differences between the two situations is our absorption in the driving task or the amount of attention that we devote to it. In this particular case, the amount of attention allocated to the driving task is determined by the situation — it increases as the driving demands are increased and decreases with corresponding decreases in the demands of the environment. Many people once thought that one of the primary goals of the highway designer is to reduce the environmental demands by making the driving task as easy as possible. However, from personal experience, we all know that an environment that places minimal demands on the driver — often synonomously labeled as monotonous — may also be dangerous since it fails to elicit a sufficiently high level of attention necessary for the driving task.

For the most part, however, we are able to appropriately vary the amount of attention we need to allocate to the driving task in accordance with the situational demands. In one study in which drivers were asked to drive under various conditions of traffic and close their eyes for as long and as often as they felt safe, it was found that people were willing to maintain their eyes closed for longer periods of time when driving under open road situations than when driving in dense traffic (Safford, 1971). In another study, using a laboratory simulator, Robinson (1975) devised a situation in which subjects were asked to perform a car-following task. Occasionally the lead car that they were following would stop and then their task was to brake in order to avoid an accident. However, to study attention, the view of the two cars and the gap between them was made available to the subjects only on request. Each look cost the subject a small amount of money, and each accident cost the subject some money. The costs were deducted from the subject's pay at the end of the experiment. Thus, the subjects had to trade off paying a little each time they wanted to see the position of the two cars, against not looking enough and then paying much more when an accident occurred. In this situation, Robinson found that subjects resisted viewing the cars most of the time, but requested more "looks" as the gap between the two cars was decreased. In a limited sense, this study demonstrated that unless the driving is conducted under extremely stressful situations, some spare attentional capacity apparently does remain. Studies by Brown and his associates conducted in England (cf. Brown, 1965) demonstrated that under conditions requiring low attentional demands (e.g., light traffic) drivers were able to perform additional mental tasks without any impair-

Table 4.1   The Ability to Recall Different Signs Correctly Shortly After Passing Them

SIGN	PERCENT DRIVERS CORRECTLY RE-CALLING SIGN
50 km/h speed limit begins 300 m ahead	78
Police control	63
Breaks in the road surface (due to frost) from here 1 km ahead	55
General warning	18
Pedestrian crossing 300 m ahead	17

Adapted from Johansson and Rumar's 1966 data.

ment in the primary driving task. However, when conditions became stressful then deterioration was observed in either the primary driving task or the additional mental task.

If the allocation of attention is a demanding task, then it is possible to view the driver as an information processor who continuously strives to reduce the effort involved, as long as the amount of risk that he or she is willing to tolerate does not exceed a certain point. The ability to vary attention according to the perceived risk was demonstrated in the same study reviewed before by Robinson (1975). As he decreased the cost of a look relative to the cost of an accident the subjects requested more looks; and vice versa, as he increased the cost of a look relative to the cost of an accident, the subjects requested fewer looks and were willing to tolerate a greater risk of having an accident. How subjective risk or importance can influence the attentional level in real driving situations is illustrated by Johansson and Rumar's (1966) study of sign perception. In this study drivers were stopped 700 yards after passing different signs, and asked to report on the last sign they passed. They found that the percent of correct responses was generally low, and differed for the different kind of signs as indicated in Table 4.1. This pattern of results is very interesting since it suggests that the percent of correct answers may be related to what can be labeled as the subjective importance of the sign or the risk involved in violating its message. This leads to a puzzling result: in order to perceive a speed limit sign more accurately than a pedestrian crossing sign, we must first interpret the meaning of the sign but this can only be done if the sign is in some sense read or at least interpreted based on a combination of physical cues such as shape and color. This finding indicates that we are able to process a lot of information to quite a high degree, that once this information is perceived as unimportant it may be immediately discarded and forgotten. Thus, the amount of processing that we allocate to the different objects on the road can vary as a function of the importance that we allocate to them. This is a very adaptive system since it allows us to vary the amount of attention in a more or less continuous fashion rather than in an all-or-none fashion in which we are either attentive or nonattentive to anything.

If the driving task does not require — or in any case does not receive — all of our attention, what then do we do with our spare attentional capacity? Much of that capacity is kept in reserve so that when the driving demands increase, we can increase the attention that we allocate to the task without having to sacrifice our driving speed. A case in point is passing another vehicle — a maneuver that requires more attention than open road driving. When the conditions are particularly difficult (e.g., narrow road, passing a large truck) the release of tension on completion of the pass can actually be felt. The reason we do not allocate all of our attention to the driving task all the time is simply because it requires an effort that is greater than the perceived risk of being involved in an accident at any given moment. This process is adaptive most of the time because we are able to vary the amount of attention as a function of the importance of various situational cues and demands. Furthermore, the more driving experience we gain without being involved in accidents, the more we are reinforced for that adaptive behavior. (More theoretical discussions of the relationship between attention and importance and between attention and effort can be found in Norman, 1976; and Kahneman, 1973, respectively.)

Distribution of Attention

The distribution of attention is somewhat analogous to the beam of a searchlight. It can be distributed over a large area, providing a little light everywhere, or focused on a small area, highlighting everything there. Furthermore, it can be selectively moved from one spot to another. This analogy is relevant to two important features of our attentional capability: we can either *divide* our attention among various objects of interest, or selectively *focus* our attention on a single area or object of interest and ignore the rest of the environment (this focusing ability has been dubbed as the "cocktail party phenomenon" based on our ability to carry a conversation with one other person in a roomful of ongoing conversations; Cherry, 1953). The analogy breaks down, however, when we consider the fact that attention can be distributed over inputs from all sensory modalities rather than just vision.

Both divided and selective attention are important in driving. In the visual domain, in driving we typically focus most of our attention on the road area ahead of us. Yet some attentional capacity must be allocated to the periphery since critical events happening immediately off the roadway may also influence our behavior. A car switching lanes, traffic entering our road from a side road, a child jumping off the curb, are just a few examples.

One of the effects of experience in driving is the gradual learning of how to distribute attention in order to maximize performance while minimizing effort. Thus, to effectively attend to all the relevant sources of information, the novice drivers tend to allocate all of their attentional capacities to the driving task (have you ever tried to maintain a conversation with a beginning driver in dense traffic?). Experienced drivers are much more adaptive in their distribution of attention and consequently able to devote less of the total amount to the driving task and more to nondriving tasks. Yet even among experienced drivers, differences in the ability to distribute their attention effectively appears to be an important determinant of their driving safety. Two studies that tested this hypothesis found a significant relationship between the capacity to quickly shift attention from one source to another and accident involvement. In the first study, by Kahneman, Ben-Ishai, and Lotan (1973), experienced Israeli bus drivers were asked to listen, through headphones, to two different messages presented simultaneously, each one to a different ear. The drivers' task was to shift their attention back and forth from one message to the other upon the presentation of an auditory cue. The researchers found a significant and positive correlation between accident rate and performance on the attention task: the higher the accident rate a driver had, the more information he tended to miss and the more errors he made in the selective attention task. In the second study, by Mihal and Barrett (1976), a similar test was administered to American utility company drivers. This study too, found a large and statistically significant correlation between the drivers' accident frequency and performance on the selective attention test. Note that in both studies all the information was auditory rather than visual. Thus, the relationships found support the argument made above that a limit in our ability to process information exists at some level beyond the specific sensory organ — and as such both visual and auditory inputs compete for the same limited resources (Shulman & Fisher, 1972).

VISUAL SEARCH

The eyes have been poetically called the windows to the mind. The observable eye movements — the visual search — are often a good indication of where the mind is, or where attention is directed. Since only those objects that are projected on the fovea are in sharp focus, the focus of our attention is typically on the objects that are in focus on the fovea (except when we are purposefully trying to see from the "corner" of our eye). If our perceptions are so selective, how can we maximize the amount of information gained through the visual search process? Two mechanisms control this process: one external and one internal. External control is in evidence whenever the blurred image on the periphery is highly conspicuous and is considered (by the brain) worthy of focused attention. The internal control is a function of our expectations concerning where in the visual field most of the information is located. Most often the two mechanisms operate in harmony. For instance, in approaching curves, successive visual fixations (looks) are governed by expectations on where the road should be as well as by the roadway edge markings, which constitute high-contrast targets capable of attracting the driver's visual fixations. In a somewhat simplified manner we can make the statement that visual fixations tend to concentrate in the most informative parts of the visual field (Mackworth & Morandi, 1967).

Which are the informative parts of the driver's visual field? Where does he or she concentrate his or her attention most of the time? Using eye movement measuring and recording systems, such as the one depicted in Figure 2.3, researchers can directly observe where in the visual field the driver's eyes are pointed. Again, since maximum visual acuity is located in the center of the eye (the fovea), it is reasonable to assume that that place in the visual field to which the fovea is directed represents the area towards which most of the driver's attention is directed. While this assumption is not always valid, it is appropriate under stressful situations in which the driver's spare attentional capacity is minimized.

Where, then, is the driver's attention focused most of the time? There are two ways to describe the driver's visual world. First we can describe the visual scene ahead of the driver in terms of degrees from a certain center. This is illustrated in Figure 4.2. In this visual field, the center (0,0) is chosen as that point where the lane markings of a straight road appear to converge. This point is called the focus of expansion because, to the moving driver, the visual field appears to expand from it. Thus when the driver fixates his or her eyes at the focus of expansion he or she is staring at the horizon. Lowering the eyes by one degree brings them to approximately 180 feet ahead of the car and, lowering the eyes two degrees below the focus of expansion, brings the look to within 100 feet of the car. After a series of studies on drivers' eye movement behavior, spanning a period of

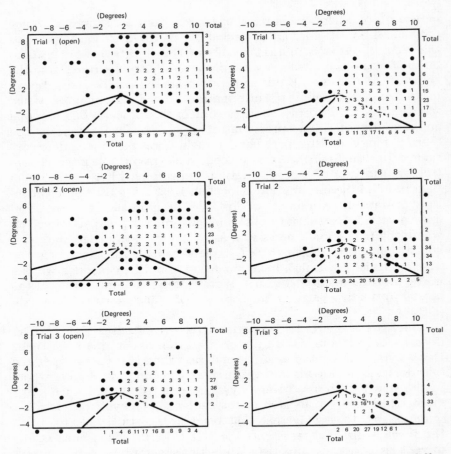

Figure 4.2. Distribution of percentage of time spent by a driver fixating different areas of the visual field when attending to all the road signs (trial 1), only the ones relevant to the designated route (trial 2), and when not reading any of the signs (trial 3); in open road driving (left figures) and when car-following (right figures). The numbers in the figures indicate percent time spent viewing that area, a dot (·) signifies less than 1 percent (from Mourant et al., 1969).

almost 10 years, Rockwell (1972b, p. 317) concluded, concerning the nature of drivers' visual search behavior, that

> *Our research on driver eye movement suggests that most eye movements in driving are less than six degrees travel and most eye fixations are between 100 milliseconds and 350 milliseconds in duration. In driving it can further be determined that some 90% of the observed fixations fall in a small region, within plus or minus 4 degrees from the focus of expansion.*

Keeping attention directed toward events in the focus of expansion is a highly appropriate strategy since it provides the driver with maximal time to prepare for information appearing on the roadway ahead. In order not to go off the road while attending to potential emergencies ahead, the driver must also attend to the vehicle's position within the lane. Here we find that the experienced driver is able to do so by relying on the less-sensitive peripheral vision (Bhise & Rockwell, 1971).

The second way of describing drivers' visual fixation habits is by noting the amount of time they spent viewing different objects in the visual field. Thus, in a study by Mourant, Rockwell, and Rackoff (1969 — see Figure 4.2) in open road driving drivers spent approximately 50 percent of the time looking straight ahead, 20 to 27 percent of the time looking at the scenery to the far right or left, 6 to 8 percent of the time looking at other vehicles, 7 to 8 percent of the time looking at bridges, and only 2 percent of the time looking directly at either the road surface close to the car or the lane markers.

Many variables can influence the driver's visual fixation pattern: individual differences such as personality, alcohol intoxication, fatigue, and driving experience; as well as situational variables, such as open road driving versus car following; and needs relevant to the driving task, such as seeking particular road signs. Since the effects of individual differences have already been discussed in the previous chapter, only the effects of situational variables and needs are discussed here. A study that investigated both variables was conducted by Mourant, Rockwell, and Rackoff (1969). In their study, drivers were asked to either drive on an open road, or to follow another car at a fixed distance. On the first trial the driver was asked to read all the road signs. On the second trial the driver was to read only the ones that pertained to his or her designated route. On the third trial the driver was asked to avoid reading any of the signs unless "necessary to complete the route successfully." As can be seen from Figure 4.2, the most apparent difference between the open road (left figures) and the car-following situation (right figures) is in the location of the visual fixations and the compactness of their distribution: when following a car, the fixations are more concentrated and closer to the car than when driving in the open road. In addition, the effect of roadway familiarity and instructions (it is impossible to separate the two effects here) are reflected in fewer and fewer fixations away from the road. Thus, although we are not consciously aware of our eye-fixation pattern, it nonetheless reflects our information-processing needs.

Another situational variable that influences the driver's fixation pattern is the geometry of the roadway. Only on a straight road does the focus of expansion and the perceptual end of the road coincide.

On a curved road, at any time, the focus of expansion is somewhere off the roadway, and consequently events there have no bearing on the driving requirements. Furthermore, when negotiating a curved road the lane markings assume added importance since the driver must make repeated steering corrections to maintain his or her position within the lane. It is therefore not surprising that in a study of eye movements in curve negotiation, Shinar, McDowell, and Rockwell (1977) found that just before entering a curve, and then while negotiating it, drivers tend to shift their fixations back and forth between the edge marking just in front of the car and the end of the road further ahead. These results provide strong support to the notion that the driver's information processing capacity is severely limited so that, when under stress, at any one time the driver can attend to *either* the directional cues (end of the road, up ahead) *or* the lateral positioning cues (edge marking close to the car) but not both simultaneously.

In summary, it can be stated that our visual fixation patterns reflect our information acquisition process, as well as (as has been discussed before) the impairments in these processes. The experienced driver is able to fixate — and presumably pay most of his or her attention to those areas in the visual field that are most relevant to his or her needs. In the least-taxing environment, the open straight road, drivers tend to concentrate their fixations on the focus of expansion. When the situation becomes more demanding through either self-imposed tasks (car following, sign reading, or just scenery watching) or changes in the roadway geometry, the visual fixation pattern changes accordingly. By knowing where and for how long drivers look at different objects in the roadway environment we can understand better the visual cues that they utilize, and perhaps be able to aid them in the driving task through improved roadway and sign designs (see Chapter Six for a discussion of design implications).

PERCEPTION AND PERCEPTUAL JUDGMENT

Perception can be defined as the meaningful experience of the objects surrounding us. This experience is made up of the combination of the information received from our senses (typically the eyes) and our expectations (typically based on past experience) on what we "should" see. When we perceive an object we restructure and interpret the information collected from the individual fixations. Thus, in the context of driving, even when the driver does fixate on the most important parts in the visual field, the brain must still interpret the sensory inputs. It is only when these inputs become meaningful that we have a perception of a roadway, cars, signs, pedestrians, and so on, rather than a conglomerate of differently colored and shaded areas.

Perception of Roadway Geometry

Most of the time our perception of the roadway ahead is sufficiently accurate so as to enable us to negotiate on it safely. However, there are limited data to suggest that under some circumstances some form of visual illusions may be acting on the highway to confuse drivers. While the data here are meager, the experience is common enough. To illustrate, how often have you approached a curve and adjusted your speed to what you thought would be the appropriate speed, only to realize (too late?) that the curve is sharper than it appeared to be from some distance ahead? Laboratory research has repeatedly demonstrated that people underestimate curvature the smaller the visible portion of the curve (Virsu & Weintraub, 1971). On the roadway, however, the underestimation may occur even though the curve is completely visible from a long distance ahead. In a series of experiments aimed at studying this illusive curve phenomenon, Shinar (1977) examined how drivers view curves. In one part of this study, people were presented with photographs of curves similar in geometry but differing in their accident history. In every pair that the subject viewed, one curve was associated with at least three daytime accidents in the previous three years, while the other curve was associated with no accidents at all. When asked to compare these geometrically matched pairs of high- and no-accident curves, the subjects tended to misperceive the high-accident curves as closer, wider, and more visible than the low-accident curves. Furthermore, the subjects did not perceive them as more dangerous and did not indicate that they would slow down more for these high-accident curves than they would for the no-accident curves. The high-accident curves did differ from the no-accident curves in some more subtle measures of curvature but the subjects — and apparently the drivers who actually had their accidents there — were not sensitive to these cues. Eye movement studies indicate the drivers utilize the roadway edgemarkings as cues to curvature (Shinar, McDowell, & Rockwell, 1977). Thus, one way to sensitize drivers to illusive curves may be to make appropriate changes in the edgemarkings themselves (Shinar, Rockwell, & Malecki, 1975; see Chapter Six).

Other cues that contribute to our perception of roadway geometry are auditory and kinesthetic cues. Although our perception of the road ahead is based almost solely on visual cues, once we enter a curve, the screeching of tires and/or swaying of the body in response to the centrifugal force provide us with feedback on whether or not we misjudged the curvature. If this feedback is not too late, we can use it to modify our driving by slowing down. As it turns out, there is a limit to our psychological tolerance of lateral acceleration (the effect of the centrifugal force), beyond which we prefer to slow down. This limit was demonstrated by Herrin and Neuhardt (1973) who had their subjects drive an instrumented vehicle on a winding rural road. They found that drivers' tolerance of lateral acceleration is not a constant but rather changes with the driver's needs and the situation. Thus, a driver "in a hurry" will tolerate more lateral acceleration than a person on a leisurely drive, and a driver familiar with the roadway will tolerate and drive at a speed that will result in a greater lateral acceleration than a driver unfamiliar with the roadway. Depending on the conditions, up until a speed of 40 mph drivers will adjust their speed to maintain a lateral acceleration of 0.25-0.40 g's (g is the acceleration of gravity = 32.2 ft/sec). This level of discomfort that drivers are willing to tolerate may also reflect their perception of risk (i.e., beyond that level of discomfort they may fear losing control of the car). It is fortunate that for most normal drivers this level is significantly below their vehicle's emergency handling capabilities (Koppa & Hayes, 1976).

Perceptual Judgments of Time, Distance, and Speed

Since driving is a time-dependent process, the accurate judgment of time, distance, and speed is critical for safe maneuvering on the highway. One of the most demanding and often performed tasks is that of passing other cars — often in the face of opposing traffic. In this situation we continuously judge and update estimates of headway, clearance, and relative velocities between ourselves, the vehicle we intend to pass and any oncoming traffic. How good are we at this task? Considering the high frequency of such maneuvers and the low frequency of accidents occurring in this context, we must be either fairly good or at least sufficiently conservative most of the time to leave a wide safety margin.

The perception of our own speed is gained mostly through the movement of the scenery in our peripheral field. Thus, in one study (Shinar, McDowell, & Rockwell, 1974) when drivers in an instrumented vehicle were instructed to maintain a nominal speed of 60 miles per hour without looking at their speedometer, they drove at an average speed of 57 mph on an open road segment compared to an average speed of 53 mph on another, tree-lined segment of the same road. The lack of peripheral cues probably also accounts for underestimation of speed when the road movement is projected on film as when it is viewed from a real moving car, since, on film, all movement is limited to the area subtended by the screen (Näätänen & Summala, 1976). Our sensory systems, and thus our perceptions, are most responsive to changes in stimulation. Compared to driving on a desert road, a tree-lined road provides the driver with rapid changes in the visual field. Another type of change that occurs over a longer period is related to our level of adaptation. When entering a freeway, a speed of 55 mph appears to be very fast, but after driving at that speed for some time it seems — intolerably, to some people — slow. Consequently, our experience of any given speed is different depending on whether we decelerate or accelerate in order to reach it. This has a significant implication for safety since, when slowing down from a high speed we are likely to overestimate our deceleration. This is a familiar experience we all have when exiting from an expressway: almost invariably we slow down to less than the recommended speed yet feel that we have already slowed down to a snail's pace. This phenomenon was also demonstrated in an experiment by Schmidt and Tiffin (1969). In their study they first had their subjects drive a car at 70 mph and then asked them to slow down to 40 mph (without looking at the speedometer). They found that the longer the drivers drove at 70 mph, the higher their elected speed was once they slowed to their estimate of 40 mph. Thus, when accelerating from a full stop the average driver's estimate of 40 mph was 41 mph. However when required to decelerate after driving for 40 miles at 70 mph, the average driver decelerated to 53 mph — a significantly, and potentially dangerous, higher speed than the driver's estimate of 40 mph.

For car-following tasks (such as driving on a busy expressway), more relevant than the driver's own speed is the judgment of headway to the car ahead and relative velocity (the speed differential between the two cars). Using aerial photography, Lee (1971) noted that on expressways the minimum headway separation was equivalent to approximately 2 seconds. With shorter headways drivers prefer to pass the car ahead, and in preparation for a pass a following driver may narrow the gap to as little as 0.5 second (Rockwell, 1972a). The use of time as a measure of headway separation is much more meaningful in light of our time-dependent information processing limits, which (as discussed below) clearly make a 0.5-second gap extremely dangerous. Surprisingly, while our ability to estimate headway changes is somewhat poor, our ability to perceive changes in relative velocity is extremely good. To illustrate, in one study subjects sat as passengers in a following vehicle and were only allowed a 4-second glimpse of the car ahead. Under these conditions subjects were able to judge the direction of the relative motion of the two cars with an accuracy of 99 percent with relative velocity of only 3 mph (Evans and Rothery, 1974). Note, however, that these results demonstrate a perceptual capability rather than actual use of this capability on the highway. As such we are dealing here with a measure of driver performance rather than a measure of driver behavior. The high frequency of rear-end accidents attests to the fact that typically we do not allocate much of our attentional capacity to perform such fine perceptual judgments.

Perhaps the most complicated perceptual judgments in driving are those involved in performing a passing maneuver on a two-lane highway. To successfully pass another vehicle we must have a sufficient clearance and perceive it to be such. If the clearance is underestimated the penalty is rather small — loss of a few minutes at best, until the next opportunity arrives. If the clearance is overestimated we may have to abort the pass halfway, cause the oncoming car to go off the road or possibly have a head-on collision. To compare drivers' ability to judge available passing distance, Gordon and Mast (1970) required their subjects to follow a control car that was moving along an experimental track at different speeds. In one condition the drivers were asked to estimate the last possible point at which they could pass the leading car and return to their lane before the end of the track. In the other condition the drivers were instructed to actually pass the car by accelerating as fast as they could and then return to their lane as soon as safely possible. The results indicated that, whether driving their own car or whether driving an unfamiliar government vehicle, drivers underestimated the minimum distance needed for passing, with the errors of estimation ranging from 20 to 50 percent of the actual overtaking distance. Furthermore, while the actual magnitude of underestimation was smallest for the highest speed used (50 mph), the percent of drivers underestimating the required distance increased with increasing speed.

In studies conducted on unsuspecting drivers on two-lane rural roads, Farber (1969) found that drivers will pass a slower moving car with a greater likelihood the greater the available passing distance, and the lower the speed of the lead car. Interesting differences were found between daytime and nighttime passing: drivers were more conservative and variable in the passing distances that they were willing to accept during the night than the day. It is obvious that the reduced nighttime visibility and elimination of many of the distance cues that are available to the driver during the daylight hours were responsible for both the smaller distances tolerated and the greater variability. Less expected was the fact that the speed of the opposing traffic did not seem to influence the driver's decision to pass. Under both day and night conditions a driver was as likely to pass when an oncoming car was traveling at 60mph as when it was traveling at 30 mph. This lack of sensitivity may be better understood if we stop and realize that the average passing maneuver requires at least 8 to 10 seconds — depending mostly on the speed of the lead car (Crawford, 1963). We can then easily calculate that at the combined speed (of the two cars approaching each other) of 80 mph the distance between the oncoming car and the driver intending to make a pass is over 1100 feet at the start of the maneuver — a distance at which it is very difficult to perceive the speed of the oncoming car.

In light of the poor distance judgment capabilities observed by Farber (1969) and by Gordon and Mast (1970), why is the frequency of overtaking and passing accidents relatively low compared to other types of accidents (rear end, right angle)? Gordon and Mast suggest that several safety factors operate here. "The driver may avoid danger by not passing at high speeds, and he may insist on an adequate safety distance. If a wrong decision is made, he may drop back to the original lane, and the overtaken and oncoming cars may slow down and move to the shoulder " (p. 170). In most cases these small accommodations by the other drivers are sufficient since, based on Farber's data, "the acceptance of truly hazardous passing opportunities is a consequence of small errors of judgment made by drivers who have short passing-opportunity distance thresholds (i.e., pass with short distances and small safety margins) rather than of large errors made by more conservative drivers" (Farber, 1969, p. 22). In any case, passing behavior illustrates how perceptual judgments operate to combine perceptions based on sensory data with expectancies about time-distance relationships and knowledge of vehicle-handling capabilities.

DECISION AND DECISION TIME

As may have become apparent from the discussion of how drivers judge distance and speed, the distinction between perception and decision may be very vague. For convenience only, let us consider decisions based more on experience, expectations, man-made rules and other nonsensory information as decisions proper. Thus we make a perceptual judgment on the distance between ourselves and opposing traffic whenever we want to pass a slower vehicle and then we make a decision to pass or not to pass. Another example, we can perceive a red light up the road but then we make a decision whether or not it's a "stop" light or some other (possibly irrelevant) red light. As may be expected, individual differences in decisions are much greater than in perception and perceptual judgments, simply because people often have widely different levels of knowledge, past experience, expectations, and so on. These factors affect our decisions in two ways: the time needed to make them and the interpretation which we make of the perceptual data, that is, their meaning.

Decision and Reaction Time

To perceive, make decisions and respond takes time. Furthermore this time — known as perception reaction time or simply reaction time — increases as the difficulty of the decision increases. Aspects of difficulty that have been shown to affect reaction time to a particular stimulus are the level of experience or amount of practice a person has had in responding to the stimulus, the degree of compatibility between the stimulus and the response, and the uncertainty associated with the stimulus. We discuss each separately, but concentrate mostly on the concept of uncertainty.

Experience. We all believe in the adage that "practice makes perfect," or, to be more exact, performance improves with practice (but only as long as it is accompanied by feedback). One significant source of that improvement is the reduction in time spent on making decisions. Hesitancy in making decisions is an easily observable characteristic of the beginning driver. An experienced driver can decide faster than a novice driver whether to cross an intersection or stop short of it once the signal light has turned from green to amber. One process that accounts for the saving in time is the automation of many responses so that less of a decision is involved in making them (Fitts, 1964).

Stimulus-Response (S-R) Compatibility. A relationship between a stimulus and a response to it is said to be compatible, whenever the association between the two is direct and "appears natural." Compatible S-R relationships are turning the steering wheel clockwise in response to a right curve in the road, and turning it counterclockwise in response to a left turn; moving the signal lever in the car up to turn right, and down to turn left; pressing the accelerator in response to a green light, and so on. Reversing the S-R relationship in all of the above examples would reduce the S-R compatibility, slow down reaction time, and cause more errors as well as more accidents. Note that some of these relationships appear direct and obvious (e.g., turning the steering wheel) and some are natural only because they have been overlearned (e.g., red means stop). In either case the effect is the same: the more compatible a relationship is the faster the appropriate decision. S-R compatibility principles have implications for both vehicle and environmental design. Whenever an obvious relationship is not apparent one approach is to standardize the design so that through exposure and experience one S-R relationship will eventually become the most compatible. That different systems can be just as compatible is demonstrated by the fact that in response to a two-lane road the English driver "naturally" picks the left lane to drive on, while the American driver — just as naturally — picks the right lane.

Uncertainty and Expectancy. The concept of uncertainty requires a brief explanation since it has a technical meaning that is somewhat different from its meaning in everyday usage. In the context of the mathematical theory of communication developed by Shannon and Weaver in 1949, uncertainty is inversely related to the probability of an event or a set of events. In addition, the probability of an event is typically in close correspondence with our expectancy of the occurrence of that event. Thus we expect a fair coin to turn up heads approximately 50 percent of the time. A large body of experimental data has been amassed showing that uncertainty in the mathematical sense and expectancy in the psychological sense affect reaction time (cf. Fitts & Posner, 1967). The more expected a target is, the quicker we are able to respond to it. Conversely, the less expected a target is, the longer it will take us to respond to it — or even to perceive it correctly. Thus, we need more time (and are more likely to miss) an exit ramp that departs from the left lane than from the right lane of an expressway. That "second look" that we colloquially say we take when "we can't believe our eyes" may be a very real and time-consuming effort. It does take longer to realize that the car ahead on a one-way street is coming toward you (going the wrong way), than it takes to realize the same thing on a two-way street — even though the sense impressions may be identical.

The most immediate relevance of decision time to driving is in its effect on braking. Braking often takes place in the context of emergency with very little preparation. A reaction time delay of one second when traveling at 60 mph is equivalent to 88 feet of travel — which is often more than is available. In a classic study conducted in 1934 by the Massachusetts Institute of Technology (reported by Matson, Smith, & Hurd, 1955), drivers' reaction time was studied as a function of various conditions that were hypothesized to affect reaction time. In this study the driver's task was to follow a lead vehicle and respond to its' signal by braking. What changed between conditions was the nature of the signal and the expectancy of the subject. The conditions and the reaction times are listed in Table 4.2. Note first that reaction time was shorter when the two vehicles were standing rather than moving. The longer reaction time of the moving driver is due to the additional attentional demands of driving. As

Table 4.2 Brake-Reaction Time in a Car-Following Situation as a Function of
Signal Quality, Driver Status (Standing or Moving), and Expectancy

CAR MOVEMENT	STIMULUS	STARTING FOOT POSITION	REACTION TIME (SECONDS)
Standing	Audible	Brake pedal	0.24
Standing	Bright light	Brake pedal	0.26
Standing	Stop light	Brake pedal	0.36
Standing	Audible	Accelerator	0.42
Standing	Bright light	Accelerator	0.44
Moving—normal road conditions	Audible	Accelerator	0.46
Standing	Stop light	Accelerator	0.52
Moving—test conditions	Stop light	Accelerator	0.68
Moving—normal road conditions	Stop light	Accelerator	0.82
Moving—test conditions	None—stop light hidden	Accelerator	1.34
Moving—normal road conditions	None—stop light hidden	Accelerator	1.65

From *Traffic Engineers* by Matson, Smith, and Hurd. Copyright 1955. McGraw-
Hill, New York. Used with permission of McGraw-Hill Book Co.

might be expected, braking reaction time is also longer when the foot
starts from a resting position on the accelerator than when it is already on the brakes. Thus, when the driver is moving and is expecting the lead car to stop, the reaction time to the brake light is 0.68
seconds — enough to cover approximately 50 feet when traveling at
60 mph. However when not expecting the car to stop, mean reaction
time increases to 0.82 seconds; and if the brake lights of the lead car
are not working — and the only cue the following driver has is a
change in headway — then reaction time goes up to 1.65 seconds. In
an emergency situation 1.65 seconds may make the difference between a near accident and a real one. Lest we assume that human
reaction time has changed much in the last 40 years, results of a
study conducted more recently (Johansson & Rumar, 1971) essentially coroborated the data in Table 4.2. In this study Swedish drivers
who volunteered to participate in the experiment were warned that
"sometime during the next 10 kilometers" they would hear a loud
horn at the side of the car, and their task would be to brake as quickly as possible. Reaction time was obtained by measuring the time
difference between the horn and the appearance of the brake light.
Note for Table 4.2 that reaction time to a sound is shorter than it is
to a light. Still, 50 percent of the drivers had a reaction time of 0.66
seconds or more and the slowest drivers needed 2 full seconds to

respond. After allowing for a correction factor for expectancy, Johansson and Rumar concluded that in a sudden emergency situation median driver reaction time can be expected to be 0.9 seconds. Note how close this estimate is to the 0.82 seconds for the similar condition in Table 4.2. Fortunately, although as drivers we do not respond any faster today than 40 years ago, our cars are more responsive, but then again we drive faster to begin with . . . .

In discussing reaction times we noted that we need more time to respond to an unexpected event than an expected one — but we made no attempt to quantify expectancy. If we measure expectancy as the probability of any event, then we can note that the greater the number of possible events that could occur the lower our expectancy concerning the actual occurrence of any one particular event. Thus our expectancy for either side of a fair coin would probably be 1/2 whereas our expectancy about any side of a fair die would be only 1/6. (Actually subjective expectancy differs from objective expectancy but for our present discussion we can equate the two.) It turns out that there is a direct relationship between reaction time and the quantifiable measures of uncertainty: reaction time increases as uncertainty (or the number of potential outcomes) increases. This is true even when the physical stimulus is the same. To illustrate, the response to a red light takes more time if on any trial any one of four colors (including red) may appear, than if only red or green may appear. Thus the increase in reaction time is said to reflect a longer decision time rather than the time needed to pick up the sensory information and make the appropriate motor responses, which remain the same in both situations (cf. Fitts & Posner, 1967, for a review of the literature in this area).

In driving, we often face the following type of uncertainty: many things can occur at any one time. A signal light may change from red to green to a green arrow, or it may change only for the opposing traffic; the car ahead may turn right, left, or go straight at the next intersection, etc. One would therefore expect that the faster a person can respond to changes in the situation — that is, the faster decision maker that person is — the better he or she would be able to cope with emergency situations. Many studies that attempted to show this by comparing drivers' reaction time to their accident and violation records failed to isolate the decision time component from the sensory and motor components and consequently found no relationship between driving performance measures and reaction time. However, using a more sophisticated approach to study the information-processing rate, Fergenson (1971) was able to demonstrate a relationship between accident involvement, violation history, and decision time. For his study Fergenson first, by questioning 875 people, identified

Table 4.3 Decision Time of Drivers (in seconds — based on the difference between simple and choice reaction time) as a Function of their Accidents and Violations Record

ACCIDENTS	VIOLATIONS		
	ZERO	HIGH	MEAN
Zero	0.038 (5)	0.026 (3)	0.031 (8)
High	0.047 (3)	0.064 (4)	0.054 (7)
Mean	0.043 (8)	0.038 (7)	0.039 (15)

Numbers in parentheses indicate number of subjects in each group (calculated from Fergenson's, 1971, data).

four mutually exclusive groups of people matched in their driving experience. One group of people had zero violations and zero accidents in the previous three years. The second group had two or more violations and two or more accidents in the previous three years. The third and fourth groups had either two or more accidents and no violations in the previous three years, or two or more violations and no accidents in the previous three years. The subjects selected for the study were given a simple reaction-time task, in which they were required to push a button whenever a red light appeared; and a choice reaction-time task, in which any one of three lights could appear and the subject's task was to push a different button for each of the lights. By measuring the difference between the two reaction times Fergenson argued that he obtained a measure similar to decision time, since the two tasks were identical in terms of the sensory inputs and the motor responses. Fergenson's results are summarized in Table 4.3. In this table the shorter the decision time, the better the information-processing ability, and presumably the quicker the driver can respond to an emerging critical situation. Since, in driving, the amount of information that needs to be processed varies over time, (as illustrated in Figure 4.1), those individuals with longer decision time can be expected to encounter more situations in which their processing capacity is exceeded and thus the probability of their being involved in an accident increases. Thus, as Fergenson's results in fact indicate, drivers who had both high accidents and high violation rates yielded the longest decision times and were the slowest information processors. Most interesting, however, is the fact that the high-violation and zero-accidents drivers showed the highest rate of information processing. Being aware of their driving ability, these drivers were probably involved in more "critical situations due to their driving habits, but still avoid accidents because their information processing ability is not overloaded due to their large channel capacity" (p. 175).

Perhaps the most conclusive demonstration to date about the relationship between decision time and accident involvement is the result obtained in Indiana University's study of accident causes (Treat et al., 1977). In this study the difference between simple reaction time and choice reaction time was calculated for three groups of drivers: at-fault drivers — drivers whose reaction time was measured within a week after being involved in an accident in which they were judged to have committed a human error (see Chapter Five for a discussion of the definition of human errors in accidents) that caused the accident; mixed drivers — who had an accident within the past week but were judged to have committed no errors which could have caused the accident, together with drivers who have had one or more accidents within the past two years (but not within the past week); and accident-free drivers — who had not had any accidents within the past two years. The difference between the simple and choice reaction times — the decision time — was found to increase from 0.052 seconds for the accident-free group, through 0.078 for the mixed group, to 0.97 for the at-fault group. This pattern provides a more definitive link between reaction time and accidents since it highlights the role of decision time in actually causing accidents. Note, however, that both Fergenson's study and this study are based on observational rather than experimental data. Still, in light of the importance of information-processing concepts in theories of driver behavior, these data provide very strong evidence that information-processing capabilities and limits affect driver effectiveness, and individual differences in information-processing rate may be one more factor that differentiates the safe from the unsafe driver.

Decision and Meaning

Despite the best intentions of design engineers, road users often do not use the information provided to them as expected by the highway designer. Thus, drivers tend to use advisory speed signs before curves as a caution sign calling for close evaluation of the curve ahead, rather than slow down to the recommended speed (Shinar, 1973). Similarly, flashing yellow signal lights require the driver to slow down prior to the signalized intersection, but do drivers slow down when approaching a flashing yellow signal? In a study designed to see how drivers respond to various lights, Bleyl (1972) manipulated the traffic light in a rural intersection so that the approaching drivers encountered either no signal, a green signal, a flashing yellow signal, or a signal that changed from red to green. The only significant difference between the four conditions was observed for the drivers who had no signal at all. These drivers crossed the intersection at 3 to 5 mph more than the drivers exposed to the signals. Thus no advantage was gained with the flashing yellow light in comparison with the green light. This is despite the fact that most drivers know the meaning of the flashing yellow light and the required response to it. It is safe to assume that drivers respond to various roadway stimuli according to their expectations and their understanding of the system (e.g., that when they have a flashing yellow light, the cross traffic would have a flashing red light and therefore stop) rather than according to the intent of the system designers.

The problem is more complicated when uncertainty exists as to the meaning of a signal. An illustrative case of this problem is the signalization of left-turning traffic. In a laboratory study, using color movies and color slides, Plummer and King (1973) presented subjects with 19 signal configurations used to indicate a left turn involving combination of arrows (green or yellow) with or without additional "ball" light (red, yellow, or green). As might be suspected, not all systems were as effective in conveying the same message. The differential effectiveness was indicated by both the accuracy in responding and by reaction time. Thus the less obvious the interpretation, the longer the decision time and the greater the likelihood of a wrong decision. In accordance with our stereotypes for the meaning of red and green light, the best systems were those combining a green ball with a green arrow on a fourth light source.

To summarize, to facilitate driver performance a primary goal of the highway engineer should be to design the system in ways that will reduce driver uncertainty, both with respect to the occurrence of an event and with respect to its meaning. Furthermore, as Bleyl's study indicates, even when all drivers tend to respond to a stimulus in a similar manner — suggesting a commonality in its meaning — the meaning and the resultant behaviors may still be different than those intended.

RESPONSE CAPABILITIES

Most of the overt driving behavior can be categorized as belonging to one of two categories: lateral control through steering and longitudinal control through acceleration, deceleration, and braking. In addition to the hand movements involved in steering and the foot movements involved in braking and acceleration, there is also the movement involved in shifting the right foot from the accelerator to the brake pedal or from the brake pedal to the accelerator pedal. In this section we discuss the implications of our response limitations in terms of speed and accuracy of movements, and some of the research conducted in steering and braking behavior.

Movement Time and Accuracy

In performing the movements needed for manipulating the steering wheel and the foot pedals, accuracy as well as speed is critical. Studies of human movement capabilities conducted by Fitts (Fitts, 1954; Fitts & Peterson, 1964) have demonstrated that movement time remains unchanged as movement extent increases provided that the desired accuracy is decreased proportionately. According to what has become known as Fitts' law, movement time remains constant as long as the ratio $A/0.5W$ — in which A is the desired movement extent or amplitude of the movement, and W is the width of the error tolerance — remain the same. To illustrate, if it takes 0.5 seconds to move a lever of a distance of 10 inches with 1 inch tolerance for error, then it would take the same time to move that lever 20 inches with $\pm$ 2 inches of error. However if the accuracy requirements remain unchanged, then the greater the extent of movement the longer the time needed to perform that movement. The reciprocal relationship between extent and accuracy is due to the way we make movements: we begin a movement with a rapid acceleration to a fast "travel" between the beginning and end points, and end it with a deceleration and "adjustments" as we near the end point (Murrell, 1969). As the movement extent increases, the increases in travel speed are accompanied by an increase in the adjustment time near the end of the movement (Jenkins & Connor, 1949). For optimum design of vehicle controls, it would be desirable to adjust the extent of movement so that within the desired level of accuracy, the total movement time (travel time plus adjustment time) would be minimized. How the relationship between adjustment time and movement time has implications for design can be illustrated by considering how steering wheel movements affect the movement of the wheels. With a power steering system in order to make a quick sharp turn (e.g., in an accident-avoidance maneuver) we would like to adjust the ratio between steering control movement and wheel movement so that a small change in the steering would affect a large change in the direction of the wheels. However, for most normal driving conditions such a design would be problematic since every little involuntary steering movement would cause a drastic change in the direction of travel. Unfortunately, for the most part, these human movement capabilities have not been systematically considered in the design of all vehicle controls, as evidenced by the wide variety of steering wheel/car wheel control ratios available on different cars on the market. One area in which human movement control capabilities have been considered is related to optimizing the distance between the accelerator pedal and the brake pedal. The critical movement here is from the accelerator to the brake, and so the width of the brake pedal can be considered as the error tolerance (W in Fitts' law) that is available to the driver: the brakes will be engaged as long as the driver depresses any part of the brake pedal. Two independent studies that investigated this issue have produced similar results, indicating that for the commonly used brake pedal sizes, the optimum separation between the two pedals should be approximately 7 inches (Drury, 1975; Snyder, 1976). In contrast, the average separation on standard-size American cars is less than 4 inches — a separation that produces significantly longer movement times. Incidentally the present standard design of making the brake pedal higher than the accelerator pedal also increases the movement time, as well as "helps" our foot to slip to the gas pedal when we attempt a sudden braking response.

Steering Behavior

Hand movements are both faster and more precise than foot movements, and thus it is appropriate that lateral control where the lane width may be as little as 8 feet (compared to American cars that are approximately 6 feet wide), be governed by the hands. Aside from the large steering movements involved in making turns, we also make repeated minute back-and-forth corrections, known as steering reversals, even when driving on a straight road. This type of steering behavior has been used in many studies as a measure of driving task requirements, driving difficulty, or driver's experience. The most frequently used measure in this respect is the rate of steering wheel reversals. Various studies have shown that on both straight and curved roads experienced drivers make fewer steering reversals than poor or novice drivers (Greenshields, 1963; Kimball, Ellingstad, & Hagen, 1971). McLean and Hoffman (1975), based on a summary of previous studies, concluded that the reversal rate is affected by two forms of task difficulty: difficulties imposed by the environment and difficulties due to driver impairment. Thus, steering reversals tend to increase with increasing road curvature (up to a point), and with reduced visibility (when a given speed is maintained) on one hand, and when the driver is alcohol intoxicated on the other hand (Huntley and Centybear, 1974). However, as may be expected, fatigue, which reduces the driver's overall alertness, leads to a decrease in the reversal rate.

Braking Behavior

In terms of longitudinal control the most important for safety is driver braking behavior. As we noted above even under optimal conditions, the average driver still requires approximately half a second to remove his or her foot from the accelerator to the brake pedal.

This time, incidentally, could be shortened if — as is the case with specially designed systems for handicapped drivers — the brakes were connected to hand controls attached to the steering wheel. (Richter & Hyman, 1974). How this would affect total control of the car still has to be studied.

However, there is more to braking than reaction time. It turns out that different people have different brake reaction patterns dichotomized by Babarik (1968) as either normal — a relatively even movement from the accelerator to the brake and then increased pressure on the brake pedal — or desynchronizing — a slow initiation of the braking followed by a compensating fast movement on the brake. The latter braking pattern appears to be indicative of the likelihood of getting struck from behind by another car. Thus, contrary to the legal assumption where the striking driver in rear-end accidents is always the responsible one, the struck driver may often be the one who actually causes the accident. Babarik's study, which demonstrated this relationship, was conducted on 127 Washington, D.C., taxicab drivers. After measuring the drivers' reaction patterns, Babarik identified each of the drivers as having either a normal or a desynchronizing reaction pattern (DRP). The results showed that more DRP drivers were struck from behind in rear-end accidents than normal drivers. Forthermore, while the two groups did not differ significantly in terms of the overall number of accidents in which they were involved, fewer DRP drivers were involved in rear-end accidents in which they *struck* the other vehicle. Thus, it appears that DRP drivers, while often able to stop short of the car ahead, brake their vehicles more abruptly in a way that prevents the following drivers from missing them.

SUMMARY

To negotiate a car on the road successfully, the driver has to continuously process new information and use it to make appropriate decisions. Although at any one time most of the visual scene is available to the driver, he or she is able to attend to only a small part of it. Only the attended part is typically visually fixated and perceived. Based on the way the environment is perceived (or misperceived), decisions relevant to driving behavior are made, and eventually the driver's responses to the environmental demands (that elicited the perception and decisions) can be observed. Each of the functions that must be performed — attention, perception, decision, and response — is subject to biases and limitations that are liable to affect driving capability.

The attention we allocate to driving varies both in amount and in place. Most of the time, the experienced driver is able to give to the driving task only as much attention as it needs — and thus he or she has spare attentional capacity to devote to listening to the radio, talking, daydreaming, and the like. When the environmental demands on the driver's attentional capacity become excessive, the amount of information processed can be increased by slowing down — thereby slowing the rate at which new information enters.

The attention allocated to the driving task is not evenly distributed over the total visual scene. The selectivity of attention is manifested in our ability to "look" where we think it is "important" to look. The ability to pick up and attend to the more informative parts of the visual world is one that must be learned. In driving this learning is manifested in the changes in visual search behavior that accompany increases in the driving experience. Thus, experienced and alert drivers tend to look more toward the "end" of the road and less at the road edges close to the cars than novice drivers who seem to be preoccupied with maintaining their cars on the road.

Once information is picked up it must be interpreted. We term this process of interpreting information as perception. Typically our perceptions are relatively accurate representations of the true state of the world. On occasion — as in the case of visual illusions — we are misled by our perceptions. Of particular importance to driving are misperceptions of roadway geometry, and misestimations of speed. Either underestimating a curve in the road or our speed as we approach it can lead to an accident. Misperceptions in both can arise as a result of the visual environment adjacent to the road, or as a result of wrong expectations and inappropriate adaptation. A particularly difficult perceptual judgment task is that involved in passing maneuvers. Here drivers must estimate the spacing between themselves and oncoming traffic, and their velocity relative to the car they are intending to overtake. Although our judgment capabilities are relatively poor in this task, we appear to compensate for it by either being conservative (take less risks) or letting the oncoming traffic accommodate us by slowing down or, if necessary, by going off the road.

We act on our perceptions by making decisions. Since in driving — particularly in emergency situations — making the right decision at the right time is critical, the time it takes to make decisions is important. Our decision time is lengthened whenever we are unexperienced in the particular task, the event we are reacting to is unexpected, or the relationship between the stimulus and response is in some sense complex or incompatible. All of these factors may influence brake-reaction time so that it can vary from as little as one quarter of a second to over one and one half seconds. In addition to these external factors of experience, compatibility, and uncertainty, there are large individual differences in decision time that, based on relatively recent research, appear to link drivers with long decision times to higher accident rates or a greater likelihood to cause an accident.

Whatever the decision time, at times the decisions that drivers make may be inappropriate. In such cases drivers interpret various signs and signals differently than intended by the highway designer. It is important then to behaviorally assess how drivers respond to signs and signals.

Last in the information-processing sequence are the drivers' overt responses. Here too there are limits on the accuracy at which we can control our hand and foot movements. Any movement that we make takes time, and this time increases as we increase the movement's accuracy. In driving we maintain our position in the lane by making frequent back-and-forth steering corrections, which increase as the driving task becomes more difficult. Accuracy of foot movements is less important for safety purposes but individual differences in their braking patterns seem to make some people — who typically brake late and abruptly — more susceptible to being struck from behind.

FIVE
HUMAN FACTORS IN HIGHWAY TRAFFIC ACCIDENTS

Approximately 500 years ago, the reputed witch and prophetess Mother Shipton, wrote a poem entitled "Prophecy," which included the following vision:

Carriages without horses shall go,
And accidents will fill the world with woe

Highway traffic accidents — as a severe societal problem — have come as a by-product of the automobile. A significant aspect of vehicle design, highway development, and driver-improvement programs is safety — typically measured through accident reduction. To measure advances in safety, a wide variety of accident statistics have been developed. These statistics provide us with a picture of the accident problem, and relative proportions of types of accidents as a function of the different driver, vehicle, and roadway characteristics. They also provide some insights into the causes of traffic accidents. Any detailed discussion of the causes of traffic accidents, however, must be preceded by defining what is an accident and by explaining some of the unique problems associated with defining and assessing accident causes. These are very important methodological issues that, depending upon how they are resolved, affect the outcomes of studies of accidents and accident causation. Once we define accidents and accident causes we can then move on to examine the role of the driver in accident causation, and the role of various driver actions and inactions that contribute to accidents. Finally, it must be acknowledged that the driver does not operate in a vacuum and consequently driver errors often cause accidents only because they interact with other "causes" related to vehicle design or the environment in which they are committed.

THE SCOPE OF THE "ACCIDENT PROBLEM"

The magnitude of the accident problem varies as a function of what we care to label as accidents. Different states and agencies define highway traffic accidents in somewhat different ways and, as a result, regional accident statistics reflect different types of data bases and biases. Consequently, national accident statistics, based on pooling data from different sources, may not be a valid indicator of the true accident picture, and comparisons among countries should be considered as even more suspect.

The Definition of an Accident

Take a few minutes to review in your mind the motor vehicle accidents that you or your friends as drivers have been involved in in the past three years. Now, did you include in your review those occasions in which you hit or lightly tapped a parked car while parallel parking? Did you include those minor collisions in moving traffic in which no damage was caused? Did you include those occasions in which you ran off the road, but were able to regain control without causing any damage or injury? The answer to all three questions is probably no. However, note then that in this case your own definition of an accident is different from the dictionary definition in which an accident is typically regarded as an unintended and unpleasant event. In its broadest scope, an accident has been technically defined as "an unexpected not necessarily injurious or damaging event, that interrupts a completion of an activity; it is invariably preceded by an unsafe act or an unsafe condition or both, or some combination of unsafe act and/or unsafe conditions" (National Safety Council, 1974, p. v).

In reviewing your own accident history, chances are that you included only a subsample of what might be called accidents. Just as your tally would have been different had you counted all these less serious accidents, so would national statistics change if all traffic collisions were included in the category of accidents. What, then, constitutes an accident?

For all practical purposes, and at least for our present purpose, it may be best to define accidents as those traffic mishaps that involve as a minimum some property damage and are reported to the police. The inclusion of police notification as a criterion is simply because presently the police have the most immediate and comprehensive reporting procedures for those events we label as traffic accidents. Thus, because police files are the major source of data, most accident statistics are based only on police-reported accidents. In the United States, a new system — the National Accident Sampling System — is now being developed. This system will provide national accident statistics in which the criterion for what constitutes an accident (something that still has to be decided) will be the same for all regions.

A final comment on the use of the term "accident." In highway traffic safety literature the words "accident," "collision," and "crash" are often used interchangeably. To be exact we should note that collision and crash are simply descriptive labels for a situation whereas an accident also involves the assumption that the collision was unintended — an assumption that is not always warranted (see discussion in Chapter 3). According to another distinction between accidents and collisions, made by Shaoul (1976, p. 575),

an accident is usually defined as certain types of outcomes of a collision between two objects in the road transport system which result in damage to property and/or injury to a road user. Thus, accidents are defined by their outcomes rather than their antecedent behavior . . . . They belong to the wider class of collisions. Various factors such as: energy-absorbing bumpers, seatbelts, efficient ambulance services, and unoccupied vehicle, may

in fact prevent a collision from being classified as an accident,
because they reduce the consequence of such a collision.

Thus, although from the point of view of trying to understand driver
behavior in accident-causing situations we should really be interested
in recording collisions, practical police-reporting limitations restrict
most of our data to accidents. Note, however, that not all researchers
make the fine distinction that Shaoul does, and consequently most
often the use of the terms is interchangeable. In this text, the term
accidents is used because most of the data we have on collisions is
from police reports (hence accidents), and because it is the most
commonly used of the three labels.

Accident Statistics

The potential societal gains from increases in highway safety should
be immediately apparent from a brief review of selected highway
statistics. In the United States alone, in 1975 there were over 16
million motor-vehicle accidents in which 8600 pedestrians and
37,400 passengers and drivers were killed. In addition to the 46,000
people killed, nearly two million people were seriously injured (National
Safety Council, 1976). While these numbers should be sufficiently alarming, a better appreciation of the magnitude of the problem can be gained by comparing highway accidents to other death-
causing agents. Thus, highway traffic accidents are the leading cause
of death for Americans under the age of 40; they are the leading
cause of accidental deaths for all ages; they account for 94 percent of
all transportation-related deaths; and each year they kill more Americans than were killed in the Vietnam war in 10 years. These comparative statistics collated by the U. S. Department of Transportation
(1975) underscore the urgent need to understand the causes of
traffic accidents and to develop effective preventive and remedial
measures. Aside from the humanitarian need to reduce accidents, in
our society — where time is money and lost time and lives are trans-
lated to lost income and revenue — the financial cost of accidents is
enormous. The societal costs (in terms of property damage, medical
expenses, insurance administration, and wage loss) from 16,500,000
accidents in 1975 were estimated by the National Safety Council
(1976) to be 21.2 billion dollars — almost as much as the costs of all
other types of accidents combined. A more concrete description of
the costs of the traffic accidents in Texas is provided in Figure 5.1.
Multiply everything in that figure by 15 and you will appreciate the
national cost.

The accident situation world wide is even more alarming. If we
divide the number of accidents by the amount of driving con-

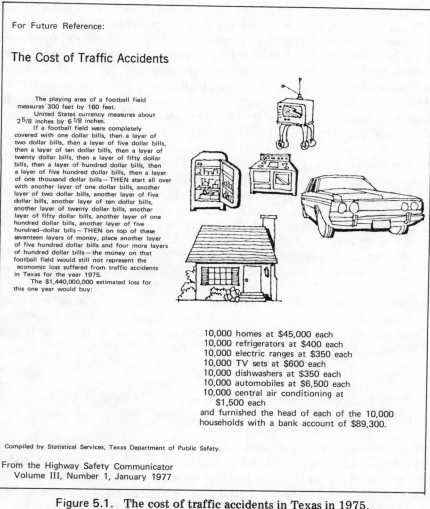

For Future Reference:

The Cost of Traffic Accidents

The playing area of a football field measures 300 feet by 160 feet.
United States currency measures about 2 5/8 inches by 6 1/8 inches.
If a football field were completely covered with one dollar bills, then a layer of two dollar bills, then a layer of five dollar bills, then a layer of ten dollar bills, then a layer of twenty dollar bills, then a layer of fifty dollar bills, then a layer of hundred dollar bills, then a layer of five hundred dollar bills, then a layer of one thousand dollar bills — THEN start all over with another layer of one dollar bills, another layer of two dollar bills, another layer of five dollar bills, another layer of ten dollar bills, another layer of twenty dollar bills, another layer of fifty dollar bills, another layer of one hundred dollar bills, another layer of five hundred--dollar bills — THEN on top of these seventeen layers of money, place another layer of five hundred dollar bills and four more layers of hundred dollar bills — the money on that football field would still not represent the economic loss suffered from traffic accidents in Texas for the year 1975.
The $1,440,000,000 estimated loss for this one year would buy:

10,000 homes at $45,000 each
10,000 refrigerators at $400 each
10,000 electric ranges at $350 each
10,000 TV sets at $600 each
10,000 dishwashers at $350 each
10,000 automobiles at $6,500 each
10,000 central air conditioning at
    $1,500 each
and furnished the head of each of the 10,000 households with a bank account of $89,300.

Compiled by Statistical Services, Texas Department of Public Safety.

From the Highway Safety Communicator
Volume III, Number 1, January 1977

Figure 5.1. The cost of traffic accidents in Texas in 1975.

ducted on the American highways (i.e., the American driver's exposure to accidents), we discover that the United States has the lowest accident fatalities rate in the world: 361 fatalities for every million vehicle-miles. For comparison purposes, the rates for other technologically advanced countries, such as Japan, are approximately three times as high. For less developed countries the fatality rate is higher. Thus, Kenya's fatality rate (based on 1973 statistics) was reported as 7500 per million vehicle-miles, that is, more than 22 times that of the United States (Borkenstein, 1973).

When we assess accident severity in terms of the number of accidents as a function of the number of miles driven by all vehicles, we get an accident rate adjusted for exposure. While this is the most common measure used, it contrasts with a more common approach used in other areas of public health and safety such as disease and crime. In these areas the fatality rate is computed per 100,000 or one million people in the population, yielding a population fatality rate. The use of different statistics can lead to different conclusions. In highway traffic accidents this is demonstrated by an apparent discrepancy noted by Klein (1976, p. 213):

> *The use of an exposure rate rather than a population rate produced, in recent years, a curious result: there was a considerable satisfaction expressed over the reduction in the fatality rate per million miles when in fact during this same period an increasing proportion of the United States population was being killed in highway crashes. From a social or public-health point of view this would not be grounds for self-satisfaction; on the contrary, efforts would be made to reduce their exposure.*

Klein's comment's should serve as a note of caution in interpreting accident statistics. Depending on the statistics used the accident problem can look grim or very grim — but as long as it exists, it cannot look good.

THE INVESTIGATION AND CAUSAL ASSESSMENT OF TRAFFIC ACCIDENTS

Three baseball referees were once discussing their different styles. The first said, "I look at the ball and if it's a strike, it's a strike and if it's a ball, it's a ball — and I call it as it is." The second one said, "I look at the ball and if it's a strike, it's a strike and if it's a ball, it's a ball — and I call it as I see it." The third one said, "I look at the ball and I call it a strike or a ball — but it ain't nothing until I call it."

In describing accidents and causes of accidents we like to assume that we act as the first referee in the above example. Unfortunately, in moments of candor we must agree that we are much more like the third one. Consequently, the results that we obtain from assessing accidents, and the conclusions that we draw from these results concerning the causes of accidents, are all determined to a large extent by our initial definition of what is an accident cause. In this section we first highlight some psychological processes that influence accident assessment and then discuss two approaches to defining and determining accident causes.

Psychological Processes in Accident Reconstruction

The process of accident investigation is by its nature a post-hoc analysis of events, since the accident has already occurred. In trying to determine either why an accident happened, or the contingencies that were involved in the accident-causing sequence, investigators must rely on their judgment. Human judgment is the basis for determining not only the accident cause, but also the basis for determining the existence or nonexistence of physical evidence left after the accident. To illustrate, there is judgment involved in measuring the length of skid marks. Skid marks are left on the dry pavement whenever the driver locks the brakes of the car. Based on the length of the skid marks, investigators can often calculate with a relatively high level of accuracy the speed of the vehicle prior to braking. However, the onset of skidding is a gradual process and the determination of where exactly the skid marks begin is based on the investigator's human judgment. Consequently, the estimate of the speed of the car prior to the accident and the speed at impact, are both subjective evaluations, even though they are based on seemingly objective information concerning skid-mark length. In evaluating all of these factors, human judges are known to have consistent biases and deficiencies that affect their judgment.

When faced with a set of circumstances that may lead to an accident, and asked to predict whether or not an accident will happen, people will judge the likelihood of an accident as much higher if they are also told whether the accident actually happened, than if they do not have knowledge of whether the accident happened or not. Once we know an accident happened, then the gift of hindsight also acts on our perceived relevance of different details that preceded the accident. This process is one that is largely unconscious and aids us in seeing our world as very deterministic: in retrospect many things appear to have been inevitable, or at least more predictable. In a paper entitled, "Hindsight: Thinking Backwards?" Fischhoff (1974, p. 12) noted:

> If we look at the past and find that it holds few surprises for us, we are essentially denying that we have anything to learn from it. Even though outcome knowledge changes our perception of specific events (by making them seem inevitable), without a feeling of surprise we'd probably feel little compunction to reevaluate the "world hypothesis" or rules with which we interpret what goes on around us.

One particularly devious bias we seem to have is that once an accident occurs, we have tendency to seek a culprit. This is also characteristic of police work: in a multiple-vehicle collision the investigating officer is required to determine which of the drivers was "responsible" for the accident. Furthermore, the more severe the accident, the greater the tendency of people to blame one of the persons involved as responsible for that accident. This was demonstrated in a laboratory experiment (Walster, 1966) in which subjects listened to a description of a single-vehicle traffic accident. There were four groups of subjects who all heard the exact same accident description, except for differences in the severity of the outcome of the accident: inconsequential damage, considerable damage, damage and near injury to a pedestrian, or heavy damage and serious injury. The results showed that the more severe the outcome, the greater the responsibility that the judges attributed to the driver. However, according to Walster, this tendency to relate the degree of blame to the severity of the accident is due not to our misperception of the behavior or the situation as much as it is due to our tendency to apply stricter moral standards in judging a person's behavior when the accidental consequences are more severe.

Another problem in attempting to reconstruct an accident and determine what in fact happened, is associated with the use of eyewitness and driver reports. Here the fallibility of memory is such that minute changes in wording of the investigator's questions can yield totally different reports. Loftus and Palmer (1974) demonstrated this relationship between language and memory by showing films of staged traffic accidents. After showing the films the subjects were queried about their estimates of the mean speed of the two cars prior to the collision. In questioning the subjects, they asked one group "about how fast were the cars going when they hit each other?" Other groups were asked the same question with a different verb replacing the word "hit"; the different verbs being "smashed," "collided," "bumped," or "contacted." As you may note, the difference between those verbs may be described in terms of the severity of the interaction between the two cars; "smashed" being the most severe and "contacted" being the least severe. The researchers found that the mean speed estimate was only 32 mph when the verb was "contacted" and rose significantly up to 41 mph when the verb used was "smashed." In a second experiment the subjects were asked to return after one week, at which time they were asked "did you see any broken glass?" This time, in the questioning immediately after the film presentation only the words "hit" and "smashed" were used. In recalling the accident a week later, 16 percent of the subjects presented with the word "hit" reported seeing glass on the road while over 50 percent of the subjects presented with the word "smashed" reported seeing glass on the road — when in fact there was no broken glass in this accident! The striking effects of semantics on the recall of visually perceived effects was explained by Loftus and Palmer by suggesting that for a complex event such as an accident, the information fed into memory is composed of two types of data: the first consists of whatever pieces of details are extracted from the actual visual occurrence during the brief time that the information is available. The second source of information is "external" information supplied after the fact. Over time the details from both sources are integrated into a coherent pattern and "all we have is one 'memory.'"

The recall problem illustrated in Loftus and Palmer's study is not unique to their experimental design. This distortion of past events can be created by the witnesses themselves in the process of repeating the accident descriptions to themselves and to others, and even in the almost immediate process of integrating the descrete glimpses that they perceived in the actual sequence of events into a coherent (and subjectively acceptable) story. Accident reconstruction based on the drivers' recall of the accident is even more suspect than eyewitnesses' reports since drivers invariably attempt to justify their behavior just prior to the accident, rather than admit — especially to themselves — that they are careless or incompetent. This phenomenon is encapsulated in a "law" attributed to J. S. Baker of Northwestern University, that "drivers tend to explain their traffic accidents by reporting circumstances of lowest culpability compatible with credibility" (Aronoff, 1971). Thus, an accident-involved drunk driver may claim he or she fell asleep and a driver who in fact fell asleep may claim a mechanical failure was the accident cause. Baker noted the amazing number of "mechanical failures" that occur at night, on open stretches of road — just after the bars and taverns close . . . . The drivers' and witnesses' biasing factors indicate that the interviewing of drivers about their own accidents should occur as soon as possible after the accidents — before elaborate rationalizations can be developed and memory is distorted — and then only by skilled interviewers.

Defining and Determining Accident Causes

In the scientific sense, the word cause implies contingency between events, and the causal explanation of a sequence of events requires a specification of one or more antecedent events whose occurrence would be necessary to bring about or "cause" the accident. Thus, sudden brake failure could be labeled as an accident cause if in the process of attempting to brake the car a previously unknown brake failure prevents an effective braking action and the driver collides with the vehicle ahead. However, note that this does not mean that brake failure is always necessary for an accident to happen, but only that in that particular situation, the accident would have been prevented had the brakes operated properly. In this sense the condition of necessity is different from the logician's definition of necessity where if a cause is necessary for an accident to occur then it should be present in all accidents. To distinguish the two, Taylor (1976) labeled an explanation of why a specific accident happened as a "reason" rather than a "cause," and further argued that because reasons are not deterministic — that is, the same explanation would not always lead to an accident — they cannot be considered as formal scientific explanations of why accidents occur. However, reasons are valuable because they can provide us with information of what kind of events and behaviors lead to accidents, how often they arise, under what circumstances, in combination with what other factors, etc. This information, in turn can be used to develop effective accident countermeasures — methods to reduce accidents (see Chapter Six). In this chapter, we use the term "cause" to describe events that precipitated accidents since this term is the one used by accident investigators and in the accident investigation literature. Nonetheless, the distinction between the scientific deterministic definition of the word cause and the more limited definition used by the accident reconstructionist should be kept in mind. Accident causes as they are described here imply only that they were necessary to cause those accidents in which they were cited as causes, and not necessarily all traffic accidents.

The process of determining accident causes is not a simple one. In the attempt to reconstruct an accident, accident investigators look for reasons for the accident that are often described in terms of driver behaviors, vehicle failures, or environmental deficiencies prior to the accident. In the absence of other sources of evidence, the driver's explanations of why he or she behaved the way they did are sometimes accepted at face value and as causes.

To overcome some of the problems in determining accident causes, two different approaches have been developed. The first approach, to which the above discussion is most relevant, involves detailed reconstruction of individual accidents. This approach, which has been labeled the "clinical" approach, has a degree of subjectivity in the assessment of causes since the evidence from which the accident is reconstructed may be both fragmentary and distorted. The alternative and more objective approach to the assessment of accident causes is based on the statistical concept of overinvolvement. This means that accident causes are those driver, vehicle, and environmental attributes that are overinvolved (i.e., more frequent) in an accident population (of drivers, vehicles, and environments) than in the general population. Thus if the frequency of alcohol intoxicated drivers is found to be greater in the accident-involved driver population than in the general driving population (and it is), then according to this approach alcohol by being "overinvolved" in accidents is an accident cause. Only by showing that a particular characteristic is more prevalent in the accident population than in the driver population at large can we infer that it causes accidents. However, the inference is only by association and sometimes is obviously inappropriate. Thus, as we noted before, young drivers are overinvolved in accidents, yet it makes little sense to think of age per se as a cause of accidents.

Although traditionally the two approaches have been applied separately, they could in fact be combined so that post-hoc accident investigation data could be used in conjunction with "exposure" data — data on the driving population at large — against which the accident population could be compared. This way, the overinvolvement of true accident causes identified in the process of accident reconstructions could be determined by observing the frequency of the same vehicle failures, environmental deficiencies, and driver errors in the general population. In this way, the clinical process could be used to identify those variables that should be investigated in the statistical approach.

SYSTEM FAILURES AS THE CAUSES OF TRAFFIC ACCIDENTS

The highway transportation system is a very forgiving one in the sense that it allows for quite a lot of variability on the part of the driver, the vehicle, and the environment before the system fails and an accident occurs. Thus, most of the time people with widely differing physical and mental capabilities, driving vehicles of different sizes and different handling capabilities, and under various degraded environmental conditions, such as rain, fog, and poor roadways, manage to function relatively well within that system. When, then, does an accident happen? An accident results whenever one or more factors — labeled as the accident cause or causes — deviate from the norm to such an extent that the system cannot accommodate it. One of the most consistent findings in accident research is that accidents are typically caused by more than one factor. Each factor cited as causal may be a cause only in the context of the other causes. To illustrate, a driver's delayed recognition of a vehicle stopping ahead may result in a delayed braking response that may be ineffective because of deficient brakes. In such a case it is possible that neither the delayed recognition nor the deficient brakes alone would have caused the accident, but given the presence of either one, the other would cause the accident.

To find out which are the driver behaviors, vehicle failures, and environmental factors that are in fact causing our highway accidents, a comprehensive five-year study was conducted by Indiana University for the U. S. Department of Transportation (Treat, Tumbas, McDonald, Shinar, Hume, Mayer, Stansifer, & Castellan, 1977). This study, the most extensive and detailed one of accident causation to date, involved the investigation by experts of over 2000 accidents. Because of the unique status of this research project in the area of accident causation, the remainder of this chapter is devoted primarily to a discussion of the results of this study. A few other studies — of more limited scope or depth — investigating the same issues, have produced similar results and are referred to in the course of the discussion. Prior to discussing the results of Indiana University's study we must first briefly describe its methodology.

Indiana University's Trilevel Study of the Causes of Traffic Accidents

Indiana University's study (Treat et al., 1977) involved three levels of accident investigation. The first level consisted of the routine police investigation of all accidents occurring in Monroe County, Indiana. These investigations yielded a total of 13,568 accident reports. At the second or "on-site" level, accidents were investigated by specially trained technicians who rushed to the accident site immediately after notification by the police. These investigators arrived at the accident site at approximately the same time as the police and were therefore able to quickly pick up evidence from the environment (such as skid marks, broken glass, etc.), the vehicle (such as tire inflation, brake condition, structural integrity, damage, etc.), and the driver (through interviews and observation). Thus, these teams were able to provide accident data on a relatively representative sample of all the police-reported accidents. Of this sample of 2258 accidents, 420 accidents were further investigated at a third and higher level of sophistication — labeled "in-depth" — by a multidisciplinary accident investigation team. The key members of this team were a behavioral scientist who interviewed and examined the drivers, an accident reconstruction specialist who examined all the evidence at the accident site and reconstructed a complete diagram of the site and the vehicles' paths, and an automotive engineer who examined the accident vehicle in a specially equipped garage. At both the on-site and in-depth levels of investigation the causes were identified as being either "definite" or "certain" (indicating the confidence level of the investigators equivalent to .95 to 1.00, in a range of .0 to 1.00), "probable" (indicating a confidence of .80 to .94), or "possible" (indicating a confidence level

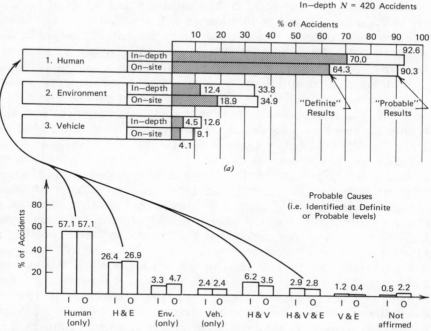

Figure 5.2. The percent of accidents caused by human, environmental, and vehicular causes (a) and the relative proportions of combinations of these causes (b). Because many accidents are caused by multiple causes the sum of the percentages in Figure 5.2a exceeds 100 percent while in Figure 5.2b the percentages add up to 100 percent (from Treat et al., 1977).

of .20 to .79). In deciding on the accident causes, both teams had a finite list of previously determined "causes" of accidents and so the process of causal assessment basically involved selecting the most appropriate causes from that list. Thus the approach was essentially one of detailed post-hoc clinical analysis. In order not to force factors into predefined categories, several pilot studies were first conducted before the final list of accident causes was compiled. Causes were classified as being either vehicular (e.g., faulty brakes, tires or steering), environmental (e.g., view obstructions, glare, or slick roads) or human (e.g., driver-delayed recognition of the critical situations, misjudgment of the situation, or improper response).

The Relative Role of Human Factors in Accident Causes

The relative frequency of human, environmental, and vehicular causes in Indiana University's study are depicted in Figure 5.2a. Only the results for the probable and definite level of confidence are noted since the results based on the possible level are more speculative and therefore less valid and reliable. The most striking aspect of the figure is the overwhelming predominance of human factors — identified as probable or definite causes in the approximately 91 percent of the accidents. This figure implies that in the majority of the accidents the driver (or one of the drivers) committed an action or failed to take an action that an otherwise alert, reasonably skilled, and defensive driver would have taken — and which would have prevented the accident. While this percentage is very high, it is consistent with the results obtained in several less comprehensive or detailed studies. Thus, the National Safety Council of America (1976) estimated (on the basis of police reports) that in 1975 "improper driving"was responsible for 85 percent of all highway accidents. Perchonok (1972), after analyzing 670 accidents, concluded that 88 percent of these accidents were caused — at least in part — by the driver. Abroad, a study conducted in England over a period of four years involving 2130 accidents also concluded that the "road user" (which could be either a driver or a pedestrian) was either solely or partially responsible for nearly 95 percent of the accidents (Sabey & Staughton, 1975). Data collated by the Finnish Insurance Information Center (1974) on 1193 accidents indicated that in 89 percent of these accidents the principal cause was a driver error. All of these studies point to the fact that — at least as far as expert opinion is concerned — approximately 90 percent of the highway traffic accidents are preceded by some information-processing failure or behavior that an alert and relatively skillful driver would not have made. This does not mean, however, that it is "normal" to remain continuously alert while driving, but only to say that at that particular moment, which preceded the accident, an alert driver would not have made that particular error.

The next point in connection with the results in Figure 5.2a is that the percentages of driver errors, environmental factors, and vehicular factors total to more than 100 percent. This indicates that in most accidents more than one factor is the "cause" of the accident. An accident may be caused by several human errors that in combination produce the accident, or by combination of a human error and a vehicular failure or by any combination of driver-vehicle-environment failure. A driver-environment combination is illustrated by the driver who detects the stopping of the car ahead too late and, in attempting to brake, skids on the wet road. This accident, then, is caused only by the combination of delayed recognition and slippery road, but not by either one alone. Figure 5.2b illustrates how human factors combined with other causes. Thus, it is somewhat comforting to note that of the 91 percent human causes (in Figure 5.2a) only 57 percent of the accidents were due to human errors without any additional environmental or vehicular factors. For the remaining 44 percent of the accidents a collision may have been prevented had a vehicular or environmental problem been corrected. Note that the most common combination is that of human and environmental causes, suggesting that a major cause of accidents is due to the interaction of human information processing difficulties in the context of environmental degradations such as view obstructions and poor signing or roadway design. Similarly, high percentages for the combination of driver and environmental factors — 30 percent and 24 percent — were obtained by Perchonok (1972) and Sabey and Staughton (1975), respectively. In contrast, vehicle failures that when combined with human errors caused accidents were relatively infrequent — or at least less frequent then many drivers would like to believe (see Figure 5.3).

PRINCIPAL HUMAN FACTORS IN ACCIDENTS

We can view the accident as an end result of an "accident process" in which we discern a causal chain of events, conditions, and behaviors that preceded the accident. A hypothetical example of such a causal chain combining both human, vehicle, and environmental elements is contained in Table 5.1 (from Fell, 1976). In this chain of events any behavior or situation can be defined as a "cause" of the following behavior or situation, which is its "effect." This effect becomes the cause for the next behavior or situation, and so on. Thus, speeding can be regarded as the "effect" of aggressive driving, and as the "cause" of delayed recognition of a dangerous situation. It is the last combination of effects, denoted in the table by capital E, that directly leads to the accident. When arriving at the scene to investigate an accident, it is easiest to identify this last combination of effects, and it becomes more and more difficult to identify the preceding events as they regress further in time. Therefore, the farther we get from the accident scene the more speculative we are in explaining the causes of the accident.

In order to remain on firmer grounds, Indiana University's study was concerned primarily with those sets of behaviors and events that immediately preceded the accident and were directly responsible for it. These behaviors were defined as human direct causes. However, to gain an insight into the relationship between direct causes and driver impairments known to affect safety, the probe for accident causes in Indiana University's study extended beyond the immediate cause into what can be labeled as "indirect causes," or causes of direct causes. These were defined as conditions or states (such as fatigue or alcohol intoxication) whose presence impaired the driver's level of information processing functions.

"There must be SOMETHING wrong with it. It keeps hitting things."

Figure 5.3. An accident may be caused by a vehicular failure or degradation — although, more often than not, it is in combination with a driver error (from *The Travelers 1954 Book of Street and Highway Data*. Illustration courtesy of The Travelers Insurance Companies.).

Table 5.1   Hypothetical Human, Vehicle, and Environmental Causal Chains that Combine in a Traffic Accident

HUMAN CAUSAL CHAIN

c:	Man fights with wife
e:	Late departure for work
c:	Late departure for work
e:	Agressive driving
c:	Agressive driving
e:	Driver speed too fast for conditions
C:	Speed too fast for conditions
E:	Driver did not immediately comprehend danger of slower vehicle ahead around curve

VEHICLE CAUSAL CHAIN

c:	Faulty inspection
e:	Worn brakes not detected
C:	Worn brakes
E:	Increased stopping distance

ENVIRONMENTAL CAUSAL CHAIN

c:	It was raining
e:	Wet roadway
C:	Wet roadway
E:	Lower coefficient of friction on roadway

Human + vehicle + environmental causal chains = CRASH

From Fell, 1976.

Human Direct Causes of Traffic Accidents

A specific description of the immediate driver error that preceded the accident is much more useful than a statement that driver error was the cause of an accident. To provide an understanding of the kind of problems that drivers have in trying to remain accident free, and the kind of behaviors that foil this, Treat et al. developed a comprehensive taxonomy of potential accident causes. Human direct causes of traffic accidents were defined as "human acts and failures to act in the minutes immediately preceding an accident, which increase the risk of collision beyond that which would have existed for a conscious driver driving to a high but reasonable standard of good defensive driving practice" (Treat et al., 1977, p. 201). These behaviors, or failures in information processing, were classified under categories similar to the ones listed in Figure 1.1, that is, perception (labeled here as recognition), decision, and response. After several pilot studies, the taxonomy of potential human direct causes illus-

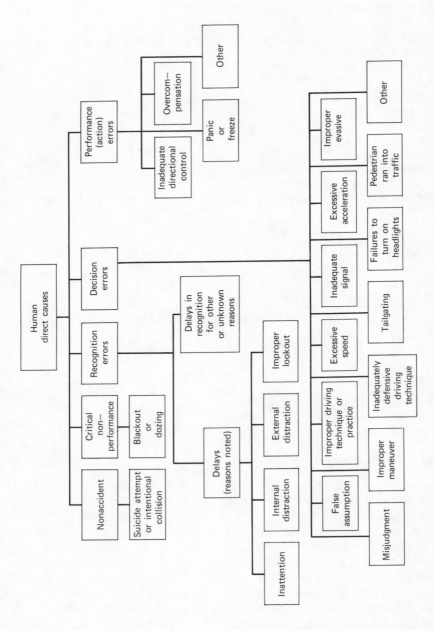

Figure 5.4. Causal factor tree for human direct causes of accidents (from Treat et al., 1977).

Table 5.2   Partial Definitions of Select Human Direct Causes

---

Critical Nonperformance: Driver blacks out or falls asleep.

Nonaccident: The collision is intentional (e.g., suicide attempt).

Inattention: Delayed recognition due to preoccupation with irrelevant thoughts or wandering of the mind.

Internal Distraction: Delayed recognition due to an attentional shift to an event, activity, object, or person *within the vehicle.*

External Distraction: Delayed recognition due to an attentional shift to an event, activity, object, or person *outside the vehicle.*

Improper Lookout: Delayed recognition due to failure to perform an adequate visual search in a situation that requires a distinct visual surveillance (e.g., in intersections and pulling out of a parking space).

False Assumption: Taking action on the basis of an assumption that is not valid — even if it is based on the traffic system rules (e.g., pulling in front of a driver who is signaling a turn but does not in fact turn).

Improper Maneuver: Willfully choosing a vehicle path that is wrong, since it increases the chance of a collision (e.g., turning from the wrong lane, driving the wrong way in a one-way street).

Improper Driving Technique: Engaging in an improper control of vehicle path or speed, in an habitual maneuver (e.g., cresting hills while driving in the center of the road).

Inadequately Defensive Driving Technique: A behavior that increases the risk of a collision *if* another driver performs contrary to expectations (e.g., crossing a one-way street without checking for cross traffic in both directions).

Excessive Speed: Speed that is excessive relative to the traffic, roadway, and ambience conditions — regardless of the legal speed limit.

Improper Evasive Action: Failing to take an emergency action that is apparent and within the capabilities of an adequately trained and alert driver (e.g., locking the brakes and as a result loosing control of the car, in a situation where steering could have prevented the accident).

Overcompensation: Improper reactions to emergency situations that cause loss of control, such as overbraking or oversteering (e.g., oversteering back into the highway after going off into the road shoulder).

From Treat et al., 1977.

trated in Figure 5.4, was developed. Each of these factors was operationally defined, and partial definitions of some of these factors are provided in Table 5.2. Taxonomies of environmental and vehicular causal factors were also developed, but a discussion of these is beyond the scope of this text (see Treat et al., 1977).

The final driver failure that makes the accident inevitable may be one of delayed recognition or perception of the impending danger, an error in the decision-making process on how to respond to that situation, or an improper response to the emergency situation. Treat et al. (1977) found — based on both the "on-site" data on 2258 accidents and the "in-depth" data on 420 accidents — that of the total driver errors, response errors were the least frequent (occurring in approximately 10 percent of the accidents). The most common errors were those labeled as recognition (present in approximately 55 percent of the accidents) and decision errors (present in approximately 50 percent of the accidents). It is difficult to compare these results to those obtained elsewhere in the United States (Perchonok, 1972) or in Europe (Finnish Insurance Information Institute, 1974; Sabey & Staughton, 1975) since the taxonomy of driver errors differed among the studies. In general, however, the predominance of attention/perception errors over response errors is common to all these studies. Thus, based on accident reconstructions and clinical evaluations, it appears that most accidents are caused by lapses in attention and impairments in the other information-processing tasks, rather than by poor vehicle-control capabilities. Given the ever-constant increase in speeds and amount of traffic on the highways and improvements in vehicle control systems, this may not be surprising.

To appreciate the specific driver errors involved in accidents better, the 10 most common driver errors cited by the Indiana University researchers are listed in Figure 5.5. Heading the list is improper lookout, followed by excessive speed, inattention, and improper evasive action. Since each of these factors was a probable cause in over 10 percent of the accidents studied, they deserve a brief discussion.

Improper Lookout. Improper lookout was the most frequent cause of accidents identified by the Indiana University study. Most of these errors (74 percent) were cited in intersections rather than in lane changes or when pulling out of a parking space. Thus, nearly one-sixth of all the accidents studied were caused by drivers who pulled into a street from an intersecting alley, driveway, or street without checking properly for the presence of other traffic. A more detailed analysis revealed that drivers cited for this error "looked but did not see" just as often as they "failed to look." Thus, merely scanning the visual field does not guarantee seeing. To see, the drivers must both look and attend. Furthermore, since view obstructions were present in only 39 percent of these accidents, it appears that improper lookout occurs independently of the presence of physical objects that would appear to make proper lookout more difficult. Instead, the most likely explanation for the predominance of improper lookout is that those situations requiring a distinct visual surveillance constitute increased environmental demands which the driver does not always respond to (see Figure 4.1). In intersections, a proper lookout also depends on adequate sensitivity in the periph-

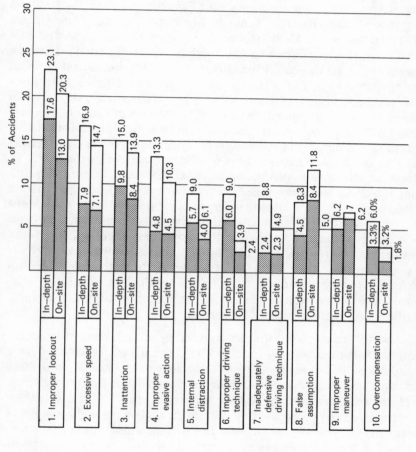

Figure 5.5. Percentage of accidents caused by specific human direct causes (from Treat et al., 1977).

eral field of view. This is a problem for older drivers who often suffer from a reduced visual field (Burg, 1968; Shinar, 1977). Indeed, Treat et al. found that drivers over 65 were twice as likely to have had their accident due to improper lookout as accident-involved drivers in general.

Excessive Speed. Excessive speed was cited as a probable accident cause in approximately 15 percent of the accidents. Similar percentages were reported by Sabey and Staughton (1975) in England (12 percent) and by the Finnish Insurance Information Center (1975) (16 percent). Most of the time, when drivers exceeded safe speed limits, it was relative to the road design rather than relative to the weather or traffic conditions. This is probably because it is much easier to perceive difficult traffic and weather conditions than poor highway design ahead of the driver — especially on rural roads. To drive safely at a high speed, the driver must proportionately increase the rate at which he or she processes all the relevant information. The results indicated that this may be an impossible task for drivers unfamiliar with the roadway who were often caught "off-guard." In contrast to the overinvolvement of older drivers in committing improper lookout, excessive speed was characteristic of younger drivers and declined with age. Interestingly, excessive speed was an accident cause twice as often (21 percent) when the driver was returning from a social event, compared to when the driver was coming from home or returning from work (11 percent). Since a familiar overinvolvement of excessive speed was observed when the driver was alcohol intoxicated compared to when he or she was sober, it is likely that alcohol intoxication was the actual instigator rather than the (abruptly terminated) reminiscences of a nice evening.

Inattention. Inattention, due to wandering of the mind or preoccupation with thoughts irrelevant to the driving task, was cited as a probable accident cause in almost 15 percent of the accidents investigated by Treat et al. The most common event that drivers failed to attend to was "traffic stopped or slowing ahead." This result reinforces the need for more alerting rear lights systems (see discussion in Chapter Six). Typically, accidents due to inattention to traffic slowing ahead involve car following situations with relatively small gaps between vehicles. To close these gaps and collide with the vehicle ahead requires no more than very brief lapses in attention. The inability to sustain attention continuously over long periods of time is a well-documented human shortcoming that may be demonstrated in some tasks after as little as one-half hour (e.g., Mackworth, 1950). Furthermore, attention to visually presented information can be impaired from nonvisual competing sources — including information retrieved from memory (Shulman & Greenberg, 1971). In Indiana's study, 57 percent of the drivers cited for inattention were able to recall a specific thought with which they were preoccupied just prior to the accident. It is also likely that a significant proportion of the remaining 47 percent simply "forgot" any thoughts they may have been preoccupied with just prior to the accident — a fairly common phenomenon known as retrograde amnesia, or the loss of recall of events just prior to a shocking experience.

Improper Evasive Action. Improper evasive action was identified as a probable accident cause in approximately 13 percent of the accidents. Most of the time it involved a situation in which the driver failed to steer or steered but the steering was ineffective because the brakes were locked and the car was already skidding. The problem here is that hard braking is the most common immediate response to an emergency situation. However, as soon as the brakes "lock" and the car starts to skid, lateral control by steering is completely lost. Thus, the appropriate response is often counter to the instinctive one of "slamming on" the brakes. One promising approach to overcoming loss of control due to skidding is incorporated in newly developed antilock brake systems. This approach appears to be more successful than training drivers to handle emergency situations (see Chapter Six).

Human Indirect Causes of Accidents

Indirect causes of accidents were defined in the Indiana study as driver conditions and states that "adversely affect the ability of the driver to perform the information processing functions necessary for safe performance of the driving task" (Treat et al. 1977, p. 212). If we can describe an accident as an end result of a chain of events, behavior, and conditions (Table 5.1), then often a direct human cause of an accident should be traceable to a predisposing condition or state. Unfortunately, to trace this chain accurately often requires the combined skills of Sherlock Holmes and Sigmund Freud. Although one or more human direct errors were considered as causes of over 90 percent of the accidents in Indiana University's study, for only 13 percent of the accidents were the accident investigators able to determine a human condition or state that they felt caused the accident (at the probable or definite level of certainty). This result does not mean that the chain-of-events hypothesis is wrong, but only that the identification of the more remote conditions and states — at least in post-hoc accident investigations — is very difficult.

The human conditions and states that the Indiana University investigators considered as potential accident causes are listed in the

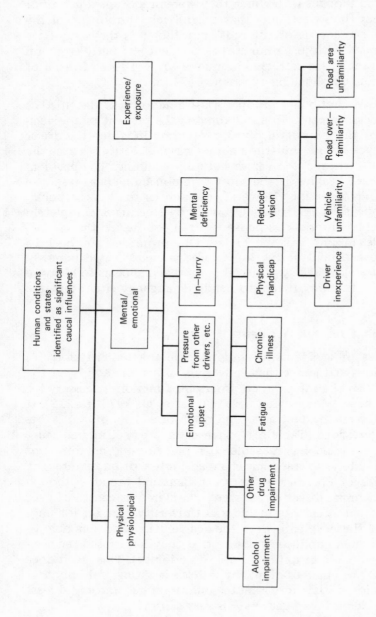

Figure 5.6. Causal factor tree of human conditions and states that cause traffic accidents (from Treat et al., 1977).

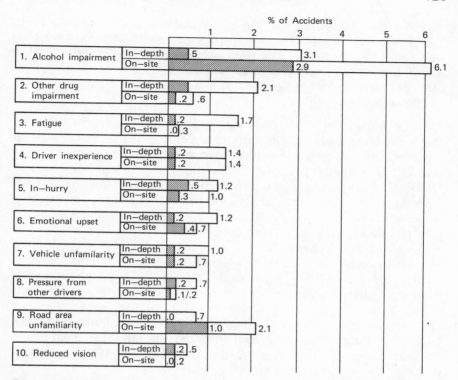

Figure 5.7. Percentage of accidents caused by specific human conditions and states (from Treat et al., 1977).

tree diagram in Figure 5.6. Three categories of impairment were considered: physical or physiological, mental or emotional, and lack of experience or exposure. Of the 14 specific categories included in Figure 5.6, the 10 most frequently cited causes are listed in Figure 5.7. Since these factors are difficult to detect and assess, it is likely that the in-depth citings in Figure 5.7 are much more valid than those of the on-site investigators. The very small percentages in which these factors were cited does not imply that the driver was not impaired in all the other accidents, but only that if driver impairments were detected, they were not assessed as causes. To illustrate, if an intoxicated driver is rear-ended by a sober driver while waiting for a traffic light to change, alcohol intoxication would not be likely to be cited as an accident cause.

It is probably more instructive to understand how these conditions and states can lead to an accident than to tabulate the driver conditions and states that cause accidents. To gain some insight into these causal chains that relate indirect and direct causes, Shinar, McDonald,

& Treat (1977) reanalyzed the 420 accidents investigated in-depth. To increase the sample size, conditions and states cited as "possible" only were also included. The rest of this section briefly describes the major findings of the Treat et al. and the Shinar et al. studies, concerning the relationship between direct and indirect human causes of traffic accidents.

Alcohol Impairment.   Alcohol was considered an accident cause by the in-depth investigators in only three percent of the accidents. This figure at first appears deceptively low in light of the previous discussion of the effects of alcohol on driving and accident involvement. However, it should be noted that Indiana University's study is based on a representative sample of all accidents rather than of only serious injury and fatal accidents; and alcohol is much more involved in injury and fatal accidents, which constitute less than 14 percent of all accidents. Second, except for the last year of their study, the Indiana University researchers investigated only accidents occurring between 11:30 A.M. and 10:30 P.M. — definitely not the late night and early morning "drinking hours" when most drinking-driving accidents occur. Teams investigating accidents on a 24-hour basis have cited alcohol as a causal factor in 12.5 percent of all accidents in England (Sabey & Staughton, 1975) and in 9 percent of total accidents in Finland (Finnish Insurance Information Center, 1974). Finland, however, has much stricter drinking-driving laws.

The most common immediate effect of alcohol in Shinar et al.'s analysis was to increase dramatically — by a factor greater than 5 — the likelihood of a critical nonperformance (most often falling asleep). This effect can be attributed to the depressant effects of alcohol on the central nervous system. To a lesser but still significant extent, alcohol intoxication increased the likelihood of being internally distracted, speeding, and overcompensating to the extent of causing an accident. The effects of alcohol on these three factors indicate how alcohol intoxication impairs the three main driver functions: perception, decision, and response.

Other Drug Impairment.   This is a catch-all category comprised of licit and illicit drugs other than alcohol. As indicated in Chapter 3, the detection, measurement, and evaluation of the effects of drugs on driving is very difficult. Even at the "possible" level of certainty other drugs were cited as causal in only 4 percent of the accidents. Sabey and Staughton (1957) cited drugs as causes in 2.3 percent of their accident sample. In the Indiana study these drugs included marijuana, depressants (such as Librium and Valium), antihistamines, and even one case of Flagyl (prescribed for vaginal infections). Because of the myriad effects that the different drugs have, no single human direct cause could be associated with this category.

Fatigue. Fatigue was cited as a possible cause in 4 percent of the accidents, a level similar to that obtained in the English and Finnish studies. Not unexpectedly, its most common effect was critical non-performance (i.e., falling asleep) and, at lower levels, it resulted in inattention.

Driver Inexperience. Lack of experience was cited as a possible cause in 2 percent of the accidents. Similarly Sabey and Staughton cited "lack of skill" and "lack of education or roadcraft" as being a cause of 2 percent of the accidents. The effect of inexperience appears to be in terms of causing inadequate directional control. Shinar et al. found that drivers cited for inexperience were almost seven times as likely to cause an accident because of inadequate directional control as drivers not cited for this condition.

Other Indirect Human Causes. The low frequency at which the remaining human conditions and states were cited, makes any discussion of them highly speculative. Still, being the only source of data that relates the effects of driver impairments to specific behaviors in actual accident situations (rather than in experimental or simulation studies), it is worthwhile to note some of the other significant relationships found by Shinar et al. Either being in a hurry, or being unfamiliar with the vehicle or roadway increased the likelihood of being involved in an accident because of speeding by a factor of between 3 and 6. This relationship, however, is partially a by-product of defining excessive speed with relationship to the vehicle and roadway limitations. Vehicle unfamiliarity was also a significant contribution to accidents resulting from inadequate directional control: of the study sample drivers, those unfamiliar with their vehicle were more than 10 times as likely to be cited for an inadequate directional control of their car.

This brief description of the relationship between direct and indirect human causes illustrates the complexity of human factors involved in accident causation. Different conditions and states make some human direct errors more likely than others. Furthermore, Shinar et al.'s analysis also suggested that some conditions and states may even suppress the likelihood of certain direct causes. Many of the specific relationships obtained in the two studies were unexpected and deserve further investigation since they may have significant implications for accident countermeasures.

SUMMARY

Highway traffic accidents have become a major societal problem in most countries. In the United States they are the leading cause of accidental deaths and the leading cause of death in general for people under the age of 40. It would therefore seem to be in everyone's interest to understand why accidents happen, or what "causes" accidents, in the hope that a better understanding of the accident generation process would help us develop accident countermeasures.

The accident investigation process is in a good part one of a post-hoc reconstruction of multiple events that happened rapidly and may not have been observed well. The accident investigator, in attempting to piece together the bits and pieces of evidence, is susceptible to many psychological processes that may lead to errors in judgment. Furthermore, just as there are several ways to define accidents, there are different ways to define accident causes — each leading to somewhat different conclusions.

In this chapter we discussed accident causes primarily in the terms of one recent and extensive study by Treat et al. (1977). In this study specially trained teams analyzed the causes of over 2000 accidents in terms of human errors, vehicle failures, and environmental problems, that had they not occurred prior to the accident, the accident would have been prevented. The results of this study revealed that in over 90 percent of the accidents the driver committed some error (that an alert and defensive driver would not have made) that caused the accident. In contrast, environmental problems were cited as accident causes in less than 35 percent of the cases, and vehicular failures were judged to have caused approximately 10 percent of the cases only. The fact that the percentages add up to more than 100, reflects the findings that in over 50 percent of the accidents more than one cause was cited. While the predominance of "human errors" as causes of accidents should serve as a humbling experience, it does not imply that the practical way to eliminate most accidents is to "fix" the driver. On the contrary, it appears that of the three major highway traffic components — the driver, the vehicle, and the roadway environment — the driver is the most difficult to change or improve (see Chapter Six).

In describing the specific human factors in accidents a distinction was made between human direct causes — behaviors and events that immediately preceded the accident and were directly responsible for it — and indirect causes — driver conditions and states (such as fatigue) whose presence caused the direct causes. The primary human direct causes of accidents — each cited in over 10 percent of the accidents — were improper lookout, excessive speed, inattention, and improper evasive action. Human indirect causes of accidents were much more difficult to assess and were cited in only 13 percent of the accidents. The primary indirect causes — each cited in more than 2 percent of the accidents, were impairments due to alcohol or "other drugs." A study on the relationship between direct and indirect causes showed that while various impairments can increase the likelihood of specific direct causes they may also suppress others. However, the results here are based on relatively small samples, and more studies must be conducted before the exact relationships can be established.

SIX
IMPLICATIONS FOR SAFETY

Efforts to improve our highway traffic system have been directed at all three of its major components — the driver, the vehicle, and the roadway. The relative effort that should be directed toward each component is a hotly argued political issue. Obviously, the automobile manufacturers would like to have a safer driver behind the wheel, while the driver would like to operate a more reliable and safer car. One argument often heard is that the driver is the only decision-making component in the system, and therefore responsible for most accidents in it. Indeed, as the studies reviewed in the last chapter indicated, perhaps as many as 95 percent of the highway traffic accidents could have been prevented had all drivers done their utmost, that is, had been attentive, defensive, with good vehicular control skills, and so on. However it is inappropriate to use this kind of statement to suggest that the best way to reduce accidents is to improve the driver. The fallacy was well articulated in a statement made by Dr. Haddon, the first director of the National Highway Safety Bureau. "The traditional safety approach of removing the nut from behind the wheel does not face the very real possibility that it may be impossible to change human nature." Thus, while attempts to improve driver performance should be pursued, we should also remain cognizant of the fact that some of our limits as information processors are inherent and are with us to stay. This chapter highlights some of the approaches taken, and some of the suggestions made to improve the overall highway safety through improvements in all of the three components.

In evaluating the success of any single safety measure, the ultimate criterion — the most significant dependent variable — is accident reduction. Unfortunately, while the reduction may be large, it may not appear as significant in the data because of the poor reliability of much of our accident data (see discussion in Chapter Five). We, therefore, must often be satisfied either with results that are statistically significant at a lower level of certainty or with significant effects on intermediate variables, that is, measures of driver behaviors that are presumed to be related to safe driving and accident involvement.

DRIVER IMPROVEMENT

There is a problem in modifying human behavior that is unique to the area of driving: everybody thinks he or she is an expert. The consequence of such an attitude is perhaps most vividly exemplified in the little effect that education, mass media campaigns, and even enforcement have had on the usage of safety belts. Although all the statistics demonstrate their effectiveness, those people who for any reason do not want to use the restraint systems rationalize their decision by resorting to their "expertise" in driving or their "knowledge" about the dangers of seat belts in accidents. Would the same people argue with an instructor on how to strap a parachute before skydiving?

For this reason it seems most beneficial to focus most of the efforts on driver improvements before a person becomes a licensed driver, and before he or she has had a chance to lapse into unsafe driving habits based on misconceptions of what the driving task and the traffic system involve. Presently, the various formal programs of driver education and training are optional. However, the next phase — licensing — is mandatory in all 50 states and most countries. All licensing programs are basically tests that evaluate the potential driver's ability to negotiate safely on the road in the presence of other drivers. Licensing is a flexible program since it does not require the same standards of all drivers, but rather allows for some driver impairments with corresponding restrictions on the license. Unfortunately, the initial training and licensing tests are not enough to guarantee safe driving. Experience with human nature makes it imperative that some enforcement of traffic laws be potentially present to ensure that all drivers — even though they may know the law, are well-trained, and do want to stay alive — observe the same rules. Thus, when training and licensing fail, the enforcement and adjudication systems provide the third avenue for driver improvement. In recent years some programs have also been developed to provide postlicensing training programs to "habitual offenders" — drivers with excessive violations and/or accidents in which they were judged legally at fault.

The high cost associated with training, licensing, enforcement, and postlicensing training has brought about much research aimed at evaluating the cost effectiveness of these programs. Since effectiveness in safety is evaluated by the nonoccurrence of accidents, most large-scale studies have been focused on the effects of the programs on crash reduction. The results of the evaluation studies are conflicting and appear to indicate that if an effect exists at all, it is relatively small. However, this should not be surprising if we recall that accidents are defined by their outcome (i.e., the crash) rather than by the behaviors that precede them, and these behaviors may be either safe or unsafe driving actions. The relationship between driver behavior and the occurrence of an accident was summarized by Peck (1976, p. 497), who noted that (1) "although unsafe driving behaviors are undoubtedly frequent events, accident occurrences are relatively rare events. Thus, the probability of a given unsafe behavior resulting in an accident is very low. (2) Safe driving behavior can be involved in accidents due to the unsafe behavior of others or when the driver task demands and external contingencies exceed normal operator capabilities." Still, if we can show the benefits of driver improvement programs on intermediate measures of safety, then the argument can be made that in the long run, with a sufficient number of drivers exposed to the program, its effectiveness in preventing accidents would also be demonstrated.

Driver Education

Driver education and training today are practically an integral part of any high school curriculum. In fact, probably 80 percent or more of the people reading this book have completed a formal driver training course. The rationale for such programs includes the fact that they involve the age group with the highest accident risk, and that they provide an intervention in the driving experience at the early and critical stage of learning the task. Beyond these reasons, there is the belief that driving, like any other perceptual-motor skill, can be improved by appropriate learning techniques and professional feedback.

Although the first driver education program was developed by Fulton in 1916, and high school behind-the-wheel training was begun by Neuhart in 1930 (Warner, 1972), only recently was a systematic study completed to specify all the component behaviors that must be learned to perform the different driving tasks. In this study, McKnight and Adams (1970) identified approximately 1500 behaviors that a driver must perform adequately in order to drive under most normal conditions. To illustrate, even the relatively simple operation of starting a car contains a sequence of eight different behaviors that must be performed correctly for the car to actually start. These behaviors include: setting the gearshift lever, depressing and releasing accelerator, inserting and turning the key to the "on" position, checking oil and generator warning light, turning ignition key until the starter is heard, and releasing the key when the appropriate engine sound is heard. While to the skillful driver all of these behaviors may seem rather elementary, to the novice driver they are descrete actions that require practice with feedback before they can be integrated into a single complex task known as starting the car.

There are at least three psychological processes that have been identified as necessary stages in the efficient learning of complex skills (Fitts, 1964). There are (1) the early intellectualization of the task (i.e., understanding how the different behaviors relate to the outcome); (2) the intermediate associative stage, in which simple stimulus-response associations are learned (e.g., releasing the key to the sound of the engine); and (3) the final autonomous stage, in which the individual associations are integrated into a single sequence of behaviors performed in reflexlike fashion. At the autonomous stage, performing a skill requires very little of our information processing capacity — as, in fact, is the case for most driving behaviors of the experienced driver.

One aspect of the driver training programs that has been shown to be productive is the training on specific subtasks of the overall driving task. To illustrate, when we considered the driver as an information processor, we noted that the driver often has difficulty in estimating distances necessary for passing maneuvers. This is a specific skill, which can be improved through training with feedback. In fact, the training for such maneuvers does not even have to be done on the road, but can be successfully performed in a simulator (Lucas, Heimstra, & Spiegel, 1973).

The effectiveness of driver education in terms of accident reduction has been subjected to various tests. Early studies indicated that students completing a high school driver education program had as much as 50 percent fewer accidents than nongraduates; that courses containing on-the-road training were more effective than classroom-only courses; and that high school courses were more effective than commercial or parent training (U.S. Department of Transportation, 1975). It was, therefore, not surprising that in 1952 Allstate Insurance Company initiated its policy of providing insurance discounts for new drivers who had completed a formal high school driver education program.

Unfortunately, the early evaluation studies were plagued with methodological problems. To begin with, many studies were initially aimed at demonstrating the program's effectiveness, rather than in documenting it objectively. Second, most studies were based on post-hoc comparisons of driving records of students completing driver education versus nontrained persons. The problem here is that students enrolling in the driver education program may have differed from the students not enrolling in the program in many other respects, such as personality, attitudes, and other self-selection factors. This was especially true in the earlier days of driver education when only a minority of the students volunteered to enroll in the program. In light of the correlations of these factors with accident involvement (see Chapter 3), it is difficult to claim that the observed reduction in accidents was due to the training per se. Finally, in many of the studies, no attempts were made to control for extraneous effects of variables that could have been controlled such as socioeconomic variables, exposure (in terms of miles driven), sex, and the like. All of these confounding variables could have accounted for the differences in accident rates.

More recent studies, that have controlled for these variables, typically fail to show any significant advantages of the drivers who have had formal driver education over the drivers who have not had driver education. In one of these studies (Coppin, Ferdun, & Peck, 1965), over 6000 California drivers were surveyed. The study showed that while the trained drivers had fewer accidents, they also drove fewer miles. Once the differences in exposure (frequency of accidents divided by miles driven) were adjusted for, the differences between the two groups in their accident rates disappeared. After reviewing these and other disappointing results, McGuire and Kersh, in 1969, concluded that it appears that "high school driver education bears no causal relationship to either traffic violations or accident frequency. It must be emphasized, however, that these studies bear repeating and the entire question should be subjected to more sophisticated experimental designs before the issue is considered settled" (p. 78).

What then can we say of the effectiveness of driver education programs today? There are some benefits to driver education — both high school and commercial — that seem relevant to safe driving behavior. Drivers who have completed a formal driver education course share attitudes that are more condusive to safe driving, and also maintain their cars better (Ohio Department of Education, 1974; Treat et al., 1977). Furthermore, with sufficiently large samples, significant effects of driver education in accident reduction can still be measured, even after controlling for many potentially confounding variables. This was demonstrated by Harrington (1971) who analyzed data of nearly 14,000 young drivers. His results indicated significant benefits of behind-the-wheel training: although the measured reduction in accidents was small, the estimated savings in societal costs (e.g., damage, lost income, medical expenses) were at least as great as the cost of the driver education program.

The somewhat confusing state of the art of driver education has led the federal government to launch a comprehensive "Driver Education Evaluation Program Study" (1975, 1976). This study is designed to randomly assign students to different driver education programs and evaluate their relative benefits. One program that is currently being evaluated in terms of its accident reduction potential involves training students to detect potentially dangerous situations and develop accident-avoidance skills. Because accidents are relatively rare events, most people are relatively unpracticed in handling accident-producing emergency situations, such as regaining control after skidding or going off the road shoulder. The final results of this evaluation program are not yet available. In any case, the sobering effect of past studies and our increased understanding of the complexity of the driving task have led to the more modest expectation that an effective program, that would reduce a person's probability of being involved in an accident "even if implemented on a massive scale, would not result in a dramatic overall crash reduction. Such a program, however, would be cost-effective" (U.S. Department of Transportation, 1975, p. 85), that is, the cost of the program would be less than the costs associated with the accidents that it would potentially eliminate or reduce in severity. Since it has been shown that even licensed drivers can benefit from improvements in their accident-avoidance skills — through the development of good visual search habits and behaviors that dispose of potential hazards before they become critical (Payne & Barmack, 1963) — there is every reason to believe that the benefits of such training should be even greater for the beginning driver.

Driver Licensing

In today's highly mobile society licensing is often more a political issue than a safety issue. We have come to regard driving as a right and not as a privilege. Upon refusal of a license, based on the present criteria, more and more applicants are demanding that the licensing authorities prove that they, the applicants, would constitute a hazard on the highway if allowed to drive. Scientific data to support present criteria are all but totally missing, and consequently there are large differences among the states in the driver examination procedures, the licensing criteria, and the requirements for taking the tests to begin with. To illustrate, the minimum driving age without special training is 21 in 1 state, 18 in 24 states, 17 in 3 states, and 15 in 2 states. Unfortunately, no data are available to "show who is right." One promising development is the increasing popularity of program evaluation studies of the various licensing programs. Perhaps the most comprehensive study to date is one conducted on 22,253 Illinois drivers (Conley & Smiley, 1976). In this study, drivers' violation records, accumulated over a period of four years, were compared with performance on the Illinois driver knowledge test. This pencil-and-paper test, which measures the person's knowledge of the rules of the road, is administered by the State of Illinois as part of the official licensing examination. The results failed to show any consistent relationships between knowledge, or lack of knowledge, of particular items and the overall frequency or types of moving violations accumulated within the first four years after passing the test. These results cast serious doubts on the validity of paper-and-pencil tests for predicting safe driving. One possible explanation for these results is that items originally missed on the tests are later learned in the course of normal driving. However, in Indiana University's study of the causes of traffic accidents (Treat et al., 1977), no significant relationships were found between being at fault in an accident and knowledge on a driver test, even when the knowledge test was administered within a week after the accident. It is more likely that the lack of relationship is due to the difference between what we labeled as driving behavior (which is influenced more by personality and attitude — see Chapter Two) and passive knowledge of the rules of the road and the legal restrictions — knowledge that may not be utilized at all in actual driving.

The absence of defensible licensing criteria is best illustrated in the

area of vision — probably the most quantifiable of all of driver capabilities. Here, a device was recently designed to enable people with
poor eyesight to pass the formal requirements of the driver vision
test (which is not the same as to improve the driving-related visual
capabilities — see Chapter Three). The device — known as bioptic telescopic lens — involves the mounting of a small telescopic lens on one
of the lenses in regular glasses. By looking through it, a person who
would otherwise (even with regular glasses) not see well enough to
pass the test can have sufficient acuity in the small area covered by
the telescopic lens. This lens, although it enables one to pass the
vision test, severely restricts vision since acuity is high only in a very
small part of the visual scene and there is a "blind" area around that
part. Thus, from a medical standpoint at least, this device has been
argued to be more detrimental than beneficial to safe driving
(Keeney, Weiss, & Silva, 1974). Many states, therefore, disqualify
people with telescopic lenses from driving. On the other hand, the
State of New York does license people with telescopic lenses, and so
far their accident and violation records have been as good as those of
the rest of the New York driving population. In one study conducted
on Massachusetts drivers, the low-vision telescopic lens wearers even
had a lower accident rate than that of the general population (Korb,
1970). How can we reconcile the medical evaluation with the empirical facts? One possibility is that these drivers compensate for their
deficiency by restricting their driving to familiar routes, daylight,
light traffic hours, and the like. If this is so, then perhaps these
drivers are not even using the telescopic part of the lenses — which is
difficult to use effectively when moving — and are only relying on
the more blurry images provided by the regular lenses in their glasses.
Now, if this is true, then we must question the present criteria for
vision in general, and not just for this small group of drivers. (See
discussion in Chapter Three.)

Another approach to licensing can be seen in attempts to develop
specialized licenses. The most common type of specialized license is
the one that defines the type of vehicle that may be operated (e.g.,
taxicab, heavy truck). A different specialized license concept that
was entertained for a short time was that of the "Master Driver
License." The plan was to reward drivers who had successfully passed
tests of accident avoidance procedures and other complicated tasks
with a privileged license that would entitle them to various benefits
such as lower insurance premiums and lower rates on tollways. To
evaluate this plan, Williams and O'Neill (1974) compared the off-
track accident and violation records of licensed race drivers belonging to the Sports Car Club of America with that of normal drivers
matched in age and sex. These race drivers had all completed ad-

vanced training in emergency driving techniques and were experienced in crash avoidance situations. Still, in two of the three states where the comparisons between these drivers and the "normal" drivers were made, both in terms of absolute number of accidents and in terms of accident rates, the race drivers were involved in more accidents than the control drivers (in the third state the difference was not statistically significant). As a result of this study, a reevaluation of the relative importance of crash avoidance skills is presently being researched. The conclusions from this study are limited, however, since it is very likely that race car drivers may also differ from normal drivers in the amount of risk taking that they allow themselves on the road. Limited data show that training in early detection and avoidance of emergency situations can reduce the accident involvement of "normal" commercial drivers (Payne & Barmack, 1963).

Enforcement

Using learning theory terminology, enforcement may be viewed as a negative reinforcer, which produces avoidance behavior. A negative reinforcer is a stimulus that a person tries to avoid, thus the threat of administering a negative reinforcer (e.g., a traffic ticket) should keep a person from committing certain behaviors. In other words, the role of the law on the road is to prevent drivers from committing behaviors for which they know they will be punished. While avoidance training is very effective in the laboratory, the issue has continuously been raised whether it is effective on the road. Two differences between the laboratory situation and the on-the-road situation are that in the laboratory, the negative reinforcement is provided consistently, according to some rule. In contrast on the road, due to practical limitations stemming from limited funds, the monitoring of the drivers by the police is not as systematic. The other difference concerns feedback. One of the best established rules of learning is that practice requires feedback for learning to occur. On the road, we do not always get feedback, or negative reinforcement, for our improper driving (e.g., when the police are not there), and when we do, the feedback is not always consistent (e.g., when we disagree with the officer concerning a violation). This makes the traffic law system a "gray area" in the sense that often neither the public nor the police officers have a very clear idea of how to behave. It is often up to the police officer to decide whether to enforce the law strictly or loosely, all the time or some of the time, and so on.

We are all familiar with that tightening of our stomach muscles whenever we spot a police cruiser parked alongside the road (see

Figure 6.1. The mere threat of enforcement is often sufficient to modify driver behavior (cartoon by Tom Wilson in
Never Get Too Personally Involved with Your Own Life,
1977).

Figure 6.1). But other than possibly interfering with digestion, does
the presence of these police cars induce a driver to drive more safely?
It would appear that this would be one instance where the presence
of this negative reinforcement would be effective. To test this hypothesis, researchers at the Highway Safety Research Center of the
University of North Carolina (Reinfurt, Levine, & Johnson, 1973)
measured the effects of a visible police car on passing drivers' speeds.
When coupled with media publicity and ticketing, the presence of
the police car led to a reduction in average speed from 38.7 mph to
35.5 mph in a 35-mph zone. More significant, though, was the reduction in the percent of speeding drivers, from 67 to 46 percent. The
mere presence of the police cruisers was also sufficient to cause
motorists to reduce their speed, but the effect was smaller in the

absence of any news media campaigns. This study illustrates the effectiveness of the visibility of the law enforcing agency as well as the benefits that can be derived using multiple approaches to safety.

The effectiveness of the presence of a police cruiser parked by the roadside has also been demonstrated on other driver behaviors such as better detection of signs appearing shortly after the site of the parked police car, and fewer crossings of the center line (Syvänen, 1968). Apparently these improved driver behaviors can be attributed to the attention getting and alerting influence of the police car. However, this attention getting effect may also be detrimental. In Syvänen's study, when the police car was parked close to a traffic sign, that sign was missed more often than when a civilian car was parked at the same place. Thus, while the police's presence can increase our overall level of arousal, it also attracts our attention away from other objects.

Enforcement, or the threat of enforcement, also extends beyond the presence of police on the roads to the court and legal system. In this connection one complaint that has been made — particularly with respect to driving under the influence of alcohol — is that the courts have not been firm enough in their enforcement of the law. An extreme case of strict laws is the one practiced in the Scandinavian countries. In some of these countries, a conviction of drunken driving leads to automatic imprisonment and loss of driver license. Does such a strong deterrent work? The answer, to date, is apparently not. A comparison of the accident statistics before these laws were put into effect with accident statistics after these laws were put into effect yielded no significant changes in either the number or the rate of fatal accidents with drunken driving (Ross, 1976).

Postlicensing Driver Improvement

A relatively recent approach to increasing highway safety is the focus on the "problem driver": that driver who has accumulated a significant number of violations and/or accidents. The desire to treat this group of drivers is based, in part, on the assumption that a small number of extreme problem drivers cause a significant proportion of all accidents. Statistical data analyzed by the U.S. Department of Transportation (1975) indicate that this assumption is false. Still, the overwhelming empirical data showing that persons with high violation rates are likely to also have high accident rates, coupled with the pervasive notion that some people under some circumstances may be more accident prone, suggest that remedial programs for such people may be beneficial.

All of the programs that have been used to treat the problem

driver assume that the problem is not due to inadequate driving performance skills but rather that driver behavior (which includes
driving habits and attitudes toward the driving task) is the culprit.
Accordingly, different programs have included various combinations
of standard and individualized warning letters, individual counseling,
and group meetings and lectures. The effectiveness of these programs
has been difficult to establish since most of the evaluation studies
conducted to date have suffered from some serious methodological
flaws (Peck, 1976). Nonetheless, based on various reviews (Nichols,
1970; Peck, 1976) the following tentative conclusions appear to
hold:

1. Less threatening interventions such as notification of violations
    and mild warnings are more effective in improving driver record
    than more threatening approaches. This differential effect is also
    commonly obtained in attitude change in other areas of behavior.
2. The effects of the program are more likely to be reflected in a re-
    duction in the violation rate than in the accident rate. This find-
    ing is consistent with our knowledge that accidents are relatively
    rare events that can be caused by a variety of factors, while viola-
    tions are more frequent events that can almost invariably be
    attributed to a driver's voluntary action.
3. When positive effects are obtained, they tend to persist for a
    short time only, generally less than a year. This is understandable
    if we realize that those driver behaviors that the improvement
    programs attempt to modify are relatively well-established habits
    that cannot be permanently extinguished by a short counter-
    measure program. This is especially so since, as we mentioned
    above, risk-taking behaviors and unsafe driving habits are often
    reinforced by the nonoccurrence of either accidents or citations.

The prominence of alcohol as a single factor that is most often
associated with fatal accidents had led to the development of educational programs aimed specifically at the drunk driver. Despite a
massive educational effort by the U.S. Department of Transportation, in its report to Congress in 1975 the National Highway Traffic
Safety Administration (NHTSA) stated that "virtually no sufficient
evidence exists to support the conclusion that such programs have
any effect whatsoever in reducing crashes. In fact in a review of more
than 40 such programs, Nichols and Reis (1974) suggest that purely
lecture-oriented courses may have a *detrimental* effect on the more
severe problem drunken types" (p. 52). This is despite the reported
improvement in driving knowledge and attitudes. One explanation
for this dismal result has been offered by Nichols (1977) who noted

that those drivers who have previously been identified as drunk drivers (based on previous accidents and violations) constitute only a small proportion of the drivers involved in serious accidents. Thus, any program that deals exclusively with these people cannot have a significant short-term impact on the total accident picture. Still — although this may at first appear to be a radical approach — one is led to suggest that as long as we are unwilling to get the drunk driver off the road (which according to the Scandinavian experience, does not work either), and seem to be unable to change this driver's behavior, we may be better off if we started to design our vehicles and highway to be responsive to the needs and limitations of the drunk driver. As we will see below, one vehicle design modification that follows this approach is already in the advanced development stage.

In summary, given the various methods used to affect driver behavior, the information gathered to date suggests that shaping and modifying driver behavior is a difficult task. The most promising educational methods are those that involve specific-skills training. Licensing, while not a method of improving driving, is an effective method of regulating the system so that minimum standards common to all those using the roads are established. Systematic — and visible — enforcement of the traffic laws can lead to significant reductions in violations and accidents. The apparent reasons for the ineffectiveness of court-enforced laws may be due to the fact that the punishment associated with them is both inconsistent and too far removed (in time) to affect the actual behavior on the road. Special postlicensing programs seem to be relatively ineffective in treating problem drivers either because they are too short to change well-established habits or because they do not offer these drivers an alternative method to satisfy the needs that dangerous driving may fulfill.

VEHICLE DESIGN

Safety improvements through vehicle design are perhaps the most visible of all safety-oriented programs. The increased density of vehicles on the road, contributing to the increased number of accidents each year, has led the government to regulate the automotive industry more and more. This has resulted in a change in design orientation from aesthetics to safety, or at least to aesthetics with safety. In parallel, the consumer's awareness of safety issues has been sharpened greatly by the numerous government standards and manufacturer advertisements. This is the first decade in which automobile manufacturers are attempting to sell cars on the basis of their safety features and human factors design principles (see Figure 6.2). Vehicle

OF ALL THE THINKING THAT WENT INTO VOLVO, THIS IS WHAT WE THOUGHT OF MOST.

These days, you find a lot of car makers copying each other's designs. In building a Volvo, we're more influenced by yours.

Man takes in seven quarts of air per minute. Volvo's 12-outlet ventilation system keeps it continuously fresh.

On a Volvo, the width of each front roof pillar is less than the normal distance between human eyes. So eyes see around it.

Human hand more accurate than human foot. So Volvo puts headlight dimmer switch on steering column instead of floor.

To protect your body, Volvo's body has crumple zones to absorb impact of collision before it reaches passenger compartment.

To reduce muscle tension, Volvo's footrest keeps left foot on same plane as right.

Volvo's bucket seats adjust in eight different directions to satisfy dimensional requirements of 97% of adult population.

Sitting puts more pressure on spinal discs than standing. To relieve pressure, Volvo has adjustable lumbar support for small of back.

Before the average driver can move his foot from the gas pedal to the brake in a panic situation, a car will travel 56 feet (at 55 m.p.h.). So Volvo puts power disc brakes on four wheels, not just two.

VOLVO. THE CAR FOR PEOPLE WHO THINK.

© 1976 Volvo of America Corporation

Figure 6.2. Would people buy a car based on its human factors and safety features? Manufacturers are beginning to think so. Do you? (copyright 1976, Volvo of America Corp.)

design improvements can be directed toward either the prevention of accidents or better ability to sustain the accidents. In designing for crashworthiness (the ability to withstand impact from an accident), the emphasis is on structural integrity, occupant restraint systems, and energy absorption devices such as the padded dashboard covers and the newly required energy-absorbing bumpers. In this section we discuss only the precrash factors since crashworthiness issues evolve around a different and highly complex area of man-machine dynamics and energy absorption. In designing for precrash improvements, modifications can be aimed at aiding the driver in picking up information — through improvements in mirrors, vehicle lighting and signalization, and display design — or in providing more responsive vehicular controls — through improved and power assisted steering and braking systems.

Visual Displays and Communication Systems

The predominant mode of driver-environment interactions is visual. The position of the car in the lane, the direction of the road ahead, and the behavior of other drivers are all conveyed visually. Typically, car horns — because of their alerting and nondirectional characteristics — are used only in emergency situations. The purpose of most visibility-related systems is, therefore, to improve the quality of information presented in any one area of the visual field (e.g., with better headlights) as well as to increase the size of the visual field available to the driver by increasing window areas and adding mirrors. In the following discussion we describe briefly some of the research and innovations in mirror designs, headlights and rear signal lights, and in-vehicle displays.

Mirrors.   At the driver's eye level, much of the car's body is surrounded by an envelope of glass. Tinted or untinted, when the car is moving this glass provides the driver with a view of a constantly changing environment. While most of the time the driver's vision is directed straight ahead, many accident-producing events are likely to first appear in the peripheral areas of his or her visual field, or even outside of the visual field (e.g., behind). To supplement the driver's field of view, interior and exterior mirrors are added. Their function is to provide the driver with a visual field that otherwise would be available only by turning the head, a costly procedure in terms of energy, vehicle control, and time. If we look at the driver's potential visual field in the horizontal plane as a circle of 360 degrees, then the usefulness of the mirrors becomes immediately apparent by comparing the available visual field without them versus the available visual field with them, as illustrated in Figure 6.3.

The importance of having a good field of view to the side and behind the car for various critical maneuvers, such as passing and turning, has resulted in the development and testing of various rear vision

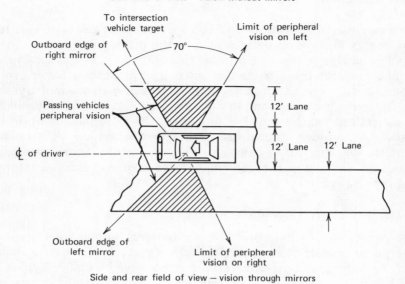

Side field of view — vision without mirrors

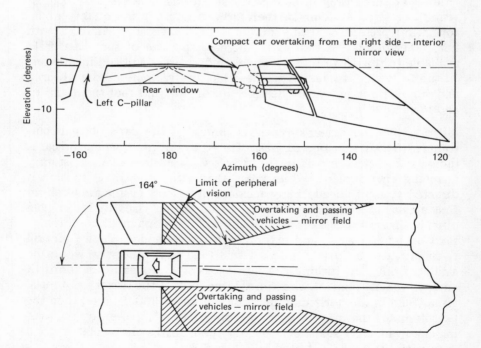

Side and rear field of view — vision through mirrors

Figure 6.3. Driver field of view to the side and rear without and with mirrors (from forbes, 1973).

devices. In a recent article entitled "What's Ahead in Rear Vision Devices?", Burger (1976) evaluated 12 different rear-vision systems, including convex mirrors, mirrors with fresnel lenses (special lenses that diffuse light and increase field of view), and periscope mirrors that are mounted above the roof of the car. In his study, the dependent measures were the number of glances at the mirror, and time spent in viewing the mirror during a maneuver. The rationale was that the more time used to view the mirrors, the less effective the mirror system is since less time is left to devote to the actual maneuver. Of the 11 innovative systems, 5 were significantly better than the conventional system, all providing the driver with a larger — and undistorted — field of view. In general, the larger the horizontal field of view available, the less time spent checking the mirror. Increasing the field of view by using the convex mirror (such as those often found attached to the side mirrors on trucks) yielded shorter fixations but more of them per maneuver, resulting in more time spent on the mirrors. This curious result is easily understandable in terms of the information processing role of the driver. Despite the fact that the curved mirrors do provide a large field of view, that field is distorted, and as a result requires a greater ability to judge the relevant distances. Distance judgment being a highly complex task to begin with, is then made much more difficult requiring frequent reevaluation on the part of the driver, manifested in frequent looks at the mirror.

The most frequent situation in which mirrors are resorted to is lane-changing and passing maneuvers. The experience of attempting to start such a maneuver only to hear the horn of another vehicle right next to us is too familiar to be ignored. Both convex mirrors and periscope mirrors can provide the needed additional degrees of visual field to overcome the problem. Because of the much greater ease of installing additional convex rather than periscope mirrors, most of the studies have focused on the potential benefits of the convex mirrors. It appears that these mirrors do not pose a serious problem to distance judgment as long as their curvature is relatively low (radius of curvature greater than 30 inches; Mortimer, 1971). To enjoy the benefits of both the large field of view of the convex mirror, as well as the undistorted image provided by the presently used plane mirrors, trucks currently employ a combination of both. One experimental system, developed by Liberty Mutual Insurance Co., has been designed so that as long as a vehicle is detected in the convex mirror a lane change is unsafe. Thus, this system relieves the driver of the most difficult decision involved in lane changing — whether to do it or not.

The emerging conclusion of the research conducted to date is that our present mirror system can be improved to increase safety. However, as recently stated in a U.S. Department of Transportation solicitation for further research in this area (U.S. Department of Transportation, 1977), "the major deficiency of past research is the lack of common measures defining the performance capabilities of the various systems tested and the lack of a common criterion for measuring their effectiveness in presenting rearview information to drivers. As a result it is not possible to pool data across studies and arrive at generalized design principles."

Headlights. Thanks to technological lighting innovations, we no longer have the problem of having insufficient illumination for relatively fast nighttime driving. Instead, the major impediment to nighttime driver visibility is the glare produced by headlights of oncoming cars. Thus, any further improvements in headlight systems must demonstrate increased visibility in the presence of the glare produced by the headlights of an oncoming vehicle. Glare is any light entering the driver's eye that reduces the visibility of the target. Glare increases as the intensity of the glare source increases and as the angular distance between the target and the glare source decreases. Thus, glare produced by an approaching vehicle increases at first as the distance between the two vehicles is reduced (and the amount of light reaching the eyes increases) and then decreases as the oncoming car's headlights start moving away from the center of the field to the left. Representative findings on how glare affects visibility distance are presented in Figure 6.4 (from Mortimer & Becker, 1973). Note that just before meeting the oncoming car the visibility with the high beam is no better than with the low beam, indicating that keeping the high beams on reflects a combination of arrogance and ignorance. The improvement in visibility, once the two cars pass each other, is gradual because the eyes require time to become dark adapted again. Because — as the last section demonstrated — driver behavior is very difficult to change, several suggestions have been made to improve the present headlights system in ways that would reduce glare from high-beam headlights. Perhaps the most notable of the various systems involve the use of polarized headlight beams and the addition of a third light beam — labeled the midbeam — that would supplement the present high and low beams.

Polarized light is light that is filtered through a medium so that all of its rays are parallel to each other. One of the most common consumer applications of polarizing filters is in glare-reducing sunglasses. Now, an interesting effect can be achieved by sandwiching two such filters: by rotating one of the filters, the amount of light passing through both changes so that when the two polarizers are crossed

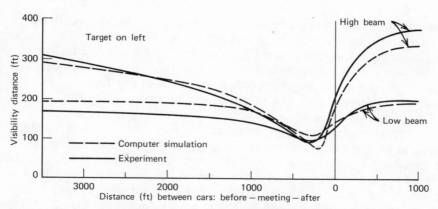

Figure 6.4. Field test results and computer simulation results showing the visibility distances for targets (with 12 percent reflectance) on the left side of the driving lane, in high- and low-beam meetings (from Mortimer and Becker, 1973).

almost all the light that passes through one filter is blocked by the second filter, and when the two filters are in "parallel" all the light passing through one filter passes the other filter too. The effect obtained is analogous to the effect one gets by holding the two hands in a praying position with the fingers slightly apart — so that some light passes between them — and then rotating one of the two hands. This effect was utilized in a study by Tsongos and Schwab (1970). In their experiment, cars' headlights were covered with a polarizing filter (at 45 degrees to the horizon) and the drivers viewed the scene with a "parallel" filter, attached to the sun visor. Thus, when encountering the headlights of an oncoming car the headlight filters of each car were crossed with the viewing filters of the opposing driver. Aside from the dramatic glare reduction, with polarized filters, drivers were able to use smaller and less variable time gaps in crossing intersections. Although in terms of glare reduction, the polarized high beams were superior only to the conventional high beams and not the conventional low beams, polarized systems could replace the present two beam systems with a one beam system. This would constitute both a simplification in design and a simplification in the night driving task, since drivers would not have to switch between beams. Unfortunately, to be effective, all the cars on the road would have to be equipped with properly aligned polarizing filters on both the headlights and the windshields or the visors.

A proposed headlight system that appears to be gaining more and more popularity is one including a midbeam that is aimed higher than the low beam but "spills" less light to the left of the driving lane than a high beam. Because the light of the proposed midbeam is aimed more to the right than the light from the present highbeams, on a straight road the visibility distance for targets located at the right side of the lane is 25 percent greater than the visibility with the present low beams. Furthermore, the glare intensity from an oncoming car equipped with the midbeams is approximately the same as that produced by the present U.S. low beams (Mortimer, 1976). Finally, the luminance of overhead retroreflective (glass beaded) signs is four times greater with the proposed midbeam than with the conventional low beam (Woltman and Youngblood, 1976). This increase in brightness makes the signs more visible — especially for older and alcohol-impaired drivers — and allows drivers to respond to them earlier than they could with the poorer, low-beam illumination. There is also experimental evidence that drivers utilize the advantages provided by the midbeams. Using a new eye-movement recording system (in which the driver is totally unaware of the fact that his or her eye movements are being recorded), Graf and Krebs (1976) measured the location on the road of drivers' fixations, under daylight conditions and with a variety of headlights. During daylight hours drivers looked at an average distance of approximately 800 feet ahead of the car. At night, drivers concentrated their fixations much closer to the car, but the average distance was the greatest with the midbeam (approximately 300 feet) and smallest with the present high- and low-beams (approximately 130 feet).

One major obstacle on the way to improving headlight systems is the criticality of proper headlight alignment. Lights that are misaimed so that their beams are projected upward by only one degree (as might occur with two rear-seat passengers or with a full trunk) can increase the glare intensity by a factor of 4 to 18 (Mortimer, 1976). Headlight misalignment can also occur as a result of hitting a bump or a pothole in the road. In light of the finding that as many as 60 percent of the vehicles entering a periodic vehicle motor inspection are likely to be rejected for faulty headlamp aim (Terry, 1973), perhaps it would be more fruitful to improve headlight stability first.

Rear Lights. Rear lights communicate the position of the car, its behavior (braking), and the driver's intentions (to turn) to other drivers on the road. Of these functions, the most important and most deficient is the information conveyed about the vehicle's behavior, that is, whether the vehicle is coasting, accelerating, or braking. Consider the following situation with a woman in one car following a man in another car: while the lead car's driver drives along, he observes a potential danger source. The driver's initial response is to lift his foot off the accelerator. A few (or perhaps many) seconds later he decides that the situation requires braking, so he brakes. Now, let's observe the information available to the following driver; and to make the case more striking, let's assume that it is nighttime. In front of her she can see the rear red lights of the vehicle ahead. Nothing about these lights, which provide the sole source of information about the behavior of the car ahead, changes until the lead car driver actually brakes. In that interim period, the gap between the two cars is significantly reduced, but this information may be lost to the following driver. It is very likely that this relatively poor ability to communicate deceleration and braking is responsible for a significant percent of all rear-end collisions caused by delayed recognition of the lead car's behavior by the following driver.

In addition to the quality of communication, the present brake-light system can be criticized on many other factors: at night, the color red is used to indicate both "go" conditions (in accelerating or coasting) and "stop" conditions; the use of brightness changes to indicate braking (rather than, say, color change) is not an optimal choice given human abilities for judging intensity differences (a ten-fold increase in intensity is needed to perceive a twofold increase in brightness; Stevens & Stevens, 1953); and viewed from the same distance, red lights appear further away than green or blue (Safford, Rockwell, & Banasik, 1970). For these reasons, the major issue according to Safford et al. is "not whether a better rear-end signal system can be designed but which of the many alternative systems is best" (p. 2).

Several alternatives to the present system have been considered. Common to all of the proposed improvements is that they provide more levels of information, typically by differentiating between coasting with the foot off the accelerator and maintaining speed (or accelerating) with the foot on the accelerator. In one study (Rockwell & Treiterer, 1968), two innovative systems were compared with the present one. One system, labeled "trilight" had red lights to indicate braking, yellow lights to indicate coasting, and green lights to indicate foot on the accelerator. The second system provided the driver with an acceleration information display (AID). Horizontal rows of red and green colors were used to indicate levels of deceleration and acceleration respectively. Thus, the harder the driver braked the more red lights flashed. Both systems reduced the reaction time of following drivers in response to slight deceleration of the lead car. However, in response to braking, which in the current system is indicated by increased intensity of the rear lights, no differences were found between the three systems. Thus, in the more critical situations that involve braking, the new systems did not constitute an improvement.

Given the many arguments for the relative inferiority of the present system, why are the "improved" systems not more effective? Most of the studies used to evaluate rear signal lights — both in the laboratory and on the road — used volunteer subjects who were aware of the purpose of the study, alert, and cooperative. It can, therefore, be concluded that once a driver is alerted to observe changes in the behavior of a lead vehicle, the added information provided by the new systems, or their improved visibility, is of little significance in responding to braking by the lead driver.

The key to total system improvement may be in combining the increased information with an attention-getting device. Perhaps the most interesting development in this area has been the use of a variable flashing deceleration light that flashes at an increasing rate, the greater the pressure applied to the brake. This system not only provides the following driver with very exact information on the deceleration rate of the lead vehicle, but also acts as an attention getter. Using such a device with a yellow flashing light, four times the intensity of the present stoplights, on a fleet of approximately 500 taxicabs in the San Francisco area, Voevodsky (1974) was able to demonstrate a reduction of 50 percent in the involvement of these vehicles in rear-end collisions. That these drivers did not behave differently because they were aware of their participation in the study was convincingly demonstrated by the fact that their involvement in all other types of accidents did not decrease or increase significantly during that period. There is one sour note to this otherwise extremely promising approach. Although the drivers equipped with the deceleration light signals were enthusiastic about their effectiveness, the high levels of intensity caused enough glare to following drivers to motivate many of them to send letters of complaints. The task is to refine the system so that it retains its alerting qualities without causing glare. This is not a simple task because it appears that any light intensity needed to provide good visibility and alert the driver's attention during daylight hours, is high enough to cause discomfort glare at night when the eyes are adapted to lower levels of illumination. Perhaps the solution may be to provide different daytime and nighttime systems, the latter one being activated whenever the headlights are turned on.

In-Vehicle Displays.   In-vehicle displays provide us with information that either cannot be observed directly (e.g., gas level) or to aid us in sensing information that is beyond our threshold. Thus, we are usually able to estimate our speed within ±10 mph, but find it difficult to estimate speed within the accuracy requirements of the law. This, in fact, is what probably makes a speedometer the most frequently used vehicle display. Rather than review the various displays with which most drivers are familiar, this section illustrates two experimental vehicle displays and the rationale for incorporating such displays in future vehicles. Note that the function of both devices is to aid the driver's information processing task rather than to actually replace a driver by a totally automated system. As such, their design is based not only on the transportation system requirements, but also — and perhaps more so — on the driver's perceptual limitations.

Master Warning Light. The proliferation of various indicators on the instrument panel has lead some automobile manufacturers to propose the installation of one more display that would, in effect, reduce rather than increase the time spent on scanning the various instruments. The function of this master warning light would be to alert the driver whenever any one of the other warning indicators is triggered. Thus, rather than scan the whole array of warning indicators every once in a while, all the driver would need is to glance from time to time at one indicator to know that all systems are functioning properly. The master warning light may be particularly beneficial for the elderly drivers, for whom the visibility of present displays is often insufficient (Mourant & Langolf, 1976). However, the overall effectiveness of this device may be minimal since, when operating under stress produced by increased environmental demands (e.g., heavy traffic, curve negotiation, etc.) drivers rarely scan the instrument panel, and thus the reduced scanning time is irrelevant. On the other hand — and this still remains to be empirically tested — a sufficiently alerting master warning light could be a cost-effective device if it would alert drivers earlier than current systems do to engine overheating, loss of brake fluid pressure, and so on.

Heads-Up Display (HUD). As its name indicates, the HUD is a display that does not require the driver to lower the head or eyes to the instrument panel. The typical eye and head movement to the instrument panel and then back to the outside visual field requires almost a whole second (and more for older drivers), which in fast driving may be critical. With the HUD, information is presented in line with the driver's gaze on the windshield, but focused at infinity so that no occular accommodation is required. The usefulness of providing information in such a way is illustrated in the following two applications: car following and curve negotiation. Car following requires the driver to adequately judge the relative velocity and headway distance between himself and the car ahead. We encounter this kind of situation most commonly on expressways, where during congestion hours cars appear to be traveling bumper to bumper at 60 mph. As the occasional chain accidents demonstrate, this can be an extremely dangerous combination of speed and headway distance. Part of the danger arises not so much from the close distances between the cars, but from the variability in those distances, which tends to create a shock wave. In other words, if the first driver slows down a little, the second driver will compensate; but his or her reaction will be delayed. This delay increases with each additional driver, creating a shock wave that leaves less and less time to the people further and further down the line until it reaches the point where a collision is inevitable. In such high-speed car-following situations, the HUD can provide the driver with a very accurate signal on whether he or she is maintaining a given headway distance, closing a gap, or widening a gap. Drivers utilizing an experimental HUD were, in fact, able to reduce the variability in their headway distance (Harrass & Mourant, 1970). The second application of HUD has been to project the speedometer image, so that in curves with advisory speed signs drivers, without removing their eyes from the road, would be able to ascertain their own speed. An evaluation of the system on a sample of 63 volunteer subjects showed that it caused a small but statistically significant speed reduction compared to cars without it (Rutley, 1975). Presently, the applications of HUD are still in their developmental stages. Based on a few studies, it appears as a promising tool in the search for new approaches to aiding the driver's information acquisition process.

Vehicle-Control Systems

Innovations developed to aid the driver control the vehicle have been channeled in two directions: improving the responsiveness and ease of handling of vehicle controls such as the steering wheel and brakes, and improving the handling capabilities of vehicles so that they can tolerate more driver errors before skidding or rolling over. The most familiar improvements of the first kind are the power steering and the power brakes. Both provide the driver with better control by reducing the vehicle's resistance. Note, however, that the present power-steering and power-brake systems differ from the first ones where much of the kinesthetic feedback was missing. Present power-steering systems provide the driver with much-needed force feedback that is proportional to the lateral acceleration of the car so that the sharper the turn, the more resistence the driver feels. Thus, the driver is provided with all of the cues present in the totally mechanical system, but is relieved of most of the work. Still, there is room for more improvements. We have already mentioned Drury's (1975) and Snyder's (1976) research on optimal spacing between the brake and accelerator pedals.

In this section we discuss the innovative braking systems geared to compensate for the difficulty in maximizing the brakes' stopping capabilities. We also evaluate the effects of improvements in vehicle-handling capabilities. These have gone unnoticed for the most part because most of us, most of the time, do not test the limits of our car. Finally, a third type of vehicle-control system is one that is so radical that it, in fact, redefines part of the driving task. The most innocuous in this category is the now standard antitheft steering wheel lock device that must be released before the car can be started. The most ominous device in this category — to be discussed below — is probably the alcohol ignition interlock that prevents a legally drunk driver from starting his or her own car.

Antilock Braking Systems. Braking correctly is not an easy task, especially in emergency situations. Consider the design of the brakes: to activate the brakes you must first push the foot several inches before any effect is noticable, and then, within a distance of one more inch you move from a light-braking mode to a hard-braking mode. Learning to make the appropriate discriminations is a trying experience for the novice driver as well as his or her passengers. Even most experienced drivers cannot adjust their braking to the level of "just before skidding," especially in an emergency situation, when the most common instinctive response is to brake as hard as possible. This type of response typically results in skidding, which produces suboptimal friction between the tires and the pavement, increasing in turn the car's stopping distance. More serious in emergency situations, is the fact that all steering control is lost once the car starts skidding, and consequently avoidance maneuvers that could have been effected by steering become totally ineffective.

To prevent cars from skidding various systems have been developed. A recent study compared the relative benefits of 10 different combinations of radar warning lights (activated whenever a car closes the gap too much), radar activated brakes and antilock brakes that prevent the car from skidding and thus prevent loss of control, were assessed. In this study Tumbas, Treat, and McDonald (1977) analyzed a sample of 215 accidents in Indiana, and concluded that given the behavior of the drivers just prior to the accident (e.g., whether they braked at all, tried to steer, etc.), as many as 38 percent of the accidents could have been prevented with a combination of radar-activated warning light and a four-wheel antilock system. The potential benefits of two-wheel antilock systems alone — which are presently available on some luxury cars — were less than 2 percent, but a four-wheel antilock system yielded an estimate of 8 percent accident reduction. In any case, these results demonstrate the tremendous room left for vehicle improvements for increasing safety and reducing accidents.

Vehicle-Handling Improvements. Whenever safety margins are increased, through either vehicular or highway improvements, one potential counter effect is that the drivers, once accustomed to the new systems will take new and added risks, thereby nullifying the potential benefits of the improvements. This can be easily observed by noting that we all tend to drive faster on wider, better-delineated, and better-paved roads than on poorer-quality roads having the same speed limit. Often, highway improvements are followed by an increase in accidents (Lauer, 1960). In automobiles, the improvements are not visible so readily and therefore drivers are less likely to exploit them by driving more recklessly. This was demonstrated in a study by Koppa and Hayes (1976) who had their subjects perform various expected and unexpected emergency maneuvers in four different cars: a subcompact, a standard sedan, a "personal" car, and a semiluxury car. The four groups of subjects who drove these cars were matched in terms of age, sex, driving experience, and pretested driving skills. The hypothesis was that if drivers are sensitive to the widely different control capabilities in this range of four different cars, they would adapt their driving behavior to exploit these differences. Instead, the results revealed that for the most part drivers do not adjust their steering, brake, and acceleration inputs to exploit the vehicle's capabilities. Furthermore, only on rare occasions did the drivers drive their vehicle to "its limits," though occasionally this did happen. These results are interesting but need to be replicated on a larger sample of drivers in their own cars, with which they would be more intimately familiar, and thus more likely to adapt their behavior to their cars' capabilities. On the positive side some degree of risk taking present in this study would probably not be present in the natural environment, since in this study the test vehicles were equipped with antiroll supporting bars, and the drivers wore helmets and fire-resistant clothing.

A safety feature that has been shown to be effective in testing conducted unobtrusively on regular road users is the studded snow tire. In a study conducted in Sweden; Rumar, Bergrund, Jernberg, and Ytterbom (1976), used a traffic-analyzer device to measure speeds of cars going through two rural curves under both dry (high friction) and icy (low friction) road conditions. Only cars whose movement was not impeded by other vehicles were included in the study. The results, as summarized by the authors (p. 454) indicated that

drivers with vehicles with studded tires drive somewhat faster than do drivers of vehicles with unstudded tires in icy (low friction) road conditions. They do not, however, make use of all the increased friction for higher speeds. In icy road conditions they are driving with higher safety margins than are drivers without studs. In dry road conditions no clear speed or safety differences were found. Drivers seem to use the extra safety margin in icy conditions to increase their safety, rather than their speed, which is a finding of vital general interest.

Note that no difference in speed was obtained on the dry road, suggesting that the difference in speeds and safety margins on the icy roads was not due to some basic personality difference between the drivers using studded tires and the drivers using unstudded tires.

Alcohol Interlock. Another direction in the search for vehicle improvement has been in the design of totally new systems that would not simply aid the driver, but in fact redefine a part of the driving task. The one system that has received most publicity has been the alcohol ignition interlock device (AIID). The AIID has been suggested as a countermeasure to prevent the drunk driver from operating a car. Common to all the AIID systems is a perceptual motor task that the driver must perform before the ignition system can be successfully engaged. In the search for such a system, several requirements had to be met: (1) the task had to be relevant to driving; (2) the task had to be one that requires little time and effort; and (3) the task had to be one that is highly related to blood alcohol levels so that it would discriminate those drivers who have a BAL above 0.1 percent (and thus are considered legally drunk) from those drivers that have a BAL below 0.1 percent. One AIID, evaluated by Tennant (1973), involved a critical tracking task in which the driver had to maintain an unstable needle centered in a display through the use of the steering wheel. The driver's performance measure in this task is the length of time that he or she is able to keep the needle from going off the scale.

Since the system to be implemented cannot be one that would also prevent the sober drivers from driving, the effectiveness of the AIID has to be judged on the percent of intoxicated drivers that fail the test, *given* that none of the sober drivers fail. By determining the passing criterion at that point at which all the sober drivers passed the test, the percent of intoxicated drivers failing the test can be determined. Using such an approach, Tennant was albe to show that with the critical tracking task 50 percent of the people with BALs at or above 0.1 percent and 75 percent of the people with BALs at or above 0.14 percent failed the test. Thus, while the incorporation of such a system would not keep all the drunk drivers off the road, it would keep a good proportion of them in their parked cars. There are problems with this system, however. First, people differ in their ability so that the pass/fail criteria would have to be individually adjusted. This, however, would create a problem for people who drive more than one car, as most of us do. Second, people vary in their abilities when they're under stress, and at different times during the day. This aspect of the AIID systems has not been tested at all yet. Third, there is the ethical issue of preventing a driver from being able to start his or her own car. Nonetheless, the general approach of keeping the drunk drivers off the road by keeping them out of the (moving) car appears to be a promising one, at least for problem drivers who have previously been convicted of drunken driving. For such drivers, a restriction to a specific car, and a requirement to install an AIID, may be justifiable.

In summary, increasing safety through improvements in vehicle systems is an ongoing process in which many improvements have already been incorporated in the past 20 years or so, and many are presently being evaluated for future models. Efforts are directed at both aiding the driver in picking up information through improved lighting, mirrors and additional displays; as well as through providing the driver with a greater margin of error through improved control systems and vehicle handling capabilities. The use of the automobile as an extention of the enforcement systems — by incorporating systems such as the alcohol ignition interlock devices — represents a new front in safety administration; one that constitutes a redefinition of the driving task and raises some ethical considerations that come back to the basic issues of driving as a right or as a state-granted privilege.

HIGHWAY IMPROVEMENTS

There is one particularly hazardous myth which boobytraps the thinking of the engineer and causes him to neglect environmental safety considerations . . . . This is the "nut behind the wheel" myth or the often repeated statement that 80 to 90 percent of all accidents are caused by driver error . . . but it is not the only factor. As an example would you consider an accident caused by a driver stopping suddenly because of a confusing directional sign driver error only? . . . There are literally hundreds of documented studies which clearly indicate the value of environmental improvements in reducing accidents (Anderson, 1976, 20-21).

Highway improvements span the whole gamut from better roadway design (wide shoulders, smooth curves, etc.) through improved communication systems (road signs) to traffic control devices (signals). As such, highway modifications can influence and aid the driver in the information acquisition process (through signing and delineation), the decision-making process (through route guidance and signalization), and even in extending the range of driver responses that will be tolerated before the car goes out of control (through increased roadway-tire friction and superelevation of the road in curves). Finally some highway signing, such as radar speedcheck signs and "good will" signs (see Figure 6.1), are even aimed at affecting the driver's attitude.

Rather than list and describe the various areas in which improvements can be — and sometimes are — made, we focus our attention here around four psychological concepts that are influenced by highway design principles, and that in turn should dictate what "good" design principles should be. The concepts around which our discussion is centered are some of the major driving-related psychological processes we have discussed in previous chapters, that is, driver expectancies, vision, and perceptual and decision-making capabilities.

Driver Expectancies and General Design Principles

How often have you encountered the following situation: you are travelling on an expressway, and upon nearing your expected exit you switch from the inside left lane to the right lane, only to discover (possibly too late) that the exit ramp leads off from the left lane. Another frustrating situation involves waiting at a signalized intersection, when you suddenly see the opposing traffic beginning to move. You may then instinctively start to move yourself, only to realize that the light on your side is still red. Both of these situations illustrate poor design, in the sense that it is counter to our expectancies. These expectancies have been built over a long period of time in which we have repeatedly responded in the same way to similar situations, often based on the *Federal Manual for Uniform Traffic Control Design*. Some of the more common driver expectancies are listed in Table 6.1. Whenever any one of these expectancies is violated, problems are likely to occur, typically in the form of "driver errors" and longer driver reaction times. These can be traced to the selective nature of perception in general, and the visual search process in particular. As we have already discussed in Chapters Three and Four, the process of selecting relevant information is to a large extent based on expectations of where the needed information is likely to be. Thus, in the search for a signal light, the Cleveland, Ohio, driver tends to look up above the center of the intersection, while the Philadelphia, Pennsylvania, driver searches for them above the curb corners. When the two cross state lines, they may at first believe that none of the intersections are signalized.

Table 6.1   Some Common Driver Expectancies

1. Expressway exits are from the right lane.
2. An exit will have fewer lanes than the continuing expressway.
3. Route guidance signs will present information in a consistent manner, for
    example, a given exit will be identified by the same name on all signs.
4. In T intersections, through-moving traffic has the right-of-way.
5. In the absence of a signal light, stop, or yield sign facing the driver, crossing
    traffic must yield the right-of-way.
6. At a signalized intersection with a flashing yellow light, cross traffic has a
    flashing red light and must stop and give right-of-way.
7. When two roads merge, traffic entering from the narrower road will yield
    the right-of-way.
8. Unless otherwise noted at each potential entrance into a street, the street is
    a two-way rather than a one-way street.

Very often there is a conflict either between driver expectations and other design criteria or among different expectancies, and so some of the driver expectancies must be compromised. This is the case when, for economic reasons, an exit ramp from the left lane is more practical than an exit from the right lane. This is also the case when traffic is given a red light in order to allow opposing left-turning vehicles to make a safe turn. The drivers facing the green arrow expect to have the right-of-way, and therefore the opposing traffic must wait despite their expectation to start moving at the same time. When such conflicts arise, the highway design engineer must assume the responsibility of alerting the drivers to the unusual situation. This is often done by providing the driver with signed information prior to the critical place. Thus, it is recommended that left exit ramps be preceded by special warning signs to alert the driver early on to the upcoming situation.

Vision and Visual Search; Signs and Roadway Illumination

With approximately 90 percent of the driving-relevant information being visual, almost every highway design consideration must involve drivers' visual capabilities, limitations, and needs. These considerations are critical in the choice of colors for signs and signals, the size and lettering design of signs, and the pattern and amount of light needed for nighttime illumination. For example, because approximately 7 percent of the male drivers are color deficient, with difficulties in discriminating between shades of red and green, the "green" light in traffic signals is not really green but rather green-blue. In this discussion we limit ourselves to reviewing some of the research conducted on driver needs for nighttime illumination and principles in sign design.

Highway Signs. To provide the driver with adequate route guidance, sign designs must be compatible with the driver's ability to process the information in them. Letter size that is too small, a sign that contains too many words, poor contrast, or poor sign location are all likely to defeat the sign's purpose. Generally speaking, signs can be described in terms of their legibility and their attention-getting value.

Factors that influence legibility are the brightness contrast between the letters and their background, the color, the styling of and spacing between the letters and the letters' size. Recommendations relevant to these factors have been made at least as early as 1932 when Lauer (in Woltman, 1976) suggested that for good legibility the sign background color should be light yellow. In this discussion we deal with letter size only. Since reading is a time-dependent process, the more information contained in the sign, the further away the driver should be in order to read it, and the larger the letter size should be. The relationship between letter size and the distance from which it is readable under normal daylight conditions is presented in Figure 6.5. The more remote the message content is from the driver's expectations, the larger the required letter size. This is because familiar words can be read even without reading all the letters, and expected words (such as when looking for a specific exit) can be identified even sooner. A legibility distance that could be recommended on the basis of this figure would be approximately 1-inch letter height per 100 feet. In other words, if a sign containing the word "exit" should be readable from a distance of 500 feet, then the letter height should be at least 5 inches. The actual legibility distances obtained for existing signs vary greatly from significantly less than the required level to levels above those required. All too often, legibility distance of many signs is reduced to below the required level when conditions are not optimal, such as night and in the presence of glare (Forbes, 1972). Furthermore, the recommended distance here is based on the "normal" driver vision, which is 20/20. This standard should probably now be changed to 1-inch letter height per 50 feet to accommodate the minimum visual acuity of 20/40 required by most states, and to be responsive to the limits of most drivers rather than to the limits of the "average" driver (Forbes, 1976).

The attention value of a sign is the degree to which it attracts the driver's attention and visual fixation. Factors that influence the sign's attention value are its location, its luminance, its contrast against the background, and its design. In general, the closer the sign to the driver's primary area of visual search, the better it is illuminated, and the greater its contrast against the background, the earlier it will be detected by the approaching driver. Good design is less simple to define, but it includes redundant coding so that a sign can be easily

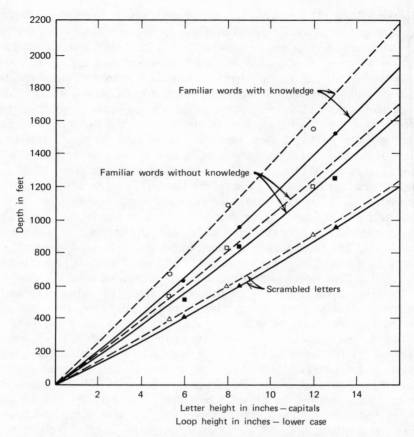

Figure 6.5. Effect of message familiarity on the legibility distance of lower-case and capital letters (from Forbes, 1972).

detected and identified by its shape or color even without reading its content (the international STOP sign is a prime example). This type of coding enables drivers to detect signs they are searching for more quickly. In complex situations such as interchanges with unusual geometrics, diagrammatic signs that contain partial schematic drawings of the interchange are an aid to most motorists.

To derive the actual readability of a sign from its attention value and its legibility distance, the final consideration should include the speed of the approaching driver. The faster the driver is going, the less time he or she will have to evaluate the sign. Given all these factors, the job of evaluating road signs becomes immensely complex. One of the more sophisticated attempts to evaluate road signs' effectiveness was made by Bhise and Rockwell (1972). Using driver eye-movement behavior as their basic means of measuring reading behavior, they developed a computer program that combines the eye movement pattern, the vehicle's lane position, the visual acuity of the driver, design features of the sign, and roadway geometry to yield a measure that would indicate the first time the driver is able to read a given sign. Then, given the knowledge of the driver's speed, an estimate can be made of whether the sign legibility or attention value should be increased in order to provide the driver with more time to read the sign.

Roadway Illumination. The greatest difference between daytime and nighttime driving is the reduced illumination and visibility during the night hours. To supplement the very restricted area illuminated by our own headlamps, it is considered good practice to install permanent lighting at high traffic density areas, high accident sites, and points on the roadway that involve maneuver changes and decisions on the part of the driver. A common juncture for all of these is the intersection. Illuminating an intersection can give the approaching driver an early warning about the location of the intersection, and the potential need to slow down in order to turn or when other traffic is present. The importance of this information for increased safety is demonstrated in a study by Walker and Roberts (1976) who noted a 49 percent reduction in nighttime accidents after lights were installed over 47 intersections in Iowa. Furthermore, the reduction was greater in the more complex intersections where more light poles were installed. Partial illumination, especially when it is inappropriately placed, can be worse than no illumination since it may confuse the driver (Rockwell, Hungerford, & Balasubramanian, 1976). One indication of good roadway illumination may be drivers' eye movements — they become almost the same as during the daytime.

Perception and Roadway Markings and Signs

Roadway Markings. Most of the time our perception of the environment surrounding us is sufficiently accurate to enable us to adequately move in it. To aid us in perceiving the geometry of the roadway ahead, most U.S. roads are marked by yellow (or sometimes white) stripes along the edges of the road. These are particularly useful in nighttime driving as indicated by both drivers' eye movements (Rackoff & Rockwell, 1973) and by their effects on the vehicles' paths (Hagen, 1970). Still, even with modern delineation markings every once in a while we are mislead by our perception. A case in point is a study by Shinar, Rockwell, and Malecki (1975) on driver behavior in approaching high-accident curves. To evaluate different approaches to affect a change in drivers' entry speeds, five curves were selected for in-depth study, and the speeds of approaching vehicles were measured before and after a modification was made. In two curves, the modification involved painting stripes on the road surface in such a way that would affect the approaching driver's perception of the road width (making it look narrower) or sharpness (making it look sharper) at the curve. In both cases, a significant reduction in both the average speed and the proportion of people speeding was obtained. On the other hand, the installation of a curve warning sign before two other curves failed to result in any significant speed reductions. Unfortunately, even with the striping the effect was transient. The curves studied were used primarily by local drivers, and after 30 days the effects of the stripings on the drivers' speed wore off. The authors concluded that "perceptual modifications may be an effective tool to affect the behavior of transient drivers unfamiliar with the high accident curves." The advantage of the perceptual modifications over the warning signs was attributed to the fact that "the verbal message is an instruction that leaves the driver the choice of attending to it or not (since it's off the road) and heeding it or not (since the driver can rely on his false sense impressions in the case of an illusive curve) . . . . On the other hand, the perceptual modifications operate directly on the driver's perception of the curve demands and are therefore more difficult to ignore."

An even more dramatic demonstration of how markings can be manipulated was provided in another part of the same study by Shinar et al., as well as by Denton (1973) in England. In this case, stripings perpendicular to the direction of the road were painted with decreasing distance between adjoining stripes. Thus, to the driver going over these stripes, they would appear to be moving at a faster and faster pace. Since the rate at which the scenery moves in our visual field is a principal cue to speed, it was hypothesized that these stripes would mislead the drivers to believe that they were accelerating, and would cause them to slow down. Indeed, in both studies the stripings resulted in significant speed reductions. Furthermore, in England where the markings were left for a period of over a year, an accident reduction from 14 in the year before the striping to only one in the year since striping, was recorded (Rutley, 1975).

Activated Signs. One disadvantage of most signs is that their message is fixed and not responsive to changes in the environment, and consequently, drivers often do not respond to them. To make them more relevant to drivers' needs and to make them perceived as more valid, recent innovations in signing include programmable and activated signs that display different messages under different conditions. The effectiveness of signal-activated signs over regular, fixed-display signs was demonstrated in a study by Hanscom (1975). The signs used were warning for icy bridges that were either standard WATCH FOR ICE signs or signs with flashing lights above the words ICE ON BRIDGE WHEN FLASHING. Although both types of signs yielded significant speed reductions from the normal conditions, the effect of the signalized signs was significantly greater. In interpreting his findings, Hanscom concluded that the signalized signs did not simply relieve the drivers of deciding whether the road was icy or not, but that "motorists were made more aware of the icing probability as a result of the cue afforded by the signing" (p. 33). Thus, according to Hanscom, the flashing lights were actually used as one more cue for making the perceptual judgments. An alternative explanation is that the major function of the flashing lights was simply to attract the drivers' attention to the sign. This explanation is consistent with Johansson and Rumar's (1966) finding that drivers attend much less to what can be considered unimportant signs than to important signs. The flashing lights may then make the sign more attention-compelling or may make it more important.

Decision and Traffic Signal Lights

In addition to easing the traffic flow at intersections, signalization eases the driving task by relieving the driver of some additional visual search prior to entering an intersection (looking for other approaching cars) and of second guessing the intention of other drivers. Just like signs, they provide the driver with information, and just like signs they may or may not be responded to appropriately. Although they are usually considered safety devices, their indiscriminate installation does not necessarily reduce accidents (Highway and Vehicle Safety Report, 1974). In complex intersections signals may be misunderstood (e.g., when opposing traffic is provided with delayed left turn) and even in the common "cross" intersection with a three-light signal configuration there may be complications. The complications stem from the fact that while the signals reduce conflicts with cross traffic at the intersection, they sometimes increase conflicts with other vehicles traveling in the same direction. More simply, drivers stopping for a red or yellow light may be hit from behind by drivers who expect them to cross and would like to cross the intersection themselves. In part, this situation can be attributed to what has been termed the "amber light dilemma." With the timing of many amber lights there is often a situation in which when the light turns from green to amber a driver is caught in a predicament of being too close to the intersection to stop safely, yet too far away to pass through it before the light turns to red. This can happen only with short amber phases. By considering the driver reaction and decision time, and adding factors such as vehicle speed and width of intersection, Gazis, Herman, and Maradudin (1960) developed a formula to compute the minimum duration of the amber phase that would eliminate the amber light dilemma. A subsequent empirical evaluation of both the function, and actual driver behavior at two different intersections, led Olson and Rothery (1961) to recommend an amber light duration of 5.5 seconds, which would be practical for a wide range of speeds. In their study they observed drivers' behavior at two intersections at different thoroughfares with different amber light durations: 3.00 and 4.75 seconds — both short enough to cause the amber light dilemma. Both signals had been operating at these durations for a long time so the assumption was made that drivers could have had the time to adapt their behaviors to the different durations. In fact, no difference in drivers' behavior was observed between the two intersections, thus dispelling the fear that drivers regard a long amber phase as an extension of the green light phase and, therefore, misuse the safety margin the amber light is designed to provide. At signalized intersections in which travel speeds are even higher, an alternative approach to an excessively long amber light phase is an all-red phase, that is, a brief period when traffic in all directions of travel has a red light. Another approach, adopted in Israel, involves a flashing green light. In this fashion, the continuous green light is followed by several flashes of the green light and only then the amber light appears. The rationale behind this approach is to provide high-speed approaching drivers with more temporal cues concerning the cycle phase. Initial evaluation of this system suggests that it is not preferable to the standard three-phase cycle. Furthermore, it appears to amplify individual differences in time-speed estimation among approaching drivers, since it causes an increase (compared to standard signalization) in rear-end collisions between cars approaching the intersection. Thus, in urban intersections the flashing green signal light was accompanied by a 71 percent increase in rear-end accidents and only a 40 percent reduction in right-angle accidents (Mehalel & Hakkert, 1975).

In summary, highway improvements can be a significant factor in accident reductions. Human factors that should be significant in implementing any change in the highway environment are driver expectancies, visual capacities, and decision-making capabilities. Driver expectancies are often shaped by present standards and deviations from these standards can lead to increased driver confusion resulting in erratic maneuvers and accidents. The driver visual capabilities and visual search behavior should dictate the design and placement of signs, signals, and roadway illumination. In this context it should be emphasized that the design considerations should be based on the expected capabilities of most drivers, rather than on the expected capabilities of the average driver. Hence, the letter size and illumination should be greater than that needed by the average driver. Good design principles should also consider the potential existence of visual illusions and possible means to counteract these illusions, preferrably by modifying the driver's visual environment. Finally, highway signs and signals should be so designed as to simplify the driver's decision making problems through unambiguous signs and traffic signals, as well as through the inclusion of human factors considerations in the timing of traffic signal lights.

SUMMARY

Highway safety can be increased by improving any one of the three major components of the highway traffic system: the vehicles, the roadway environment, and the road user — typically the driver.

Driver improvement begins even before licensing a person to drive, at the driver education stage, and can be continued by imposing valid criteria for measuring driver behavior at the driving test, by providing effective enforcement of the traffic laws, and by requiring problem drivers (with many violations and accidents) to take remedial courses. Attempts to improve driving safety have been made in all four phases. Driver education is practically an integral part of any high school curriculum. This state of affairs reflects our assumption that structured driver education and training is useful. At the same time, because driver education is so prevalent, it is difficult to evaluate its impact on accident reduction. Some large-scale evaluation studies are presently being conducted. On the other hand, driver training has been shown to be an effective method for improving specific driving skills, such as distance estimation. In the licensing domain the present trend is to view driving as a necessity of everyday life and to allow as many people as possible to obtain a license. This often results in lower standards for passing — especially in visual performance. For the licensed driver, enforcement is a means of pressuring him or her to drive according to the rules, that is, not exceed the speed limit. To the extent that the driver perceives the existence of enforcement — often obtained by parking a police cruiser on the road shoulder — it is indeed effective. Finally, for those drivers who, despite all of the other efforts mentioned above, still repeatedly violate the laws or cause accidents, there are postlicensing remedial programs. The effectiveness of these programs in reducing accidents and violations vary as do the programs themselves. Most of these programs, however, still need further testing of their effectiveness.

In the area of vehicle design, many safety features are obvious.

However, most vehicle improvements have been directed toward increasing crashworthiness — the ability to withstand accidents once they occur — rather than to help the driver avoid getting into accidents in the first place. Effective driver aids aimed at avoiding accidents have included various means of increasing the field of view — innovative mirrors and headlight systems — as well as information systems designed to supplement the driver's perceptual capabilities — such as rear deceleration lights and heads-up displays. Better vehicle control can be achieved through improved handling capabilities, but there is a question as to whether drivers in fact are aware of these improvements and utilize them effectively. Systems that are geared to increase safety — with or without the driver's cooperation — are antilock braking systems that, as their name implies, prevent the brakes from locking, and consequently allow the driver to maintain effective steering even while braking hard. Finally, we are now seeing vehicle changes that are aimed at improving safety even at the cost of the driver's own desires. Most notable is the alcohol ignition interlock device, a system that gives the driver a perceptual motor test that is able to differentiate between the sober and intoxicated driver. Further improvements in the reliability of the alcohol ignition interlock device may lead to a new generation of cars and a new philosophy of traffic control — an approach aimed at serving drivers even against their wills.

Highway improvements include various systems that help the driver in the information-processing task. These include standardized design features that are congruent with driver expectancies, signs and roadway illumination that supplement the driver's perception and increase his or her visibility, and activated signs and signals that aid the driver's decision making. Driver expectancies — shaped through repeated experience — should serve as a guide to making highway design decision. Whenever driver expectancies are violated, traffic conflicts and accidents are likely to increase. Driver vision and visual search behavior is relevant to most highway design features beginning with the dimensions of letters on highway signs and the sign location in the driver's visual field and ending with roadway illumination as a supplementary light source to the vehicle's headlights. The driver's perception of the roadway geometry is greatly influenced by the contours formed by the road against its background, as well as by the total visual scene. The accuracy of this perception can be increased by improvements in the roadway delineation systems (markings and point stripes). Other elements — typically a repetitious pattern immediately off the road and parallel to it — influence speed perception. Misperception of either roadway geometry or speed can be countered by careful design and may even be exploited to influence driver behavior toward greater safety. Finally the driver's decision making can be helped by devising signals that are easy to interpret and reduce uncertainty. In connection with signal lights, driver uncertainty — whether to stop or proceed — is greatest during the amber phase of the signal cycle. Human factors analyses have shown that this uncertainty can be reduced by increasing the duration of the amber phase.

SEVEN
THE PEDESTRIAN

The driver is not the only road user. Other road users — often ignored by the drivers — are passengers, bicyclists, pedestrians, and even animals. To obtain a safe traffic system, all of these road users should be accommodated. Perhaps because passengers are relatively passive users of the system, and animals are relatively uncontrolled, the focus on nondrivers has centered on cyclists and pedestrians. Although the difficulties that cyclists may have in merging with the four-wheel vehicles may be intuitively obvious (poor visibility relative to cars, lower speeds, no licensing criteria for the riders, young riders, etc.) only in the very recent past have their problems been scientifically studied, and environmental design solutions been seriously considered (for recent studies and surveys on bicycle riders and usage, and on environmental design implications, see Bergman, 1976; Roy, 1976; Snelson, 1976). This last chapter therefore focuses on the most often encountered and most widely studied nondriver road user — the pedestrian.

"The pedestrian is a humble man, who has been pushed around first by a man on horseback, then by a man in a carriage, and now by others in cars and trucks" (Bird, 1969). While many people identify with the driver role, most people tend to think of the pedestrian as somebody else. Apparently, this line of thinking has led to what by now may be described as severe negligence in the design of the highway system to accommodate the pedestrian. Signalized intersections are designed to accommodate the vehicle traffic; many otherwise expensive suburbs do not have sidewalks; and in many new development areas, the roads are designed to accommodate more and more vehicles while the sidewalks are designed to accommodate fewer and fewer people. In spite of all this, we are amazingly quick to assume the role of righteous pedestrians eager to claim our rights when we are put into that position.

The increasing concern about the pedestrians as part of the traffic system is due to their vulnerability compared to the drivers who are protected by the shield of their car. Although, in the United States, pedestrian accidents accounted for only 1.6 percent of all motor vehicle accidents they accounted for 4 percent of the traffic fatalities, and constituted 19 percent of the nearly 40,000 fatal accidents recorded in 1975 (National Safety Council, 1976). Also, perhaps less expected and less known, is Balasha's (1977) finding that traffic conflicts involving pedestrians are more severe than traffic conflicts among cars only, in the sense that they involve more violent braking and swerving maneuvers on the part of the driver. Presumably this is due to the suddeness at which pedestrians often enter the roadway.

In this chapter we first define who is the pedestrian in general and who is the accident-involved pedestrian in particular. Next we discuss the causes of pedestrian accidents and finally we review some potential countermeasures.

IDENTIFYING THE VULNERABLE PEDESTRIAN

The pedestrian is more than just a driver out of the car. Drivers, because of regulations and licensing requirements, constitute a much more homogenous group of people than pedestrians. The most obvious difference between the groups is the age distribution. Along the age continuum we can distinguish among three categories of pedestrians — differing from each other in their capabilities to interact with the total traffic system. The first category consists of young children, not old enough to drive. The second and largest category includes people who are older and may be licensed to drive but are not in a car at a particular time. The last group — the elderly — are people who due to old age experience various problems in interacting with the traffic system. Accident statistics indicate that it is persons in the first and last groups who are the primary victims of pedestrian accidents. To illustrate, a survey of pedestrian accidents in the Baltimore, Maryland area over a three-year period revealed that almost three-fourths of the fatally injured were either less than 10 years old, or over 65 years old, or under the influence of alcohol (Baker, Robertson, & O'Neill, 1972). A similar survey by Kentucky's Department of Transportation (Zegeer & Deen, 1976) found that although most people who were killed in traffic accidents were between the ages of 15 and 44, pedestrian fatalities were highest for the ages under 9 and over 64. Similar results have been reported for other countries such as England (Smeed, 1976) and Australia (Avery, 1974). Furthermore, in the English study, when accident involvement was measured relative to the amount of walking that people in different age groups do, it was found that old people (65+) were three times as likely to have an accident as young adults (30 to 39 years old) for every mile walked; while children under the age of 10 were eight times as likely to have an accident as young adults for every mile walked.

The statistics above seem to suggest that at the two extremes of the age distributions people may have specific deficiencies that make them more likely to be involved in accidents. Fortunately, drivers also perceive these two groups as the most vulnerable. This was demonstrated in a survey conducted in Switzerland in which drivers were stopped and shown a picture of a pedestrian wanting to cross the road. Of the 417 drivers interviewed, 47 percent considered a little girl to be the most vulnerable to traffic, 44 percent considered an elderly woman to be the most vulnerable, and the remaining 9 percent judged a mother with a child, a middle-aged man, or a young man to be the most vulnerable (Zuercher, 1976). Since young children are faster on their feet and the awareness that they must be protected is greater in the context of highway traffic safety, more attention has been directed to children than to elderly people.

The Child Pedestrian

Children represent a particular hazard since they may lack the skills and habits, that are typically acquired at a later age, which enable people to behave safely on the road. Unintrusive observations of children walking to and from school have led to the realization that the child pedestrian, particularly under the age of 10, lives in a different conceptual world than the adult pedestrian. Some of the generalizations that have been repeatedly made concerning child pedestrians are that their perception and ways of thinking is still egocentric; they have only a fragmentary understanding of the rules and structure of the traffic system; their attention level fluctuates and they are easily distracted; and their knowledge of traffic signs is incomplete — and for young children, practically nil. In light of all of these limitations, Sandels (1975), who pioneered the systematic observations of children in traffic, concluded that it is impossible to fully adapt the small child to the complex traffic environment of the 1970s. Instead, she argues we should design the traffic system with these constraints in mind.

After performing a street-crossing task analysis, and analyzing the sensory, perceptual, judgmental, memory, and motor functions involved in a relatively simple street crossing operation, Avery (1974) concluded that many of these functions have a "developmental trend" in the sense that they improve with age so that prior to a certain age a child is not capable of performing them adequately. Thus, although the static visual acuity of young children does not seem to improve beyond the age of 1 year, the ability of 5-year olds to effectively search their visual field for predetermined targets is poorer than that of adults (Liss & Haith, 1970). Children also have more difficulties in judging distances. Zwahlen (1974) found that while on the average the distance judgments of young children were not less accurate than those of adults, the variability that the children exhibited in their judgments was twice as large, that is, they were much less consistent in their judgment. Thus, it is possible that under the same circumstances a child on one occasion may decide not to cross the street, while on another similar occasion the same child may decide to cross it.

How a child's cognitive limitations can hamper misguided efforts to increase children's safety is illustrated by two studies; one conducted in England and one in the United States. In England, as part of a safety program the children were taught a drill or jingle that was supposed to serve as a mnemonic (memory improving) device to use the proper visual search procedures prior to crossing the street (e.g., "Look to the right, look to the left, etc.). In their evaluation of the drill's effectiveness, Pease and Preston (1967) found that first, many children believed that simply repeating the jingle protected them from potential hazards (what is known as magical thinking). Second, many children under six years old tended to regard "right" and "left" as certain parts of the environment rather than directions relative to their own body position. In the second study conducted in the United States, Salvatore (1974) asked children of ages 5 to 14 to estimate the speed of approaching cars as "fast," "medium," or "slow." He found that the ability to assess speed correctly improved with age for cars that actually were going at a "slow" or "medium" speed but paradoxically, the likelihood of correctly identifying fast moving cars decreased with age. A closer inspection of the data revealed that the younger children were simply more conservative in their estimate, classifying many more cars as fast. As an explanation for this bias, Salvatore suggested that "these younger children were responding to parental dicta concerning the dangers of the road and ignoring the actual sensory cues" (p. 122).

Even a complete awareness of the child's world is not enough. There also remains the problem of knowing what to teach. It appears that the "correct" behavior we preach to children is not the same as our own and so the child who is also taught to imitate us is caught in a bind. This dilemma was aptly stated by Routledge, Repetto-Wright, and Howarth (1976) who filmed and then analyzed the behavior of children and adults in traffic, in Nottingham, England. In the authors' own words (p. 701):

Adults assess the crossing situation as they approach the kerb, while children pay little attention to the crossing situation until they arrive at the kerb, and are therefore less well prepared to take advantage of favourable traffic configurations. Having stopped at the kerb to wait for a gap in the traffic children are slower to start and seldom anticipate when they cross through a chosen gap, while adults take most advantage of gaps in traffic by anticipating their arrival. Children learn to adopt these adult strategies without instruction and indeed contrary to the way in which they have been taught. There appears to be a mismatch between the information they receive from parents, schools and safety programmes and the information they gain from their own experiences and from observation of adult pedestrians.

Other differences between children and adults are manifested in the way they utilize gaps in the traffic. Routledge et al. (1976) discovered that even though the mean size of the gap in traffic that children five to ten years old accepted for crossing was larger than the gaps accepted by older children or adults (9 versus 7 and 4.5 seconds), the way they utilized the gap was less efficient. The older children and adult pedestrians seemed to anticipate the arrival of the gap, and crossed closely behind the car defining the beginning of the gap. This is a strategy that we all commonly employ yet it is not explicitly taught to children.

Finally, to compound the problem of child safety in the streets, it should be noted that children also use the streets differently than adults. While it is probably safe to assume that most adults cross the road for the same reasons the proverbial chicken does, that is, to get to the other side, this is not true for children who often use the streets as play areas. In the United States, of the five- to nine-year-old pedestrian children killed by moving vehicles 8.6 percent were playing in the roadway (National Safety Council, 1976). It is therefore not surprising that a significant reduction in children pedestrian accidents was noted in urban areas following the installation of playgrounds (Bartholomew, 1967).

The Aged Pedestrian

The problems of the aged and handicapped pedestrians are different from those of children. They are cognizant of the dangers inherent in crossing the streets but may have reduced sensory and motor capabilities that prevent them from quick maneuvering between cars. The deterioration in their visual field and dynamic visual acuity is likely to cause delayed detection of approaching traffic as well as poorer judgment of vehicles' speed and time available for crossing. In addition, the perceptual abilities of older people who also suffer from difficulties in walking may be further reduced due to the tendencies of these people to glance at their feet (Rodstein, 1969). Finally, the aging process may affect mental capabilities needed for safe behavior. Weiner (1968) found that elderly pedestrians are often confused by the traffic signal lights, and base their judgments on when to cross the street on the perceived traffic movement — a perception that may already be impaired.

The most obvious motoric impairment of the aged is their reduced walking speed. For traffic engineering purposes, a walking rate of 4 feet per second is assumed (U.S. Department of Transportation, 1971). However, approximately 35 percent of all pedestrians walk at slower speeds (Bruce, 1965; Sleight, 1972). The average adult and elderly person walk at a rate of approximately 4.5 feet per second. Although the elderly are not slower as a group, they are more variable. Some walk much faster than most adults while some walk much slower than most adults. This increase in individual differences with increasing age is typical of most sensorimotor functions. In any case, for safety purposes the mean of the group is not the most appropriate measure since it might eliminate (literally) approximately 50 percent of the population. A more realistic estimate, then, would be one that would enable most (e.g., 95 percent) people to cross. Such an estimate based on a study conducted in Sweden (reported by Sleight, 1972) is 2.2 feet per second for adults but only 1.8 feet per second for the elderly; that is a speed approximately half as fast as the 4.0 feet per second assumed for design purposes. Thus, for a relatively narrow street that is only 30 feet wide, the duration of the WALK cycle that would accommodate the elderly pedestrian should be almost one quarter of a minute.

The predicament of the elderly pedestrians is particularly acute because drivers — despite their realization of the elderly pedestrians' vulnerability — do not tend to accommodate them. This was found by Zuercher (1976) who observed drivers unobtrusively and noted whether they stopped or did not stop for a pedestrian intending to cross the street at a marked crossing (where the pedestrian has the right-of-way). When the pedestrian was a young woman "attractive but not conspicuous, dressed in boots, a coat and carrying a handbag" an average of every sixth driver (more men than women) stopped to let the pedestrian pass. When, however, a policewoman was made up to look like an old woman, "dressed in an old fashioned coat, short boots and carrying a shopping bag," an average of only one out of every eight drivers stopped to let the woman pass. When asked to reflect on her experience the policewoman said "as an old person I was just left standing there; I was completely ignored and pushed aside . . . . The expressions on the passing drivers' faces said: I am really very sorry for you, but I am not the one to help you" (p. 7 E 5).

THE CAUSES OF PEDESTRIAN ACCIDENTS

Although the highway traffic system is designed to prevent interactions between pedestrians and vehicles, the recurrence of pedestrian accidents is testimony to failures in this area. The overwhelming majority of these accidents occur when pedestrians step into the roadway rather than when drivers run their cars off the road. Thus it can be said that most often it is the pedestrian who encroaches into the territory of the driver — a somewhat expected result since pedestrians must step into the road in order to cross streets while drivers are rarely compelled to mount curbs. As soon as a pedestrian steps off the curb, he or she increases the risk of being involved in an accident. To develop effective pedestrian accident countermeasures, it is important to first understand what specific driver and pedestrian behaviors cause these accidents.

In this section we focus our discussion on the results of a study by Snyder and Knoblauch (1971). This study involved post-hoc analyses of 2157 pedestrian accidents that were recorded in 13 major U.S.

cities in the years 1969 to 1970. Some similarities between the results of this pedestrian accident study and the results obtained in Indiana University's study of accident causes (see Chapter Five) will be mentioned in the course of this discussion. However, because of differences between the two studies in the way accident causes were defined, many otherwise interesting comparisons are difficult to make.

To identify the circumstances under which pedestrian accidents occur, Snyder and Knoblauch developed a taxonomy of accident types — categories that describe the nature of the pedestrian behavior and the circumstances prior to the accident. They found that 34 percent of all accidents occurred after the pedestrian darted out into the street from the curb or from between parked cars — and not in an intersection. In all of these cases, they agreed, the driver, traveling at a normal rate of speed, did not have time to stop after detecting the pedestrian (typically a child). In contrast with the high frequency of the midblock "dart-out" situation, intersection dart-outs, classified as an "intersection dart" occurred only in 9 percent of the 2157 accidents analyzed. Common to both types of dart-outs, is the very short time available to the driver to respond to the pedestrian. In the case of a midblock dart-out the effective time to respond is further shortened because of the driver's low expectancy to encounter a pedestrian there (see Snyder & Knoblauch, 1971, Chapter Four, Figure 4).

In order to avoid an accident, the driver and the pedestrian must be able to effectively communicate their intentions. To do so, they must both perform effectively the following tasks:

Select a proper course of movement.

Visually search for the presence of each other.

Actually detect each other and their relative locations.

Evaluate the actions and intention of each other.

Decide on a proper course of action.

Make the proper response to avoid an accident.

An accident could happen whenever either the pedestrian or the driver fails to perform adequately any one of these tasks. The relative contribution of failures on each one of these tasks to accident causation is listed in Table 7.1. Note that the total number of factors cited by Snyder and Knoblauch is almost twice as large as the number of accidents in the sample. This is because approximately 25 percent of the accidents were caused by a combination of two or three factors. In Table 7.1, the second column represents the percent of times that

Table 7.1   Frequency of Primary Pedestrian Accident Causal Factors

FACTOR GROUP	NUMBER OF TIMES SELECTED	PERCENT OF FACTORS SELECTED	PERCENT OF ACCIDENTS SELECTED
Ped course	1206	30.6	55.9
Ped search and detection	1166	29.4	54.1
Ped detection	238	6.0	11.0
Ped evaluation	158	4.0	7.3
Ped decision	17	0.4	0.8
Ped action	19	0.5	0.9
Driver course	181	4.6	8.4
Driver search and detection	510	12.9	23.6
Driver detection	292	7.4	13.5
Driver evaluation	82	2.1	3.8
Driver control-action	75	1.9	3.5
Driver and ped interaction	9	0.2	0.4
Total	3953	100.0	—

Based on a sample of 2157 accidents. Adapted from Snyder and Knoblauch, 1971.

each factor was cited out of the total number of factors cited (3953) while the entries in the right column represent the percent of times each factor was cited out of the total number of accidents.

Either way the results are viewed, two findings are conspicuous: First, the pedestrians — who are much more vulnerable than the drivers — are the ones whose actions precipitate the majority of the accidents. When only one precipitating or causal factor was identified, 60 percent of the times it was a pedestrian factor. When two or three factors were identified, the percentage of pedestrian factors rose to 75 and 68, respectively. Second, poor choice of a street-crossing course and inadequate visual search of the roadway are the pedestrian's primary failures. Of the driver failures, the most common cause was an inadequate visual search. In this respect, Snyder and Knoblauch's findings are very similar to Treat et al.'s (1977) conclusions that the single most common cause of traffic accidents is improper lookout.

A closer look at the pedestrian and driver errors revealed that the most common pedestrian course errors involved increased risk taking by running across the street at an unexpected place or time, and crossing the street against the light. The following extreme example of the first type of improper course selection by pedestrians was provided by Baker (1977, p. 117) in a study of pedestrian accidents in Rio de Janeiro.

*One densely populated area was divided by a highspeed high-
way, some 15 miles long. In certain places pedestrians could
cross safely by climbing a long flight of stairs to a foot bridge.
Perhaps because of the long distances between these "passa-
rellas" and the difficulty of carrying bicycles, children, and
packages up the stairs, many pedestrians could be observed
running across three lanes of traffic to the 3-foot high concrete
barrier in the center of the highway, climbing over the barrier —
often with bicycles and children — and then running across the
second traffic stream. In 1970, 27 of the 115 pedestrians in the
10% sample were killed on this highway.*

A close runnerup to improper pedestrian course was improper
visual search and detection. In a post-hoc analysis of already existing
records, it is very difficult to reconstruct what kind of visual search
error the pedestrian committed. Consequently, Snyder and
Knoblauch were unable to identify the nature of the visual search
failure in a significant percentage of the accidents. Nonetheless, of
those identified, the most common were "inattention" and "inadequate search" which together accounted for 24 percent of the accidents, while the least frequent were overload and distraction by
traffic or traffic signals, which together accounted for less than 2
percent of the accidents. Thus, as with poor pedestrian course selection, the primary problem appears to be lack of care in performing
the street crossing task. In their study of the causes of traffic accidents in England, Sabey and Staughton (1975), attributed nearly
50 percent of the pedestrian accidents to the pedestrian's lack of care
— a rather loose catchall category which at the very least implies a
lack of awareness of the potential risks involved in street crossing.

The most common driver errors were inadequate visual search and
delayed detection of the pedestrian due to parked cars restricting the
driver's field of view. Obviously pedestrian "dart-out" accidents
would be drastically reduced if it were not for the parked cars behind
which the pedestrians wait to dart into the road. These visual search
failures correspond closely to those accident causes labeled by Treat
et al. (1977) as improper lookout and delayed recognition due to
view obstructions. The similarity between the two sets of results
despite the many differences in the accident samples and causal
assessment procedures, underscores the importance of the visual-per-
ceptual surveillance, and the relatively high frequency of its failures.

As we noted above (and in Chapter Five), the majority of accidents are precipitated by a combination of two or more causes,
which *together* cause the accident. Thus, the mere listing of individual factors provides a somewhat misleading perspective of why
accidents happen. To provide a more accurate picture, Snyder and

Table 7.2   The Most Common Combinations of Pedestrian Accident Causes

COMBINATION OF CAUSES	PERCENT OF CASES
Ped course, ped search, driver detection	13.6
Ped course, ped search	11.3
Ped search, driver search	9.9
Ped course, ped search, driver search	6.3
Ped course, ped detection, driver detection	5.7
Ped search, driver detection	3.9
Ped course	3.7
Driver search	3.6
Ped search	3.6
No factors identified	8.1
Other factors (each combination less than 3%)	30.3

Based on a sample of 2157 accidents, from Snyder and Knoblauch, 1971.

Knoblauch also tabulated the most frequent combinations of factors. These combinations are listed in Table 7.2. Note that five out of the seven most frequent combinations accounting for nearly 40 percent of the accidents, involved both the driver and the pedestrian. These accidents typically happened when the pedestrian selected an inappropriate crossing course and failed to search sufficiently, while the approaching driver, for one reason or another, was delayed in detecting the pedestrian. However, in 21 percent of the cases the delayed detection and visual search failures were associated with view obstructions attributed to parked cars. In Indiana University's study of all accident types, view obstructions from parked cars were cited in only 3.3 percent of the cases, indicating that they are a much more serious problem in driver-pedestrian interactions than in driver-driver interactions.

With respect to human indirect causes of accidents (i.e., human conditions and states) Snyder and Knoblauch were able to evaluate only alcohol and old age (as manifested in an overall reduction in various driving and walking related skills). Although the percent of times in which alcohol could be definitely described as a causal factor was relatively low, it was still twice as high for pedestrians (3.8 percent) than for drivers (2.0 percent). This result should not be misinterpreted as an indication that when drunk it is safer to drive than to walk. It probably reflects a greater tendency of drunk pedestrians to walk off the curb and into the road (without any heed to proper course and visual search procedures), than a similar tendency of drunk drivers to run off the road and strike pedestrians — as it is, the intoxicated driver is already overinvolved in injury producing accidents with other moving vehicles.

To study whether in fact intoxicated pedestrians are overinvolved in accidents, Clayton, Booth, and McCarthy (1977) first analyzed the BALs of 344 pedestrian fatalties and then conducted roadside interviews and measured the BALs of a control group consisting of a matched sample of pedestrians (not involved in accidents) crossing the same streets and at the same times that the accident sample did. They found that in the control group only 4 percent of the pedestrians had BALs equal to a greater than 0.10 percent, whereas in the accident group 19 percent had BALs equal to or greater than 0.10 percent. This pattern of results is similar to that obtained for drivers (see Chapter Three), suggesting that the saying "if you drink don't drive" should be revised to "if you drink stay off the street."

THE PREVENTION OF PEDESTRIAN ACCIDENTS

As with other types of highway traffic accidents, pedestrian accidents can be prevented by modifications in the highway environment, changes in vehicle design and features, and driver improvements. In the particular case of pedestrian accidents, an additional accident countermeasure is pedestrian improvement — after all, the data indicate that in the majority of the accidents the pedestrian is more at fault than the driver. Since vehicle improvement and driver improvement have already been discussed (Chapter Six), we will focus our attention here on pedestrian-oriented highway system modifications and on pedestrian improvement.

Highway Designs for Pedestrian Safety

The ultimate goal of any pedestrian safety feature is to minimize the interactions between pedestrians and drivers. The most familiar — and least expensive — pedestrian accommodation is the marked crosswalk at intersections. Its purpose is to channel pedestrians into specific points for crossing the street, and to alert drivers to the potential presence of pedestrians there. However it remains up to these road users to actually observe these rules. Since it turns out to be a difficult task to train drivers and pedestrians to appropriately attend to each other, respect each other's rights and behave accordingly, then a more appropriate solution is to physically separate vehicle and pedestrian movement. The separation can be done either in time, through the use of a "pedestrian only" phase in the signal cycle, or in space, by building pedestrian overpasses and underpasses and by creating "pedestrian only" zones. As might be expected, the effectiveness of the different measures varies; though not necessarily in a direct relationship to the cost involved.

Pedestrian Crossings. The white markings of pedestrian crosswalks can provide visual cues to both drivers and pedestrians, ostensibly increasing the alertness of drivers to the potential presence of pedestrians. The uniform placement of these crossings next to intersections should also help to alert the drivers. Indeed, studies conducted in several European countries and Israel have demonstrated that the risk of an accident — defined as the ratio between the number of pedestrian accidents in a particular location and the number of pedestrians crossing the street at that location (during a particular time period) — is approximately two to five times higher in unmarked sections than in the marked crossing sections (Jacobs & Wilson, 1967; Katz, Elgrishi, & Guttman, 1972; Older & Grayson, 1976). Accordingly, channeling pedestrians into crosswalks adjacent to intersections by installing guardrails extending from the ends of the crosswalk has proved to be an effective way to both control pedestrian roadcrossing behavior as well as reduce pedestrian accidents (Katz et al., 1972).

There remains a question, however, of whether the markings themselves or the mere proximity of the intersection — which raises the driver's level of alertness to crossing cars as well as pedestrians — is the cause of the lower accident rate. While detailed analyses of the European studies indicate that the marked crossing by themselves contribute to the lower accident risk, at least one extensive and carefully controlled study conducted in San Diego, California, throws some doubt on this conclusion. In this study, by Herms (1972), pedestrian behavior was observed at 400 unsignalized intersections, each having one marked and one unmarked crossing. The results showed that crosswalks did in fact induce pedestrians to use them. Almost three times as many pedestrians crossed the street in the marked section versus the unmarked section. However, the results on the more important measure — accident rates — were quite disappointing. Over a five-year period, 177 pedestrians were hit in the marked crosswalks compared with only 31 pedestrians hit in the unmarked crosswalks. Even after adjusting for the rate of usage, twice as many pedestrian accidents occurred in the marked crosswalk compared with the unmarked crosswalk. The large number of intersections observed, and the long span of time studied, make these results difficult to ignore, or discount as spurious due to sampling error. Nonetheless, Herms concluded that the high accident risk in the marked crosswalks was "not due to the crosswalk being marked, as much as it is a reflection on the pedestrians' attitude and behavior when using the marked crosswalk . . . (since marked crosswalks) may cause pedestrians to have a false sense of security and to place themselves in a hazardous position with respect to vehicular traffic . . .

cause the pedestrian to think that the motorist can and will stop in all cases, even when it is impossible to do so . . . may cause a greater number of rear-end and associated collisions due to pedestrians not waiting for gaps in traffic" (p. 12). Some of these pedestrian expectations are apparently known to the approaching driver. In a study conducted in Israel, drivers were observed to slow down or stop more often for pedestrians when the latter crossed in a marked crosswalk or when the pedestrian did not look in the direction of the approaching car! (Katz, Zaidel, & Elgrishi, 1975).

Pedestrian Signals. Since the added safety provided by the marked crossing is often minimal, an alternative approach is to provide pedestrian signals. These signals are assumed to provide an added safety margin because they coordinate the movement of *both* vehicular and pedestrian traffic. Here, too, the studies conducted in Europe yield lower risk values for signalized than for nonsignalized intersections. In Detroit, Michigan, Mortimer (1973) compared pedestrian behavior at signalized intersections with and without pedestrian signals. He found that compliance with the traffic signals was greater at those intersections with the pedestrian signals, than at those having traffic signals only. There were nearly 35 percent fewer illegal crossing (entering the roadway against the traffic light) in those intersections having the pedestrian signals.

The benefit of the pedestrian signals would be even greater if pedestrians were to comply with them as much as drivers comply with traffic signals. In a recent survey of pedestrian compliance in seven cities in the United States, the rates varied from 82 percent (in Tempe, Arizona) to 42 percent (in Buffalo, New York) (Robertson, 1976). As may be expected, when the compliance is minimal so is the advantage of the signal. In New York City, in a comparison of the number of accidents at 11 intersections before and after the installation of pedestrian WALK signals, 27 accidents were recorded before and 25 accidents were recorded after the signal installation (Fleig & Duffy, 1967). In the same study, however, an observation of pedestrian behavior at one of these intersections showed as many pedestrian violations after the signal's installation as before its installation. While the disregard for the pedestrian signal may be characteristic of the New Yorkers, the relationship between signal effectiveness and level of compliance is probably true anywhere.

The introduction of new traffic regulations permitting vehicles to turn right on red signals, makes the safety benefits of the present pedestrian WALK signals very questionable. According to Sleight (1972), "the WALK light that is on when vehicles are permitted to turn the corner can be a hazard, because it may delude pedestrians into thinking that they have the freedom to move without vehicle interference. Furthermore, their attention is focused in large part on the light that has given them this information and they may thus be relatively inattentive to traffic in the vicinity" (p. 244). A case in point is a finding in a study conducted in New York City in which out of 172 pedestrian accidents in intersections, the only fatal accident was caused by a left-turning vehicle when both the pedestrian and the vehicle had the green light (Fruin, 1973). An innovative approach to circumvent the problem, has been to use a flashing green WALK signal whenever both pedestrians may cross and vehicles may turn. However the intuitive meaning of the flashing WALK is apparently not clear enough. Of over 1000 pedestrians interviewed by Robertson (1976), 44 percent said they would not expect turning vehicles when they crossed on a flashing WALK signal.

Spatial Separation of Pedestrians and Drivers. The reluctance of pedestrians to comply with walk signals and the existing desire of traffic engineers to improve vehicular flow by allowing right turn on red lights, point to the ultimate solution of separating drivers from pedestrians in space rather than in time. This can be achieved through the use of pedestrian foot bridges (overpasses), tunnels (underpasses), and pedestrian-only zones.

In the case of pedestrian overpasses and underpasses one cannot simply assume that they force the separation of pedestrians from drivers. A case in point was quoted from Baker's study (see p. 178). Therefore the effectiveness of these facilities depends on their degree of utilization by pedestrians. In one study comparing the utilization of eight pedestrian overpasses (Zaidel, Algarishi, & Katz, 1976) a wide range of utilization rates was observed. Fortunately, across all locations, children, mothers accompanied by children, elderly, and handicapped people, who are the most susceptible to pedestrian accidents, used the bridges more frequently than young adults. Being physically more capable the young adults are apparently willing to assume a greater risk rather than lengthen their route by climbing up and down the steps or ramps of the overpass. Perhaps not surprising, Zaidel et al. discovered that of those using the overpasses 95 percent felt it was safer than crossing at grade with the traffic, whereas of those crossing at grade with the traffic — often right under the footbridge — only 59 percent admitted that using the overpass is safer.

How can utilization be assured and pedestrian safety be guaranteed? According to Zaidel et al. (1976), the most important factor that determines the utilization rate is the bridge's location and geometric design. "When a bridge is built in a natural and direct link between activity centers, most pedestrians will cross there, even if there is no strong basic need for a crossing aid .... The details of the bridge's architectural design will not have a significant effect, as long as the comfort of crossing the bridge is reasonable" (p. 7 F 7). In other words, in deciding whether or not to use a bridge, young and physically able people will base their decision more on expediency needs rather than safety needs — especially if they can rationalize that crossing on a bridge is not safer than crossing on the highway.

Pedestrian bridges are most commonly seen over high speed and high density roads, where there is ample space to construct the bridge and its ramps or stairs, and where it is considered impractical or costly to stop the traffic flow. Because of these requirements we rarely find pedestrian bridges in busy downtown areas. An extension of the concept to urban areas of high pedestrian concentrations — typically downtown shopping centers — are the pedestrian skywalks or underground tunnels that connect and flow through busy shopping and commercial centers. Again, it is their strategic locations in downtown areas (e.g., Minneapolis, Minnesota, and Philadelphia, Pennsylvania) that make them effective in both reducing vehicular downtown traffic, and separating pedestrians from automobile traffic, as well as in providing an economic boom to the centers they connect. When the construction of a parallel pedestrian flow system is not a practical solution, creating pedestrian malls seems to be a good alternative. Currently, supported by the federal government, 30 urban areas are in the process of developing new traffic management strategies that include pedestrian zones (U.S. Department of Transportation, 1977).

The Pedestrian's Responsibility

The results of the analysis of the causes of pedestrian accidents, the fact that relative to the level of pedestrian traffic, intersection crossings are safer than midblock crossings, and the fact that pedestrians walking along the edge of the road are more likely to be involved in accidents when they walk on the right side of the road (so that their back is turned toward traffic approaching their side) than when they walk on the left side of the road; all indicate that pedestrian safety could be greatly enhanced if the pedestrian behavior could be modified. Aside from regulating the pedestrians through the use of guardrails and separate pedestrian elevated or underground crossings, there have been attempts to modify pedestrian behavior by effective information campaigns. The federal government has, in fact, issued a Safety Program Standard requiring all states to provide

programs for training and educating all members of the public as to safe pedestrian behavior on or near streets and highways:

A. For children, youths and adults in schools beginning at the earliest possible age.
B. For the general population via the public media.
(Highway Safety Program Standard 14, U.S. Department of Transportation, 1968).

This federal decree underscores the point that although pedestrians are not licensed and are less regulated than drivers, they are nonetheless traffic units that interact with the rest of the traffic. Consequently, just like drivers they too must assume some of the responsibility for maintaining safety. At the very least, the pedestrian should be aware of the rules that govern the vehicular traffic. Hopefully, that knowledge is provided for children through school education and for adults through the mass media.

One problem that may cause many pedestrian nighttime accidents, is that many people — when they are acting as pedestrians — overestimate their visibility to approaching drivers. A review of all the pedestrian accident records occurring in one year in the State of Indiana revealed that in 87 percent of the nighttime accidents, the drivers claimed they did not see the pedestrian in time (Hazlett & Allen, 1968). In contrast, pedestrians seem to think that they are more visible than in fact they are. In one field study (Allen, Hazlett, Tacker, & Graham, 1970), pedestrians with normal vision, standing by the edge of an unlit rural road, were asked to estimate when they felt certain that they were visible to the driver of an approaching vehicle. Of 26 pedestrian observers, only the most pessimistic one closely estimated his true visibility at 175 feet. The average pedestrian thought that he was visible from as far away as 345 feet, while four pedestrians were certain they were visible from more than 500 feet away. Obviously, as long as the gap between the driver's capabilities and the pedestrian's expectations of the driver remains, so will the problem.

To avoid a collision, the approaching driver must detect the pedestrian within a sufficient distance. Based on the stopping distance for various speeds, Hazlett and Allen (1968) calculated the "critical visibility distance" — the minimum distance needed to detect an object in order to stop when proceeding at a given velocity. Using the visibility distance as a criterion, Hazlett and Allen found that when wearing black or gray clothing, the pedestrian can be detected by an oncoming vehicle less than 50 percent of the time when the driver is traveling at a speed of 40 miles an hour or more. In Allen's (1972) words:

Unfortunately, the motorist usually has no warning of the pedestrian because of the normal low reflectivity of clothing.

An illustration of the difficulty is the following incident which occurred early in our testing of pedestrian visibility. The experimenters found that cardboard boxes, spray-painted black, were visible at considerable distances because of surface reflections. To evaluate quickly the visibility of cloth, one of the graduate students volunteered to stand in the roadway while a second student approached in an automobile at 20 miles per hour. The plan was to stop as soon as the driver saw the pedestrian's dark clothing. The pedestrian stood in line with the driver's side of the approaching car and waited, anticipating the driver's stop. It finally became necessary to leap out of the way as the car continued down the road at 20 miles per hour. When the driver returned to the pedestrian's location, he asked, "Where were you?" A simple question indeed, but one of great significance. Keep in mind the slow speed, the motorist's sure knowledge that a pedestrian was out there, the absence of glare, and the driver's ready-to-stop attitude.

The importance of pedestrian visibility cannot be emphasized enough. Roadway illumination — while effective in reducing nighttime pedestrian accidents (Polus & Katz, 1978) — cannot be installed over the complete roadway network. Thus, much of the responsibility for remaining visible to the approaching driver should be shouldered by the pedestrian. Also, improved visibility can be achieved quite easily. By wearing white clothing, a pedestrian is likely to be detected by an oncoming driver going at 60 mph approximately 97 percent of the time. For lower speeds or when wearing reflectorized clothing, this figure goes up to 100 percent (Hazlett & Allen, 1968).

SUMMARY

The pedestrian is a person who interacts with the traffic system whenever he or she steps off the curb and into the road. Of particular interest from the safety point of view are children and elderly people, who, for different reasons, are overinvolved in pedestrian accidents. Children may be involved in accidents because their understanding of the traffic system and their attentional and judgmental capabilities are not sufficiently developed to adequately search for moving traffic and to evaluate vehicle distance and speed. In addition, children may use the streets as play areas, thus further reducing their attention to traffic. On the other hand, the difficulties of elderly people are typically due to their reduced visual and motor capabilities. This is manifested in late detection of oncoming cars that is often coupled with slow walking speed and inability to run.

    An analysis of driver and pedestrian errors that cause pedestrian accidents by Snyder and Knoblauch (1971) indicates that, more often than not, it is the vulnerable pedestrian that causes the accident rather than the relatively protected driver. The most common accident-causing pedestrian behavior is darting out into the street in midblock, most often from behind a parked car or some other view obstruction. Under these circumstances it is often physically impossible to stop the car in time. Thus, approximately half of the accidents in Snyder and Knoblauch's study could have been prevented had the pedestrian searched the visual field adequately before stepping into the vehicle's path.

    Most of the efforts directed at the prevention of pedestrian accidents are aimed at separating pedestrians from vehicular traffic. This can be done either in time — through the creation of exclusive pedestrian walk cycles in the traffic signals — or in space — through the construction of pedestrian overpasses, underpasses, and even complete pedestrian traffic networks. Since these environmental countermeasures cannot be constructed at all potential pedestrian crossing zones, a significant portion of the responsibility for avoiding accidents rests on the pedestrian. Various educational programs and mass media campaigns have been directed at increasing the public awareness of safe pedestrian behavior, but the effectiveness of these programs is yet to be ascertained. One area in which the public's ignorance has been demonstrated is in the nighttime visibility of pedestrians. Most people overestimate the distance from which they can be detected by an approaching driver. Here the effectiveness of light-colored clothing in increasing the visibility distance is quite striking, and efforts should be directed at making pedestrians aware of this.

REFERENCES

Allen, M. J. *Vision and highway safety.* Philadelphia: Chilton, 1970.

Allen, M. J., Hazlett, R. D., Tacker, H. L., & Graham, B. V. Actual pedestrian visibility and the pedestrian's estimate of his own visibility. *American Journal of Optometry and Archives of the American Academy of Optometry,* 1970, 47, 44-49.

Alther, L. *Kinflicks.* New York: Signet, 1975.

Anderson, H. S. Let's try to dispel some highway safety myths. *Traffic Engineering,* 1976, 46, 20-23.

Aronoff, C. J. Stannard Baker, traffic safety pioneer, retires from N U Traffic Institute. *Northwestern University News,* August 27, 1971.

Avery, G. C. The capacity of young children to cope with the traffic system: A review. Traffic Accident Research Unit, Department of Motor Transport, New South Wales, June 1974.

Babarik, P. Automobile accidents and driver reaction patterns. *Journal of Applied Psychology,* 1968, 52, 49-54.

Babst, D. V., Inciardi, J. A., Raeder, P. K., Jr., & Negri, D. B. Driving records of heroin addicts. New York State Narcotic Addiction Control Commission, New York State Department of Motor Vehicles, 1969.

Baker, S. P. Pedestrian deaths in Rio de Janeiro and Baltimore. *Accident Analysis and Prevention,* 1977, 9, 113-118.

Baker, S. P., Robertson, L. S., & O'Neill, B. Drivers involved in fatal pedestrian collisions. *Proceedings of the 16th Conference of the American Association for Automotive Medicine,* Chapel Hill, North Carolina, October 1972.

Baker, W. T. An evaluation of the traffic conflicts technique. *Highway Research Record,* 1972, No. 384, 1-8.

Balasha, D. Near accidents as a measure of traffic risk at intersections. Unpublished doctoral dissertation, Technion — Israel Institute of Technology, Haifa, 1977.

Barrett, G. V. Review of automobile simulator research. *Proceedings of the International Symposium on Psychological Aspects of Driver Behavior.* Noordwjkerhout, the Netherlands, August 1971.

Barrett, G. V., Kobayashi, M., & Fox, B. A. Driving at requested speed: Comparison of projected and virtual image displays. *Human Factors,* 1968, 10, 259-262.

Barrett, G. V., Thornton, C. L., & Cabe, P. A. Relation between embedded figures test performance and simulator behavior. *Journal of Applied Psychology,* 1969, 53, 253-254.

Bartholomew, W. M. Pedestrian accidents in service areas of selected city recreation facilities. *Traffic Safety Research Review,* December 1967.

Beers, J., Case, H. W., & Hulbert, S. Driving ability as affected by age. UCLA-ITTE Report No. 70-18, 1970. (Cited in Barrett, 1971).

Beideman, L. R., & Stern, J. A. Aspect of the eye blink during simulated driving as a function of alcohol. *Human Factors*, 1977, 19, 73-78.

Belt, B. L. Driver eye movement as a function of low alcohol concentration. Engineering Experiment Station Technical Report, The Ohio State University, Columbus, Ohio, 1969.

Bergman, S. E. Pedestrian and bicycle facilities and traffic controls: Programs of the U.S. Federal Highway Administration. *Proceedings of the International Conference on Pedestrian Safety*. Haifa, Israel: Michlol, 1976.

Bhise, V. D., & Rockwell, T. H. The role of peripheral vision and time sharing in driving. In *Proceedings of the 15th Annual Meeting of the American Association for Automotive Medicine*. Colorado Springs, Colorado, November 1971.

Bhise, V. D., & Rockwell T. H. Development of a methodology for evaluating road signs. Engineering Experiment Station, Final Report Number EES 315B The Ohio State University, 1972.

Bird, A. D. How to plan for the pedestrian. *The American City*, July 1969.

Black, S. *Man and motor cars: An ergonomic study*. New York: W. W. Norton and Co., 1966.

Bleyl, R. L. Speed profiles approaching a traffic signal. *Highway Research Record*, 1972, No. 386, 17-23.

Blomberg, R. D., & Preusser, D. F. Drug abuse and driving performance. Dunlap and Associates, Inc. Final Report No. HS-800-754, 1972 (cited in Joscelyn and Maickel, 1975).

Blumenthal, M. Dimensions of the traffic safety problem. *Traffic Safety Research Review*, 1968, 12, 7-12.

Borkenstein, R. F., Fatalities per 100 million vehicle/kms. In *International Road Federation world road statistics*, 1973. As cited by the U.S. Department of Transportation (1975).

Borkenstein, R. F., Crowther, R. F., Shumate, R. P., Ziel, W. B., & Zylman, R., The role of the drinking driver in traffic accidents. Department of Police Administration, Indiana University, February 1964.

Brezina, E. H. Traffic accidents and offences: An observational study of the Ontario driver population. *Accident Analysis and Prevention*, 1969, 1, 373-395.

Brody, L. Personal factors in safe operation of motor vehicles. Center for Safety Education, New York University, New York, 1941. (Cited in Burg, 1964).

Brody, L. Personal characteristics of chronic violators and accident repeaters. *Highway Research Board Bulletin*, 1957, No. 152, 1-2.

Brown, I. D. Effect of a car radio on driving in traffic. *Ergonomics*, 1965, 8, 475-479.

Brown, S. L., & Bohnert, P. J. Alcohol safety study: Drivers who died. Houston, Texas: Baylor University College of Medicine, 1968.

Bruce, J. A. The pedestrian. In J. E. Baerwald (Ed.), *Traffic engineering handbook*. Washington, D.C.: Institute of Traffic Engineers, 1965.

Burg, A. An investigation of some relationships between dynamic visual acuity, static visual acuity, and driving record. Report No. 64-18, Department of Engineering, University of California, Los Angeles, April 1964.

Burg, A. The relationship between vision test scores and driving record: General findings. Report Number 64-24, Los Angeles: University of California, Department of Engineering, June 1967.

Burg, A. Lateral visual field as related to age and sex. *Journal of Applied Psychology*, 1968, 52, 10-15.

Burg, A. Visual degradation in relation to specific accident types. Report No. UCLA-ENG-7419, Institute of Transportation and Traffic Engineering, University of California, Los Angeles, March 1974.

Burger, W. J. What's ahead in rear vision devices. *Traffic Safety*, May 1976, 76, 22, 32.

Buttigliere, M., Brunse, A. J., & Case, H. W. Effect of alcohol and drugs on driving behavior. In T. W. Forbes (Ed.), *Human factors in highway traffic safety research*. New York: Wiley, 1972.

Cherry, E. C. Some experiments on the recognition of speech with one and with two ears. *Journal of the Acoustical Society of America*, 1953, 25, 975-979.

Clayton, A. B. The effects of psychotropic drugs upon driving related skills. *Human Factors*, 1976, 18, 241-252.

Clayton, A. B., Booth, A. C., & McCarthy, P. E. A controlled study of the role of alcohol in fatal adult pedestrian accidents. Transport and Road Research Laboratory, Supplementary Report No. 332, Crawthorne, England, 1977.

Cobb, P. W. Automobile driver tests administered to 3,663 persons in Connecticut, 1936-37, and the relation of the test scores to accidents sustained. Unpublished report to the Highway Research Board, July 1939 (cited in Burg, 1964).

Conley, J. A., & Smiley, R. Driver licensing tests as a predictor of subsequent violations. *Human Factors*, 1976, 18, 565-574.

Coppin, R. S., Ferdun, G. S., & Peck, R. C. The teen-age driver. California Department of Motor Vehicles, Report Number 21, February, 1965.

Crancer, A., Jr., Dillie, J. M., Delay, J. C., Wallace, J. E., & Haykin, M. D. Comparison of the effects of marijuana and alcohol on simulated driving performance. *Science*, 1969, 164, 851-854.

Crancer, A., Jr., & Quiring, D. L. Driving records of persons hospitalized with suicidal gestures. *Behavioral Research in Highway Safety*, 1970, 1, 33-42.

Crandall, F., Duggar, B., & Fox, B. A study of driver behavior during a simulated driving task. Bio-Dynamics, Contract No. PH103-64-79, 1966. (Cited in Barrett, 1971.)

Crawford, A. The overtaking driver. *Ergonomics*, 1963, 6, 153-170.

Denton, G. G. The influence of visual pattern on speed at M8 Midlothian. Transport and Road Research Laboratory, Report LR 531. Crowthorn, England, 1973.

Drury, C. G. Application of Fitts Law to foot-pedal design. *Human Factors*, 1975, 17, 368-373.

Duggar, B. C., Young, H. N., Budrose, C. R., & Kanter E. H. Fixed-base simulator versus skid pad practice in skid control training. Injury Control Research Laboratory, ICRL-RR-68-3, Providence, R. I., 1968. (Cited in Barrett, 1971.)

Edwards, A. L. *Experimental design in psychological research*. New York: Holt, Rinehart and Winston, 1968.

Eklund, K. The conspicuity of traffic signs and factors affecting it. Reports from Talja, No. 6, Helsinki, 1968 (as cited by Näätänen and Summala, 1976).

Ellingstad, V. S. A factor analytic approach to the driving task. *Behavioral Research in Highway Safety*, 1970, 1, 115-125.

Evans, L., & Rothery, R. W. Detection of the sign relative motion when following a vehicle, *Human Factors*, 1974, 16, 161-173.

Farber, E. Passing behavior on public highways under daytime and nighttime conditions. *Highway Research Record*, 1969, No. 292, 11-23.

Fell, J. C. A motor vehicle accident causal system: The human element. *Human Factors*, 1976, 18, 85-94.

Fergenson, P. E. The relationship between information processing and driving accidents and violation records, *Human Factors*, 1971, 13, 173-176.

Finnish Insurance Information Center, *Insurance in Finland*, No. 1, 1974.

Fischhoff, B. Hindsight: Thinking backward? Oregon Research Institute, *ORI Research Monograph*, 1974, Vol. 14, No. 1.

Fitts, P. M. The information capacity of the human motor system in controlling the amplitude of movement. *Journal of Experimental Psychology*, 1954, 47, 381-391.

Fitts, P. M. Perceptual-motor skill learning. In A. W. Melton (Ed.), *Categories of human learning*. New York: Academic Press, 1964.

Fitts, P. M. & Peterson, J. R. Information capacity of discrete motor responses. *Journal of Experimental Psychology*, 1964, 67, 103-112.

Fitts, P. M., & Posner, M. I. *Human performance*. Belmont, Cal.: Brooks/Cole, 1967.

Fleig, P. H., & Duffy, J. A study of pedestrian safety behavior using activity sampling. *Traffic Safety Research Review*, December 1967.

Fletcher, E. D. Visual acuity and safe driving. *Journal of the American Optometric Association*, 1949, 20, 439-442.

Forbes, L. Field of view from automotive vehicles. Paper presented at Automobile Engineering Meeting, Detroit, Mich., May 1973.

Forbes, T. W. Discussion of Woltman's paper on visibility factors in roadway signing. *Highway Research Board Special Report*, No. 134, 1973, 37-39.

Forbes, T. W. The normal automobile driver as a traffic problem. *Journal of General Psychology*, 1939, 20, 471-474.

Forbes, T. Visibility and legibility of highway signs. In T. W. Forbes (Ed.), *Human factors in highway traffic safety research*. New York: Wiley, 1972.

Fruin, J. J. Pedestrian accident characteristics in a one-way grid. *Highway Research Record*, No. 436, 1973, 1-7.

Gazis, D., Herman, R., & Maradudin, A. The problem of the amber signal light in traffic flow. *Operations Research*, 1960, 8, 112-132.

Goodenough, D. R. A review of individual differences in field dependence as a factor in auto safety. *Human Factors*, 1976, 18, 53-62.

Gordon, D. A., & Mast, T. M. Driver's judgment in overtaking and passing. *Human Factors*, 1970, 12, 341-346.

Graf, C. P., & Krebs, M. J. Headlight factors and nighttime vision. Minneapolis, Minn. Honeywell, Inc., Report No. 765RC13, April 1976.

Greenshields, B. D. Driving behavior and related problems. *Highway Research Record*, 1963, 25, 14-32.

Greenwood, M., & Woods, H. M. A report on the incidence of industrial accidents upon individuals with special reference to multiple accidents. *British Industrial Fatigue Research Board*, No. 4, 1919.

Hagen, R. E. Countermeasures in traffic safety. In N. W. Heimstra (Ed.), *Injury control in traffic safety*. Springfield, Ill.: Charles C Thomas, 1970.

Hanscom, F. R. An evaluation of signing to warn of potentially icy bridges. *Transportation Research Record*, 1975, No. 531, 18-35.

Harrass, J. A., & Mourant, R. R. Continuous tracking with a heads-up presentation in automobile driving. *Proceedings of the Human Factors Society 14th Annual Meeting*. San Francisco, Cal.: October 1970.

Harrington, D. M. The young driver follow-up study: An evaluation of the role of human factors in the first four years of driving. Sacramento, Cal.: California Department of Motor Vehicles, 1971.

Haviland, C. V., & Wiseman, H. A. B. Criminals who drive. *Proceedings of the 18th Annual Conference of the American Association for Automotive Medicine*. Toronto, Canada: September 1974.

Hazlett, R. D., & Allen, M. J. The ability to see a pedestrian at night: The effect of clothing, reflectorization, and driver intoxication. *American Journal of Optometry and Archives of the American Academy of Optometry*, 1968, 45, 246-257.

Heimstra, N. W. The effects of "stress fatigue" on performance in a simulated driving situation. *Ergonomics*, 1970, 13, 209-218.

Heimstra, N. W., & McDonald, A. L. *Psychology and contemporary problems*. Monterey, Cal.: Brooks/Cole, 1973.

Helander, M. Vehicle control and driving experience: A psychophysiological approach. *Proceedings of the 6th Congress of the International Ergonomics Association*. College Park, Md.: July 1976.

Henderson, R. L., & Burg, A. Vision and audition in driving. System Development Corporation, TM(L)-5297/000/00, April 1974.

Henderson, R. L., Burg, A., & Brazelton, F. A. Development of an integrated vision testing device: Phase I. Final Report No. TM(L)-4848/000/00, Systems Development Corporation, Santa Monica, Cal., 1971.

Herms, B. S. Pedestrian crosswalk study: Accidents in painted and unpainted crosswalks. *Highway Research Record*, 1972, No. 406, 1-13.

Herrin, G. D., & Neuhardt, J. B. An empirical model for automobile driver horizontal curve negotiation. *Human Factors*, 1974, 16, 129-133.

Hicks, J. A. An evaluation of the effect of sign brightness on the sign reading behavior of alcohol-impaired drivers. University of South Carolina, Traffic and Transportation Center, TTC Report No. 6, May 1974.

Highway and Vehicle Safety Report. Traffic lights are not always the solution, 1974, 1(2).

Hirschfeld, A. M., & Behan, R. C. The accident process: III. Disability: Acceptable and unacceptable. *Journal of the American Medical Association*, 1966, 197, 85-89.

Hofstetter, H. W. Visual acuity and highway accidents. *Journal of the American Optometric Association*, 1976, 47, 887-893.

Holroyd, K., & Kahn, M. Personality factors in student drug use. *Journal of Consulting and Clinical Psychology*, 1974, 42, 236-243.

Hulbert, S. Effect of driver fatigue. In T. W. Forbes (Ed.), *Human factors in highway traffic safety research*. New York: Wiley, 1972.

Hulbert, S., & Wojcik, C. Driving task simulation. In T. W. Forbes (Ed.), *Human factors in highway traffic safety research*. New York, Wiley, 1972.

Huntley, M. S., Jr., & Centybear, T. M. Alcohol, sleep deprivation and driving speed effects upon control use during driving. *Human Factors*, 1974, 16, 19-28.

Hurst, P. M. Amphetamines and driving behavior. *Accident Analysis and Prevention*, 1976, 8, 9-14.

Indiana University, Institute for Research in Public Safety. In-Depth Case Study, TAC-75-260, Tri-Level Crash Research, Contract DOT-HS-034-3-535-75-TAC, April 1975.

Jacobs, G. D., & Wilson, D. G. A study of pedestrian risk in crossing busy roads in four towns. RRL Report LR 106, Road Research Laboratory, Ministry of Transport, England, 1967.

Jenkins, W. L., & Connor, M. B. Some design factors in making settings on a linear scale. *Journal of Applied Psychology*, 1949, 33, 395-409.

Jex, H. R., DiMarco, R. J., & Wade, A. R. Impairment of moderate versus heavy drinkers in simulated driver tests. Paper presented at the 10th Annual Conference on Manual Control, Wright-Patterson AFB, Ohio, April 1974.

Johansson, G., & Backlund, F. Drivers and road signs. *Ergonomics*, 1970, 13, 749-759.

Johansson, G., & Rumar, K. Drivers and road signs: A preliminary investigation of the capacity of car drivers to get information from road signs. *Ergonomics*, 1966, 9, 57-62.

Johansson, G., & Rumar, K. Drivers' brake reaction times. *Human Factors*, 1971, 13, 23-27.

Johnson, L., & Lauer, A. R. A study of the effect of induced manual handicaps on automotive performance in relation to reaction time. *Journal of Applied Psychology*, 1937, 21, 85-93.

Joscelyn, K. B., & Maickel, R. P. Drugs and driving: A research review. Indiana University, Bloomington, Ind., Technical Report No. DOT-HS-4-00994-2, November 1975.

Kahneman, D., Ben-Ishai, R., & Lotan, M. Relation of a test of attention to road accidents. *Journal of Applied Psychology*, 1973, 58, 113-115.

Kaluger, N. A., & Smith, G. L., Jr. Driver eye-movement patterns under conditions of prolonged driving and sleep deprivation. *Highway Research Record*, 1970, No. 336, 92-106.

Katz, A., Elgrishi, A., & Guttman, L. Proposed warrants and standards for pedestrian guardrails. Report No. 1: Pedestrian behavior at locations with guardrails. Publication No. 72/7. Road Safety Center, Technion Research and Development Foundation, August 1972.

Katz, A., Zaidel, D., & Elgrishi, A. An experimental study of driver and pedestrian interaction during the crossing conflict. *Human Factors*, 1975, 17, 514-527.

Keeney, A. H., Weiss, S., & Silva, D. Functional problems of telescopic spectacles in the driving task. *Transactions of the American Opthalmological Society*, 1972, 72, 132-138.

Kimball, K. A., Ellingstad, V. S., & Hagen, R. E. Effect of experience on patterns of driving skill. *Journal of Safety Research*, 1971, 3, 129-135.

Klein, D. Social aspects of exposure to highway crash. *Human Factors*, 1976, 18, 211-220.

Klonoff, H. Marijuana and driving in real-life situations. *Science*, 1974, 186, 317-323.

Koppa, R. J., & Hayes, G. G. Driver inputs during emergency or extreme vehicle maneuvers. *Human Factors*, 1976, 18, 361-370.

Korb, D. R. Preparing the visually handicapped person for motor vehicle operation. *American Journal of Optometry and Archives of the American Academy of Optometry*, 1970, 47, 619-628.

Lauer, A. R. Motor vision. *Journal of the American Optometric Association*, 1937, 9, 317-323.

Lauer, A. R. *The psychology of driving*. Springfield, Ill.: Charles C Thomas, 1960.

Lauer, A. R., DeSilva, H. R., & Forbes, T. W. Report to the Highway Research Board, 1939 (unpublished). (Cited in Burg, 1964.)

Lee, J. The multilinear speed-density relationship and its immediate applications. Unpublished doctoral dissertation, The Ohio State University, Columbus, Ohio, 1971.

Levine, J. M., Kramer, G. G., & Levine, E. N. Effects of alcohol on human performance: An integration of research findings based on abilities classification. *Journal of Applied Psychology*, 1975, 60, 285-293.

Ling, G. M. Interaction between alcohol and drugs, and their relationship to driving. Discussion. Conference on Medical, Human and Related Factors Causing Traffic Accidents Including Alcohol and Other Drugs. 1973. (Cited in Joscelyn and Maickel, 1975.)

Linnoila, M., & Mattila, M. J. Drug interaction on driving skills as evaluated by laboratory tests and by a driving simulator. *Pharmakopsychiatrie Neuro-Psychopharmakolgie*, 1973, 6, 127-132.

Liss, P. H., & Haith, M. M. The speed of visual processing in children and adults: Effects of backward and forward masking. *Perception and Psychophysics*, 1970, 8, 396-398.

Loftus, E., & Palmer, J. C. Reconstruction of automobile destruction: An example of the interaction between language and memory. *Journal of Verbal Learning and Verbal Behavior*, 1974, 13, 585-589.

Lucas, R., Heimstra, N., & Spiegel, D. Part-task simulation training of drivers' passing judgments. *Human Factors*, 1973, 15, 269-274.

Mackworth, N. H. *Researches on the measurement of human performance*. Medical Research Council Special Report Series, No. 268, London: H.M.-S.O., 1950.

Mackworth, N. H., & Morandi, A. J. The gaze selects informative details within pictures. *Perception and Psychophysics*, 1967, 2, 547-552.

Maisto, S. A., & Adesso, V. J. Effect of instructions and feedback on blood alcohol level discrimination training in nonalcoholic drinkers. *Journal of Consulting and Clinical Psychology*, 1977, 45, 625-636.

Malfetti, J. L., & Fine, J. L. Characteristics of safe drivers: A pilot study. *Traffic Safety Research Review*, 1962, **6**, 3-9.

Matson, T. M., Smith, W. S., & Hurd, F. W. *Traffic Engineering.* New York: McGraw-Hill, 1955.

Mayer, R. E., & Treat, J. R. Psychological, social and cognitive characteristics of high-risk drivers: A pilot study. *Accident Analysis and Prevention*, 1977, **9**, 1-8.

McFarland, R. A. Health and safety in transportation. In W. Haddon, E. A. Suchman, & D. Klein (Eds.), *Accident research: Methods and approaches.* New York: Harper & Row, 1964.

McGuire, F. L. Personality factors in highway accidents. *Human Factors*, 1976, **18**, 433-442.

McGuire, F. L., & Kersh, R. C. *An evaluation of driver education: A study of history, philosophy, research methodology and effectiveness in the field of driver education.* Berkeley, Cal.: University of California Press, 1969.

McKnight, A. J., & Adams, B. D. Driver education task analysis, Volume I, Task descriptions. Alexandria, Va.: Human Resources Research Organization, 1970.

McLean, J. R., & Hoffman, E. R. Steering reversals as a measure of driver performance and steering task difficulty. *Human Factors*, 1975, **17**, 248-256.

McMurray, L. Emotional stress and driving performance: The effects of divorce. *Behavioral Research in Highway Safety*, 1970, **1**, 100-114.

Mehalel, D., & Hakkert, A. S. The influence of signalization and installation of a flashing green signal light on the number of injury accidents at intersections (Hebrew). Report No. 74/13, Road Safety Center, Technion Research and Development Foundation, Haifa, Israel, December 1975.

Mihal, W. L., & Barrett, G. V. Individual differences in perceptual information processing and their relation to automobile accident involvement. *Journal of Applied Psychology*, 1976, **61**, 229-233.

Mortimer, R. G. The effects of convex exterior mirrors on lane-changing and passing performance of drivers. *Society of Automotive Engineering*, Report No. 710543, June 1971.

Mortimer, R. G. Behavioral evaluation of pedestrian signals. *Traffic Engineering*, 1973, **43**, 22-26.

Mortimer, R. G. Drug use and driving by a university student sample. *Proceedings of the 20th Conference of the American Association for Automotive Medicine.* Atlanta, Ga.: November 1976.

Mortimer, R. G. Motor vehicle exterior lighting. *Human Factors*, 1976, **18**, 259-272.

Mortimer, R. G., & Becker, J. M. Development of a computer simulation to predict the visibility distance provided by headlamp beams. Highway Safety Research Institute, University of Michigan, Ann Arbor, Mich., Report No. UM-HSRI-HF-73-15, July 1973.

Moser, B. A., Bressler, L. D., & Williams, R. B. Collection analysis and interpretation of data on relationship between drugs and driving. Research Triangle Institute, Final Report No. HS-800-648, 1972.

Moskowitz, H., & Sharma, S. Effects of alcohol on peripheral vision as a function of attention. *Human Factors*, 1974, 16, 174-180.

Moskowitz, H., Ziedman, K., & Sharma, S. Visual search behavior while viewing driving scenes under the influence of alcohol and marijuana. *Human Factors*, 1976, 18, 417-432.

Mourant, R. R., & Langolf, G. D. Luminance specifications for automobile instrument panels. *Human Factors*, 1976, 18, 71-84.

Mourant, R. R., & Rockwell, T. H. Strategies of visual search by novice and experienced drivers. *Human Factors*, 1972, 14, 325-335.

Mourant, R. R. Rockwell, T. H., & Rackoff, N. J. Drivers' eye movements and visual workload. *Highway Research Record*, 1969, No. 292, 1-10.

Murrell, K. F. H. *Ergonomics: Man in his working environment*. London: Chapman and Hall, 1969.

Myrsten, A. L., Post, B., Frankenhaeuser, M., & Johansson, G. Changes in behavioral and physiological activation induced by cigarette smoking in habitual smokers. *Psychopharmacologia*, 1972, 27, 305-312.

Näätänen, R., & Summala, H. *Road-user behavior and traffic accidents*. Amsterdam: North-Holland, 1976.

National Safety Council. *Accident prevention manual for industrial operations*. (7th ed.) Chicago: National Safety Council, 1974.

National Safety Council. *Accidents facts*. (1976 ed.) Chicago: National Safety Council, 1976.

Nichols, J. L. Driver education and improvement programs. In N. W. Heimstra (Ed.), *Injury control in traffic safety*. Springfield, Ill.: Charles C. Thomas, 1970.

Nichols, J. L. DWI treatment efforts: Managing through evaluation. *National Traffic Safety Newsletter*, June 1977, 6-9.

Nichols, J. L., & Reis, R. E. One model for the evaluation of ASAP rehabilitation efforts. Paper presented at the Sixth International Conference on Alcohol, Drugs, and Traffic Safety. Toronto, Canada: September 1974.

Norman D. A. *Memory and attention*. (2nd ed.) New York: Wiley, 1976.

Ohio Department of Education. The development and validation of attitude, knowledge and performance tests for evaluating driver educational curricula. Columbus, Ohio, 1974.

Older, S. J., & Grayson, G. B. An international comparison of pedestrian risk in four cities. *Proceedings of the International Conference on Pedestrian Safety*. Haifa, Israel: Michlol, 1976.

Older, S. J., & Spicer, B. R. Traffic conflicts — A development in accident research. *Human Factors*, 1976, 18, 335-350.

Olson, P. L. Aspects of driving performance as a function of field dependence. *Journal of Applied Psychology*, 1974, 59, 192-196.

Olson, P. L., & Rothery, R. W. Driver response to the amber phase of traffic signals. *Operations Research*, 1961, 9, 650-663.

Owens, D. A., & Leibowitz, H. W. Night myopia: Cause and a possible basis for amelioration. *American Journal of Optometry and Physiological Optics*, 1976, 53, 709-717.

Payne, D. E., & Barmack, J. E. An experimental field test of the Smith-Cummings-Sherman driver training system. *Traffic Safety Research Review*, 1963, 7, 10-14.

Pease, K., & Preston, B. Road safety education for young children. *British Journal of Educational Psychology*, 1967, 37, 305-313.

Peck, R. C. Toward a dynamic system of driver improvement program evaluation. *Human Factors*, 1976, 18, 493-506.

Perchonok, K. Accident cause analysis. CAL Report No. ZM-5010-V-3, Cornell Aeronautical Laboratory, Inc., Buffalo, N.Y., July 1972.

Perkins, S. R. GMR traffic conflicts techniques — Procedures manual. General Motors Research Publication 895, 1969.

Phillips, D. T. Motor vehicle fatalities increase just after publicized suicide stories. *Science*, 1977, **196**, 1464-1465.

Platt, F. N. *The highway systems safety car*. Detroit, Mich.: Ford Motor Co., 1970.

Plummer, R. W., & King, L. E. Meaning and application of color and arrow indications for traffic signals. *Highway Research Record*, 1973, No. 445, 34-44.

Polus, A., & Katz, A. An analysis of nighttime pedestrian accidents at specially illuminated crosswalks. *Accident Analysis and Prevention*, 1978, in press.

Rackoff, N. J., & Rockwell, T. H. Driver eye-movement patterns during nighttime and twilight driving. Systems Research Group, The Ohio State University, Columbus, Ohio. Report No. EES3288, 1973.

Reinfurt, D. W., Levine, D. N., & Johnson, W. D. Radar as a speed deterrent: An evaluation. Highway Safety Research Center, University of North Carolina, Chapel Hill, N.C., February 1973.

Richter, R. L., & Hyman, W. A. Driver's brake reaction times with adaptive controls. *Human Factors*, 1974, **16**, 87-88.

Robertson, H. D. Intersection improvements for pedestrians. *Proceedings of the International Conference on Pedestrian Safety*. Haifa, Israel: Michlol, 1976.

Robinson, G. H. Toward measurement of attention as a function of risk preference in man-machine systems. *Human Factors*, 1975, **17**, 236-242.

Rockwell, T. H. Skills, judgment and information acquisition in driving. In T. W. Forbes (Ed.), *Human factors in highway traffic safety research*. New York: Wiley, 1972a.

Rockwell, T. H. Eye-movement analysis of visual information acquisition in driving: An overview. *Proceedings of the 6th Conference of the Australian Road Research Board*, 1972b, 6, 316-331.

Rockwell, T. H., & Balasubramanian, K. N. Carbon monoxide effects on highway driving performance. *Proceedings of the 19th Conference of the American Association for Automotive Medicine*. San Diego, Cal.: November 1975.

Rockwell, T. H., Bhise, V. D., & Mourant, R. R. A television system to record eye movements of automobile drivers. *Proceedings of the Annual Meeting of the Society of Photo-Optical Instrumentation Engineers*. Detroit, Mich.: 1972.

Rockwell, T. H., Hungerford, J. C., & Balasubramanian, K. N. Evaluation of illumination designs for accident reduction at high nighttime-accident highway sites. *Proceedings of the 20th Conference of the American Association for Automotive Medicine.* Atlanta, Ga.: November 1976.

Rockwell, T. H., & Treiterer, J. Sensing and communication between vehicles. NCHRP Report No. 51, Highway Research Board, 1968.

Rockwell, T. H., & Weir, F. W. The interactive effects of carbon monoxide and alcohol on driving skills. Final Report RF. 3332, The Ohio State University, Columbus, Ohio, August 1974.

Rodger, J. R. The sleepy driver as a preventive medicine problem. *General Practitioner,* 1956, 14, 90-94. (Cited in Hulbert 1972.)

Rodstein, M. Pathological and physiological changes in older adults: Effects on drivers and pedestrians. *Proceedings of the 3rd Triennial Congress on Medical and Related Aspects of Motor Vehicle Accidents.* Ann Arbor, Mich.: May-June 1969.

Ross, H. L. The Scandinavian Myth: The effectiveness of drinking and driving legislation in Sweden and Norway. *The Journal of Legal Studies,* 1975, 4, 285-310.

Routledge, D. A., Repetto-Wright, R., & Howarth, C. I. The development of road crossing skill by child pedestrians. *Proceedings of the International Conference on Pedestrian Safety.* Haifa, Israel: Michlol, 1976.

Roy, L. A. Bicycle safety: Everyone's responsibility. *Proceedings of the International Conference on Pedestrian Safety.* Haifa, Israel: Michlol, 1976.

Ruch, T. C., & Patton, H. D. *Physiology and Biophysics.* Philadelphia, Pa.: W. B. Saunders Co., 1965.

Rumar, K., Berggrund, U., Jernberg, P., & Ytterbom, U. Driver reaction to a technical safety measure — studded tires. *Human Factors,* 1976, 18, 443-454.

Rutley, K. S. Control of drivers' speed by means other than enforcement. *Ergonomics,* 1975, 18, 89-100.

Sabey, B. E., & Staughton, G. C. Interacting roles of road environment, vehicle, and road user in accidents. Paper presented at the 5th International Conference of the International Association for Accident and Traffic Medicine, London, September 1975.

Safford, R. R. Visual spare capacity in automobile driving and its sensitivity to carboxyhemoglobin. Unpublished doctoral dissertation, The Ohio State University, Columbus, Ohio, 1971.

Safford, R. R., & Rockwell, T. H. Performance decrement in twenty-four hour driving. *Highway Research Record,* 1967, 163, 68-79.

Safford, R. R., Rockwell, T. H., & Banasik, R. C. The effects of automotive rear-signal system characteristics on driving performance. *Highway Research Record,* 1970, No. 336, 1-20.

Salvatore, S. Effect of removing acceleration cues on sensing vehicular velocity. *Perceptual and Motor Skills,* 1969, 28, 615-622.

Salvatore, S. The ability of elementary and secondary school children to sense oncoming car velocity. *Journal of Safety Research,* 1974, 6, 118-125.

Sandels, S. *Children in traffic.* London: Elek Books, 1975.

Sanders, A. F., & Bunt, A. A. Some remarks on the effect of drugs, lack of sleep and loud noise on human performance. *Proceedings of the International*

Symposium on Psychological Aspects of Driver Behavior. Noordwijkeshout, The Netherlands: August 1971.

Schmidt, C. W., Jr., Shaffer, J. W., Zlotowitz, H. I., & Fisher, R. S. Personality factors in crashes: Age and alcohol. *Proceedings of the 20th Conference of the American Association for Automotive Medicine.* Atlanta, Ga.: November 1976.

Schmidt, F., & Tiffin, J. Distortion of drivers' estimates of automobile speed as a function of speed adaptation. *Journal of Applied Psychology,* 1969, 53, 536-539.

Schori, T. R. Experimental approaches and hardware for driving research. In N. W. Heimstra (Ed.), *Injury control in traffic safety.* Springfield, Ill.: Charles C Thomas, 1970.

Schori, T. R., & Jones, B. W. The effect of smoking on risk-taking in a simulated passing task. *Human Factors,* 1977, 19, 37-46.

Selzer, N. L., Rogers, J. E., & Kern, S. Fatal accidents: The role of psychopathology, social stress and acute disturbance. *American Journal of Psychiatry,* 1968, 124, 46-54.

Shannon, C. D., & Weaver, W. *The mathematical theory of communication.* Urbana, Ill.: University of Illinois Press, 1949.

Shaoul, J. E. The use of intermediate criteria for evaluating the effectiveness of accident countermeasures. *Human Factors,* 1976, 18, 575-586.

Sharma, S. Barbiturates and driving. *Accident Analysis and Prevention,* 1976, 8, 27-32.

Shinar, D. A survey of road user expectancies, unpublished paper, 1973.

Shinar, D. Driver visual limitations, diagnosis and treatment. Indiana University Final Report No. DOT-HS-5-1275, Indiana University, Bloomington, Ind.: October 1977.

Shinar, D., Mayer, R. E., & Treat, J. R. Reliability and validity assessments of a newly developed battery of driving related vision tests. *Proceedings of the 19th Annual Conference of the American Association for Automotive Medicine.* San Diego, Cal.: November 1975.

Shinar, D., McDonald, S. T., & Treat, J. R. The interaction between causally-implicated driver mental and physical conditions and driver errors causing traffic accidents: An analytical approach and a pilot study. *Journal of Safety Research,* 10, 1978, 16-23.

Shinar, D., McDowell, E. D., Rackoff, N. J., & Rockwell, T. H. Field dependence and driver visual search behavior. *Human Factors,* 1978, 20, in press.

Shinar, D., McDowell, E. D., & Rockwell, T. H. Improving driver performance on curves in rural highways through perceptual changes. The Ohio State University, Engineering Experiment Station, Report EES 428B, 1974.

Shinar, D., McDowell, E. D., & Rockwell, T. H. Eye movements in curve negotiation. *Human Factors,* 1977, 19, 63-72.

Shinar, D., Rockwell, T. H., & Malecki, J. Rural Curves: Designed for the birds? Or the effect of changes in driver perception on rural curve negotiation. Paper presented at the 8th Summer Meeting of the Transportation Research Board, Ann Arbor, Mich.: August 1975.

Shulman, H. G., & Fisher, R. P. Expected value as a determinant of the distribution of attention. *Journal of Experimental Psychology,* 1972, 93, 343-348.

Shulman, H. G., & Greenberg, S. N. Perceptual deficit due to division of attention between memory and perception. *Journal of Experimental Psychology*, 1971, 88, 171-176.

Silver, E. H. Report of the research department of the American Optometric Association, *Journal of the American Optometric Association*, 1936, 8, 63-69.

Sleight, R. B. The pedestrian. In T. W. Forbes (Ed.), *Human factors in highway traffic safety research*. New York: Wiley, 1972.

Smeed, R. J. Pedestrian accidents. *Proceedings of the International Conference on Pedestrian Safety*. Vol. II. Haifa, Israel: Michlol, 1976.

Snelson, P. Provision for cyclists in the medium sized urban area — Bedford. *Proceedings of the International Conference on Pedestrian Safety*. Vol. I. Haifa, Israel: Michlol, 1976.

Snyder, H. L. Braking movement time and accelerator-brake separation. *Human Factors*, 1976, 18, 201-204.

Snyder, M. G., & Knoblauch, R. L. Pedestrian safety: The identification of precipitating factors and possible countermeasures. Silver Spring, Md.: Operations Research, Report No. FH-11-7312, January 1971.

Springer, E., Staak, M., & Raff, G. Experimental studies on the absorption of small amounts of alcohol and their effect on driving. (In German.) *Beitr. Berichtl. Med.*, 1973, 31, 253-258. Abstracted in *Journal of Studies on Alcohol*, 1975, 36, 214.

Staak, M., & Brillinger, H. Experimental studies on the subjective ability to distinguish between alcoholic beverages of different concentrations (In German.) *Blutalkohol*, 1975, 12, 81-93. Abstracted in *Journal of Studies on Alcohol*, 1975, 36, 1635.

Stevens, J. C., & Stevens, S. S. Brightness function: Effects of adaptation. *Journal of the Optical Society of America*. 1963, 53, 375-385.

Summala, H., & Näätänen, R. Perception of highway traffic signs and motivation. *Journal of Safety Research*, 1974, 6, 150-153.

Syvänen, M. Effect of police supervision on the perception of traffic signs and driving habits. Reports from Talja No. 6, Helsinki, 1968 (as reported by Näätänen and Summala, 1976).

Taylor, D. H. Accidents, risks, and models of explanation. *Human Factors*, 1976, 18, 371-380.

Tennant, J. A. Drunk driver countermeasures. *Proceedings of the Automotive Safety Engineering Seminar*. Detroit, Mich.: General Motors, June 1973.

Terry, R. M. Automotive headlamp aiming intentions and results. *Society of Automotive Engineers*, Report No. 730007, 1973.

Tillmann, W. A. & Hobbs, G. E. The accident-prone automobile driver. *American Journal of Psychiatry*, 1949, 106, 321-331.

Treat, J. R., Tumbas, N. S., McDonald, S. T., Shinar, D., Hume, R. D., Mayer, R. E., Stansifer, R. L., & Castellan, N. J. Tri-level study of the causes of traffic accidents. Report No. DOT-HS-034-3-535-77 (TAC), Indiana University, March 1977.

Tsongos, N. G., & Schwab, R. N. Driver judgments as influenced by vehicular lighting at intersections. *Highway Research Record*, 1970, No. 336, 21-32.

Tumbas, N. S., Treat, J. R., & McDonald, S. T. An assessment of the accident avoidance and severity reduction potential of radar warning, radar actuated, and anti-lock braking systems. *Society of Automotive Engineers*, Report No. 770266, 1977.

U.S. Department of Transportation, Federal Highway Administration. Highway Safety Program Standard 14: Pedestrian Safety, November 1968.

U.S. Department of Transportation, Federal Highway Administration. *Manual on Uniform Traffic Control Devices for Streets and Highways*, 1971.

U.S. Department of Transportation, National Highway Traffic Safety Administration. Driving performance impairment in heavy versus light drinkers. RFP, NHTSA-2-B640, February 1972.

U.S. Department of Transportation, National Highway Safety Administration. The driver education evaluation program (DEEP) study: A report to the Congress, July 1975.

U.S. Department of Transportation, National Highway Traffic Safety Administration. The driver education evaluation program (DEEP) study: Second report to Congress, July 1976.

U.S. Department of Transportation, National Highway Traffic Safety Administration. Optimizing and evaluating rearview mirror systems for passenger cars, light trucks and multipurpose passenger vehicles. RFP NHTSA-7-A772, June 1977.

U.S. Department of Transportation, Federal Highway Administration. The federal role in aiding pedestrian traffic, 1977.

Virsu, V., & Weintraub, D. J. Perceived curvature of arcs and dot patterns as a function of curvature, arc length, and instructions. *Journal of Experimental Psychology*, 1971, 23, 373-380.

Voevodsky, J. Evaluation of the deceleration warning light for reducing rear-end automobile collisions. *Journal of Applied Psychology*, 1974, 59, 270-273.

Walker, F. W., & Roberts, S. E. Influence of lighting on accident frequency at highway intersections. *Transportation Research Record*, 1976, No. 562, 73-78.

Waller, J. A., Lamborn, K. R., & Steffenhagen, R. A. Marijuana and driving among teenagers. Repeated use pattern, effects, and experiences related to driving. *Accident Analysis and Prevention*, 1974, 6, 141-161.

Walster, E. Assignment of responsibility for an accident. *Journal of Personality and Social Psychology*, 1966, 3, 73-79.

Warner, W. L. A brief history of driver education. *Journal of Traffic Safety Education*, 1972, 19, 13-15.

Weil, A. T., Zinberg, N. E., & Nelson, J. M. Clinical and psychological effects of marijuana in men. *Science*, 1968, 162, 1234-1242.

Weiner, E. L. The elderly pedestrian: Response to an enforcement campaign. *Traffic Safety Research Review*, 1968, 12, 100-110.

Weiss, A. P., & Lauer, A. R. Psychological principles in automotive driving. Studies in Psychology, Report No. 11, The Ohio State University, Columbus, Ohio, 1930. (Cited in Burg, 1964.)

Wilkinson, R. T. Effects of up to 60 hours sleep deprivation on different types of work. *Ergonomics*, 1964, 7, 175-186.

Wilkinson, R. T. Some factors influencing the effect of environmental stressors upon performance. *Psychological Bulletin*, 1969, 72, 260-272.

Williams, A. S., & O'Neill, B. On-the-road driving records of licensed race drivers. *Accident Analysis and Prevention*, 1974, 6, 263-270.

Wilson, T. *Never get too personally involved with your own life*. New York: Universal Press, 1977.

Witkin, H. A., Lewis, H. B., Herzman, M., Machover, K. Meissner, P. B., & Wapner, S. *Personality through perception: An experimental and clinical study*. New York: Harper and Brothers, 1954. (Republished: Westport, Conn.: Greenwood Press, 1972.)

Wojcik, C. K., & Weir, D. H. Studies of the driver as a control element. Phase #2. UCLA-ITTE, Report No. 70-73, 1970. (Cited in Barrett, 1971.)

Woltman, H. L. Review of visibility factors in roadway signing. Highway *Research Board Special Report*, 1973, No. 134, 23-37.

Woltman, H. L., & Youngblood, W. P. An evaluation of retroreflective signing materials under the 3-beam-head-lamp system. *Transportation Research Record*, 1976, No. 662, 79-86.

Wyss, V. Investigations on comparative O_2 pulse values measured in car driving and in equivalent work on bicycle ergometer. *Proceedings of International Symposium on Psychological Aspects of Driver Behavior*. Noordwijkerhout, The Netherlands: August 1976.

Zaidel, D., Algarishi, A., & Katz, A. Factors affecting the use of pedestrian overpasses. *Proceedings of the International Conference on Pedestrian Safety*. Haifa, Israel: Michlol, 1976.

Zegeev, C. V., & Deen, R. C. Pedestrian accidents in Kentucky. *Transportation Research Record*, 1976, No. 605, 26-28.

Zuercher, R. Communications at pedestrian crossings. *Proceedings of the International Conference on Pedestrian Safety*. Haifa, Israel: Michlol, 1976.

Zwahlen, H. T. Distance judgment capabilities of children and adults in a pedestrian situation. Paper presented at the 3rd International Congress of Automotive Safety, San Francisco, Cal.: July 1974.

AUTHOR INDEX

SUBJECT INDEX